GROUP DREAMING:

DREAMS TO THE TENTH POWER

Jean Campbell

Wordminder Press
Norfolk, Virginia

Group Dreaming: Dreams to the Tenth Power

Published by:
Wordminder Press
PO Box 10438
Norfolk, VA 23513-0438
www.WordminderPress.com
757-853-4788

Edited by Susan M. Andrus
Cover designed by Liz Diaz

Library of Congress Control Number: 2006923797

ISBN-10: 0-9729103-2-8
ISBN-13: 978-0-9729103-2-3

Wordminder Press books are available from Amazon.com, your local bookstore or directly from the publisher.
Quantity purchases: We offer substantial discounts on bulk sales to organizations, schools, professionals, and businesses. For more information, call (757) 853-4788.

Dedicated to the dreamers of The World Dreams Peace Bridge

"You see things as they are and say why? But I dream things that never were and I say why not?" George Bernard Shaw

Contents

Part One
Dreams to the Tenth Power

Chapter One – The Experiment Begins

What would the world be like if dreams really did come true? Or better yet, what if we could consciously participate in this magical transformation of dreams into waking reality? What if we could share our dreams together while still asleep and remember the sharing of them when we awake?

I asked myself these questions over thirty years ago when, as the director of a consciousness research organization, Poseidia Institute in Virginia Beach, Virginia, I began to conduct dream research. And these questions are just as valid today.

This story has to do with dreams—shared dreams. Research conducted with ordinary people from across the United States and around the world has revealed a story of achievements made by people from all walks of life—young people, middle aged, and elderly.

In a 1984 article in *Brain/Mind Bulletin*, then-managing editor Connie Zweig spoke of Poseidia Institute's dream experiments begun in 1979, saying, "In fact, truth may be stranger than fiction. The mutual dreaming experiments of Poseidia Institute provide clues to the plasticity of human awareness in dreams."[1]

The idea for Dreams to the Tenth Power emerged during a healing experiment undertaken by a joint team of researchers from Poseidia Institute and the Edgar Cayce organization, The Association for Research and Enlightenment (ARE). As recounted in my earlier book, *Dreams Beyond Dreaming*, members of these two groups met together at the ARE building on Atlantic Avenue in Virginia Beach around Easter of 1977 with the intention of providing a "Dream Helper Ceremony" for a young woman who had come to Poseidia Institute for a medical reading from one of the psychics who worked there.

At that time, many people in Virginia Beach posed questions about the possible achievements of human consciousness. For several years a recent Princeton University graduate, Henry Reed, Ph.D., along with his mentor Dr. Robert Van de Castle of the University of Virginia, had been acting to revive the Aesculapian model of dreaming for a "patient." The model itself derived from ancient Greece where, in a temple setting, a trained dreamer would dream information pertinent to the sick person's health. The oracle at Delphi was such a dreamer. Reed and Van de Castle had conducted these Dream Helper Ceremonies with numerous groups in which the participants, without knowing the specific problem, dreamed together one night for a member of the group.

This time we proposed to up the ante of the experiment by asking a group of dreamers (selected from among staff members of the two cooperating organizations) to dream about the medical issues of someone they did not know at all and had met only briefly at the beginning of the experiment. The subject was a young woman who, as many people did at the time, came to Poseidia

Institute because she heard about the convincing accuracy of the medical readings done there. Though she didn't know any of us, she readily agreed that if she could still have the medical reading she wanted, she would happily participate in the dream experiment as well.

The morning after the Dream Helper Ceremony dreams, I climbed the stairs to the second floor of the ARE building thinking about the treasure of historic information on consciousness it housed. Psychic Edgar Cayce had purchased the rambling white building to use as a hospital, a place to provide the treatments recommended in his psychic readings. The bottom floor housed a library containing the largest collection of books about human consciousness in the world.

When Cayce arrived in 1922, Virginia Beach was a sleepy coastal town filled with family vacation houses. Now the ARE building stood alone and above them all. Behind it, knobby-kneed cypress and crooked branches of live oak trees jutted out from acres of beach grass in Seashore State Park.

In the office upstairs, the ten dreamers of the Dream Helper Ceremony sat around a well-polished mahogany table. As we read our dreams aloud, many of us were struck by the similarities in dream content. Several people dreamed about houses and even, it appeared, the same row of houses. Automobiles also figured in a number of dreams. Some people dreamed specifically about the subject of our experiment.

I came away from that meeting full of questions. As a result of this brief and basically inconclusive night of dreaming, I found myself wondering about shared dreams. Was it possible for people to share dreams whenever they wanted to? I had heard accounts of mutual dreaming, that is of people having the same dream at the same time, and had even experienced this myself—most recently with Ellen Andrews, a psychic employed by Poseidia Institute. In the middle of the night she had awakened from a dream about a fire, and when her waking awoke her husband, she told him to go back to sleep. Some time later, her husband woke and told her the dream he'd been having. It was the same dream. She looked at him and said, "You just watch. Jean Campbell will remember this dream too." And so I did. Further, I had by that time experienced what in dream literature is called lucid dreaming – the experience of being aware of dreaming while the dream is still going on.

What would happen if people tried to dream together and tried to dream lucidly at the same time? To date no experiments of the type had been conducted to answer even the question of whether people could dream together if they wanted to. Dream lucidity, though experienced by many for centuries, was still a relatively new concept to current dream research. In the field of dream research, few believed until the late 1960s that accounts of lucid dreaming could be accepted as valid. Today, much of this has changed.

The idea of shared dreaming intrigued me. Because I had the good fortune to work with a group of people whose curiosity was nearly as great as my own, it was easy to find subjects willing to participate in a series of dream experiments. We began to call the proposed research Dreams to the Tenth Power, or Dreams[10] because in addition to having ten participants, it was clear that if the group actually succeeded in its attempts to demonstrate that people could dream together, we would be suggesting that dreams could be augmented in an exponential manner.

Ten people already connected with the Institute made up the first Dreams to the Tenth Power research group. Some were staff members; others were involved in classes or programs. All participants anticipated the experiment with excitement and curiosity. By the time the selection process was completed, the group included a professional psychic, a Baptist minister, a dialysis technician from a Richmond hospital, a mathematics professor, a college student, a dream researcher, and four other professionals including myself. About half of the group had experienced lucidity in the dream state with varying degrees of success at controlling their dream awareness.

All of us had ideas about what we should do – how we might explore the possibilities entailed in dreaming together. We agreed to set up a series of meetings in the dream state over a period of approximately six months and see if we could perform certain, predetermined tasks together. The first task was to see if we could meet in dream state at all.

Before discussing the results of this first Dreams[10] experiment, let us take a brief look at the complications encountered by anyone who attempts to explore the world of dreams.

Dreams, as we generally think about them, are shimmering images which may or may not correlate with what we consider to be waking reality. Dreams occur on what has been called the symbolic level. In the dream state, while dreaming about one thing, the dreamer may picture it as another. Volumes of material have been written on the interpretation of dreams and how to understand their symbolism. Interpretative techniques range from the uniquely personal to what psychiatrist Carl Jung referred to as archetypal or universal.

Although at the time most experts tended to believe that dream symbols are best interpreted in a personal manner, some had utilized what researcher Anne Faraday describes as the gestalt technique for dream interpretation based on the work of Fritz Perls. By its nature, the gestalt technique takes in the environment of the dreamer but still is a long way from the concept of group dreaming in the sense that it focuses primarily on individuals.

Attempts to demonstrate the interface between dream reality and waking reality create obvious problems in group dreaming research. How were we to tell if we were dreaming with one another if one dreamer pictured another as a tree or a flower or an animal? And what if each of the dreamers in the group had a different symbol for each of the others in the group? Would we be able to recognize that we were dreaming together even if we managed to do so?

The dreamers in the new research group agreed on some ground rules before the experiment began. Each dreamer agreed to keep a record of *all* dreams for the six month period. We could then, we hoped, look at the dreamers' overall symbol patterns and determine whether some people accomplished the assigned tasks even if in a symbolic way.

We decided to use our intuition as well, and indicate if we felt a dream was particularly associated with the group, even if no group member appeared in recognizable form. We were exploring uncharted waters. And, as explorers have always done, we had to trust that our search would take us somewhere, if not necessarily where we originally thought we might go. After all, if Columbus had not set out to find a passage to India, Europeans might never have located the North American continent. Who knew what we dreamers might discover?

The second problem for any dream researcher involved what research terminology calls self-report. The person who records a dream recounts an experience for which there is no direct physical counterpart. Dreams only occur in the mind. And many scientists find this type of material questionable.

Some dream researchers have tried to surmount this obstacle by combining dream reports with quantitative analysis or with equipment which can record physiological functions in the laboratory while the dreamer is asleep.

The group dreaming project however, did not lend itself well to standard measurement. The dreamers would be at home rather than in the laboratory. We would write down our dreams, photocopy them, and mail them to a central point – all of this well before the age of the Internet. In order to collect data we would have to rely on the words of the dreamers, trusting both their perceptions and the accuracy of their reporting. While acknowledging that the type of qualitative research we were doing differed from the more accepted scientific norms and with the realization that the research might not be accepted as scientific, we concluded that the only thing we could do was try the experiment as we had designed it and see what happened.

As time for the official start of the project drew near, I found myself battling with anxiety. This research put a burden of considerable time and effort on an already overextended staff. Would it be worth the work? Would we have any useful results?

A few weeks before the experiment was scheduled to begin in February 1979, an incident occurred which calmed me down and gave me hope for our eventual success.

Though most of the newly-selected dream team members knew several other members of the group, no one knew everyone. To let people know who their fellow team members would be as well as to invite a couple of potential dreamers who had not been part of the planning, I mailed a letter to participants in early January.

On January 11, I received a note from Scott Sparrow, a dream researcher then on the staff of the ARE. Scott was one of the few people in the group who had already written extensively about lucid dreams.

Dear Jean,

Your letter/proposal sounds great. For a long time I've also wanted to do this, but it has always seemed that there was not enough time, or the right people. I received your letter on Tuesday the 9th. On Sunday night/Monday morning of the 7th-8th, I had a lucid dream which I feel anticipated your letter. (I recorded the dream on Monday night, before I received your letter, by the way.)

The dream shows the ambivalence which cropped up in my Dream Helper dreams: "Do I really want to be part of this group? Is what they are doing in accord with my ideals?" Even so, the central aspect of the dream was the text, which was profoundly beautiful. Such beauty has a way of dwarfing my resistances.

So what's the next step? I'm game.

Love,

Scott

Portions of Scott's rather long dream are excerpted here. Precognitive dreaming, another aspect of dreams, which has long intrigued researchers involves previewing an event before it happens in waking life. Precognitive dreaming is not uncommon. But the perplexing fact of its very existence seems to say something about the nature of time. If precognitive dreaming is possible, then events in waking time must be happening in some manner perceivable to the dreamer, prior to the waking-time event.

Even though physicists have consistently been moving away from a classical or linear approach to the description of time ever since Einstein, the ordinary person finds the notion that one moment may not simply follow another to be more than a little disquieting. For dream researchers, dream precognition, though interesting to study, has generally been relegated to the category of anomalous or extraordinary dream activity.

Still, here was Scott's dream giving him information about a project he had not even heard of yet. Christi, another member of the Dreams[10] team, to whom Scott referred in the dream, had suggested inviting Scott. Clearly Scott's dream was related to the research project though his reservations about group dreaming would emerge more fully in the months to come.

Scott's dream:

[I am]…in an office at the end of a hallway. There is a woman, the receptionist or intake person for a course in understanding or attaining altered states of consciousness. I looked at their text. It was titled: "The Nature of

Altered States According to the Cayce Readings".... I looked through the exquisitely beautiful text. Each page had a chapter or lesson title on it, and a beautiful mandala surrounded with seraphic figures....

I became lucid at some point.... I tried to sustain it (the lucidity) by simply letting it alone and "checking back" every few moments to be sure I hadn't lapsed into normal dream awareness.

The receptionist says that she has checked with the director and cleared it for me to take the course. It will take place from 2-3 a.m.! (or similar hours)....

At this point, several people emerge into the reception area. I notice Jean Campbell and another woman, whom I take for the director. Still lucid, I join them and place my hands on their shoulders in a conscious attempt to be a channel in the dream.

Finally I have to go to get in my car. I see a girl sitting on top of another car. I think she is Christi at first, but I cannot see well....

Members of the first Dreams to the Tenth Power Experiment

> Jean—Director of Poseidia Institute
> Ellen—Trance psychic employed at Poseidia Institute
> Steve—Student at the College of William and Mary
> Darius—Dialysis technician employed at a Richmond hospital
> Sid—Baptist minister
> Don—Assistant to an award-winning photojournalist
> Christi—Psychic and part-time employee of ARE
> Scott—Author of lucid dream books, employed by ARE
> Byron—Actor, artist
> Ed—College math professor

We decided to begin the Dreams to the Tenth Power project on February 14, 1979 – Valentine's Day. Because this was the first time anyone had attempted a formal study of group dreaming, we agreed to take as lighthearted an approach as possible hoping to keep performance anxiety from being another of the problems we faced.

The group would meet in the dream state at Seashore State Park in a place called The Narrows. All members of the dream team were familiar with this popular park and its walking paths. We had three goals: to see if we could get there, to see if we remembered anyone else being there, and to see if we remembered the dream upon waking. Dream lucidity had been made part of this project in only a peripheral way. All of the team members were interested in lucidity, but again we didn't want to create anxiety by setting too many difficult goals.

On this first night of the project, seven out of the ten members of the dream team remembered at least one dream. Three of the team members dreamed lucidly while the other four had non-lucid dreams which seemed to pertain to the project. Three people did not remember any dreams.

Steve said he prepared for the night's project by glancing over the names of the team members just before going to sleep. "For me, lucid dreams occur in the light levels of sleep," he said. "I often feel as though I am trying to go to sleep and I can't." In this particular lucid dream, Steve awoke (or became aware of his dreaming) in his apartment:

> In the dream I am watching a large T.V. screen or video projector. The show appears to be about the Dreams Ten experiment, but I am not sure. I have walked in during the middle of the program.... During this process, I am aware of various other team members around. They are just making visits. No one in particular—but I can't seem to leave with them. Jean Campbell appears—head and shoulders—and places both hands on my shoulders and says, "It's time. Come with me." This is <u>very</u> real. I have full sensory awareness of the touch, the voice, and the vision of Jean's presence. I'm a bit startled: my sleep level changes, but I do not wake up. I feel I can't quite leave with Jean....

In the dream, Steve goes back to watching the television program.

Darius, who did not dream lucidly, was the only one of the group who made it to a park in the dream state:

> We were walking through a park. (Someone was with me. I don't know who.) Suddenly, to the left of us on a hill, was a large, old, stately house. And to the left of this big stone house were eight or so (I did not exactly count them.) smaller stone houses that were quite old....
>
> We then walked up to the large stone house and it didn't look as if anybody lived in it, so we decided to go in and watch television....

In this dream, Darius appears to pick up on a symbolic element common to group dreaming participants – symbolizing people as houses. People seem to dream others as houses and, as particularly demonstrated in one of Don's later dreams, tend to see their own house as a symbol of their most intimate consciousness.

Darius's dream went on. As he and his companions were watching television, they heard a noise. From the hallway of the house, a woman whom he thought was Christi though he'd never met her, told him that they were expected.

> We were led outside to the enclosed porch. There were six or eight or so people sitting around. All the people had arrived as we were watching television.... I got the impression that all these people were assembled there by either a concerned individual or that a situation had developed requiring all of these people to meet....

Ed, a math professor living in Ohio, wrote that he wasn't sure any of his dreams that week had involved the dream team. On the night of the experiment, he dreamed about going to a family gathering. Several of his cousins, all close to him in age, had received excellent promotions in their jobs. As the dream closed Ed said:

> I was then told that there was a good possibility I would be offered a job as a national TV commentator based in Norfolk. The program opened, "From the Tidewater area of Virginia,".... It seemed to be a time of high energy.

Apparently several of the dreamers found a commonality in the symbol of television or projection. Ellen, who was in the process of moving to Florida, wrote that she had (as was frequently true) dreamed lucidly. In her dream, she went to meet the dream group at "a combination of Poseidia Institute's new building and my new house in Florida. The place was dark and full of unpacked boxes. Jean is there waiting for me and, since we are so early, I suggest that we go see a movie."

Ellen was the dream team member who most clearly recalled seeing others from the group while in the dream state, even though she did not find this to be very comfortable. In her dream, when she and I returned from the movies, there were two men from the team already there. One was very frightened.

> Christi arrives and these two men immediately brighten up. The scared one's aura goes back to normal. Byron arrives next, glowing as usual. He hugs Jean and then me and says, "Hello, dear," as he always does. I ask him and Jean if they want to go to the movies again....
>
> Suddenly there is a flash, a bang, a puff of smoke, and Darius appears. Jean and I crack up with laughter and everyone else just stares, dumbfounded. Darius tells us he is experimenting with ways of "telepathic travel."
>
> ...I am vaguely aware that Ed has also arrived, but is just observing. He seems to be like a ghost. His body looks less solid than everyone else's.

By this time, you might be wondering what I was doing in my own dreams during the dream group meeting, since everyone seemed to be finding me in different locations. My recall of the first dream event was this. I fell asleep thinking about a house I had designed and built a few years earlier. At a certain point, I realized I was sleeping and decided to try an out-of-body experience. OBEs, as they are commonly called, traditionally thought of as possible in dreams, happen in waking state as well. In the dream state, the individual literally perceives herself as being out of the body. It is not uncommon for me to travel when I am dreaming lucidly. Here is what I wrote when I awoke.

> As soon as I realized where I was, I thought of the Dreams Ten experiment and thought about going to wake up Ellen. But I couldn't call her, and I couldn't get out of the room! I floated out of bed all right, and I made it over to the mirror, calling "Ellen!" But when I reached the wall, I would bounce back. I knew I could get out through the wall if I'd just let go, but I was afraid I'd start whirling so fast I'd lose "consciousness."

Finally, unable to get Ellen by this means, I lay back down in bed and thought how maybe I could just <u>think</u> myself there, or maybe I could wake her up and get her to come here…. So I decided to concentrate on her face and call her name. Then I lost "consciousness."

The one encounter I did recall on the evening of the first experiment came in the ordinary dream state and it was not with any member of the dream team. Instead, I went to a restaurant where I met with psychic Jane Roberts, author of the Seth material. In the dream, I was apologizing for taking up her time saying, "I know how it is when you have ten people a day wanting you to teach them."

Jane Roberts, probably the most respected and widely published psychic of the seventies, wrote a number of books with the aid of her husband, Rob Butts. Roberts channeled these books primarily from the entity, Seth.

In *Psychic Politics*, one of the books Jane Roberts wrote from ordinary consciousness rather than delivering in an altered state, she gives one of the few accounts of group dreaming then available. In a chapter called "A Probable Class," she relates the dreams of several members of the psychic development class she was then teaching. According to Roberts, class members spontaneously dreamed with one another in a continuation of the evening's class. We will look at this phenomenon more closely in the chapter on spontaneous group dreaming.

I later learned about another dreams researcher, James Donahoe's work through his book, *Enigma*. Donahoe was conducting research similar to the Dreams[10] research at approximately the same time in California. He too took inspiration from Seth and Jane Roberts.

On the night of the first Dreams to the Tenth Power experiment, of the two remaining team members who recalled dreams, Christi (perceived by several other team members to be present at their meetings) found herself in an ordinary dream in a boat on an ocean cruise. As this dream progressed, Christi, the dreamer, became increasingly frustrated because no one seemed to be clear on where the boat was going – an indication of the uncharted waters of our research.

Finally, after more of this sailing about, Christi reports: "Then I comment, 'This isn't the dream I want. There isn't even anyone on board from the dream group. Besides, I want to become lucid now and I'm not.'"

Byron, who remembered only that he had been dreaming but not what his dreams were about, called me the next morning to ask, "Was I there?"

After this first night of the Dreams to the Tenth Power research, we recognized that something was definitely happening. Many of the group members had been conscious of wanting to meet with the dream group while in the dream state. Even those who had not been lucid reported dreams which included group members. Several had attempted to reach the meeting place or had dreams that correlated with the dreams of other team members.

As we moved toward the second meeting night two weeks later, interest was high. We were soon to find out that dreaming together might raise even more questions than it brought answers.

On February 24, the day she moved to Daytona Beach, Florida, Ellen had the following dream:

I am in a gray place that I sometimes find myself in when I am in trance or when I am meditating. It's a place where I often get information. Either I hear voices or I just simply know things I didn't know before.

People are visiting me. They are gray and shapeless. Also they have no emotion. We have quiet, short discussions that are very intellectual and rational. Suddenly I realize that I am meeting the dream experiment group. I think to myself, "This isn't very bizarre or interesting, so I must be dreaming." (Usually it's just the opposite. I notice that things are bizarre and strange and that lets me know I'm dreaming.)

The people fade away and Byron appears. Byron is surrounded by white light and energy. He looks terrific and it feels good to be close to him. I tell him about the other people I saw and he laughs....

The second dream meeting night was scheduled for February 28. Again we would meet in dream state in Seashore State Park, and this time I told group members that I would give them a message. The task was to see if they got it.

As evidenced by Ellen's letter, even before the second meeting date arrived, people had begun to have some second thoughts about the group. Quite possibly our success with the first stage of the project, obvious even to the untrained eye, had a deeper impact than any of the participants at first suspected.

Reverend Sid, who prior to the experiment had been a prolific dreamer, dried up. He stopped remembering any of his dreams, even those which came on non-experiment nights. On the day of the second team effort, Sid drove to Seashore State Park. He stood among the dunes and tall, old cypress trees to see if he could urge his dream consciousness to cooperate. He had no luck that night, nor did several of the other dreamers.

The message I sent for the Dreams Ten members to receive the night of the second group dream was "Love yourself." I meditated upon this message for about an hour before I went to sleep that night, thinking about stories I'd heard of Edgar Cayce. When the first Glad Helpers prayer healing group was formed at the ARE many years earlier, Cayce would arrive in people's sleeping consciousness to wake them up for a 2:00 a.m. meditation. Edgar Cayce I was not. Still, Virginia Beach is the ideal place for telepathic work. Many psychics believe its proximity to the ocean acts to enhance their abilities.

In the dream state this time, I at least managed to get out of my bedroom. I went so far as to arrive in the park before I again lost lucidity. Then in ordinary dream state I had a conversation with Ed. Our conversation though had nothing to do with the group dreaming project.

Other members of the group fared little better. Scott, who went to bed with a headache said: "I awoke at 3:30 a.m. with the knowledge that I'd had a dream with Jesus in it. I still felt the love and unconditional acceptance that such dreams invariably bring."

"The first dream," Scott said in the note accompanying his dreams, "certainly reflects the message you (Jean) were sending, for I rarely ever 'allow' myself to dream of Jesus." A second dream that night though showed Scott that he was feeling like an outsider to the group. In the second dream, he went to Canada to visit friends and to go on a fishing trip. When he arrived, the others had already left. Scott said he felt "hurt and surprised."

Christi wrote that she woke at 5:30 a.m. with this dream:

I am teaching a class. I feel an inflow of energy and realize I am being filled with the Holy Spirit. It is a pleasant feeling and I wonder how this fits with our Dreams[10] experiment. I can't see any connection.

On the one hand, it could be argued that Christi had a direct hit on the message I was sending the group. In her dream, she was filled with the Holy Spirit, the spirit of love. And she simultaneously wondered what this had to do with the experiment. On the other hand, it would be easy enough to believe that this dream was not a hit because Christi saw no one in the dream group, nor did she go to the designated place. It was clear that we had a lot to learn about group dreaming.

Christi did dream about groups that night, in all of the dreams she recorded—as did Ed, Byron, and Ellen. But no one dreamed specifically of the dream group or the park.

In Christi's dreams, groups met in the wilderness, which might be considered a park of sorts, and a restaurant. Ed went lucidly to a group workshop on losing body awareness while lucid, but the group he dreamed of was not the Dreams to the Tenth Power group. Interestingly enough, Ed's dream ended with Helen Keller dying in a bedroom upstairs. According to Ed, she was "dying in triumph," with music and dance. Ed saw a connection between this and the message I was sending but it was obviously at a feeling level. Without having seen Christi's dream accounts, he also dreamed the next night about eating in a restaurant with a woman named Anna Hill. Christi's entire name was Christiana, a name that she infrequently used. Still I felt it was stretching a bit to make a correlation between Ed's dreams and Christi's, or between the message I sent the group and Helen Keller dying in an upstairs bedroom.

Byron almost came the closest to meeting with the group. In his dream, he was with a group of people in a large hall or "recreation center."

We are waiting for the evening program to begin. Music is playing over the intercom system. Then I hear some kind of verbal instructions over the music. I feel I must turn these off, so I kneel down under the counter to turn down the volume... Just as I feel I have located the control dial and am reaching for it...my alarm goes off and I wake up. (Not in the dream, but I actually awaken in my bed.)

We will never know what Byron might have dreamed had he stayed asleep.

Ellen who, as she wrote, was "living amid unpacked boxes," kept telling herself in dream state that she needed to get to the Park, to the Dreams[10] experiment. But she ended up in a maze with "friends from Virginia Beach."

Darius, Steve, Don and Sid remembered no dreams the night of the experiment.

During the week that followed, a synchronistic sidelight to the Dreams[10] experiment began to take shape. On the first Thursday in March, I began teaching an Advanced Psychic Development class. One of the professional psychics who worked for us taught with me. In the class, Darius, Sid and Steve met one another for the first time in physical reality. Had we been taking a more formal approach to the dream experiment, this class could certainly have been seen as contaminating the data. But because what we were doing was exploratory research, we considered the class to be only one factor of many to be considered. As far as the Dreams to the Tenth Power research went, this meeting between participants in the experiment seemed to have beneficial results.

The day after his first class, Darius wrote, "I was with Jean Campbell for a very lengthy conversation (in dream state). There were a lot of people standing around listening to us. The theme seemed to be very serious."

That same night I dreamed I was with the psychic development class, talking particularly to Darius. I taught them all an exercise in making faces at one another so they wouldn't be so serious. Darius, who had not been having any great luck at remembering the group dreaming, spontaneously shared a dream with me, no problem.

For her own part, Ellen, who was unaware that the psychic development class was taking place until she heard about it days later in a letter, had a dream Thursday night about me and the other teacher in the class. She became lucid, thinking, "Something special must be happening because I haven't dreamed about or thought about Steve (the other teacher) in ages." In her letter to me, she went on, "Realizing that I'm dreaming, I look for you to ask if you're aware too."

Despite the growing number of shared dream events, members of the dream team seemed beset with a growing sense of discomfort. Ellen had written, almost since the beginning, of feeling uncomfortable with the project and people in it. Scott felt left out. Don and Sid had yet to recall their first dreams, and others expressed a sense of vague anxiety about the project.

The commitment to the work we were doing was still strong however, so the third dream event was set for Wednesday, March 14, 1979. Jokingly in the letter I sent to announce this date, I quipped, "Beware the Ides of March!" Little did I know how true that statement would turn out to be. Don, returning from New York where he worked part time as an assistant to a well-known author, said he felt slightly under the weather. He asked to have the group attempt a healing on him in the dream state. His letter, written the day after the third dream meeting says it all:

Dear Group:
Thank you for the healing! Rather I should have submitted myself to a voodoo rite. Arose from my Procrustean bed with an instant cold (HUZZACH!), a colitis attack, and a thumping tooth. Staggered to my mirror to see if I'd come back in the wrong body. No such luck.

After this opening, Don's letter continues with an account of his dream from the previous night, the night of the dream experiment. About his sister who appears in the dream, he says, "She has been…an alcoholic all her adult life. This was, for a period of years, very hard on me…."

"Dreamed I was in a large mansion surrounded by much activity," Don writes:

It was a social gathering, but there were other levels of activity going on at a more subtle level. I was somewhat apprehensive about these untried, untested, and barely-perceived goings on. My sister appeared as a slim and lovely girl, as she once was, radiant with health, vitality, and a kind of calm and sophisticated mastery of the situation. Felt relieved that I would fare better with her around.

Was Don symbolizing the dream group as the people in the mansion of his dream? Were his feelings about the group summarized by his perception of the "untried, untested, and barely perceived goings on"? More than once, as the experiment progressed, Don would dream of rowdy parties of people breaking into his house. For Don the experience of this target date was admittedly less than satisfactory.

Don reported that he felt the dream talked about his relationship with the dream group even though no specific member of the group appeared. In this instance, as is generally true with dream work, we must assume that the dreamer has the greatest insight into the dream.

None of the other members of the dream team wanted to claim responsibility for Don's worsened condition. No one dreamed about Don. Byron, Darius, Ellen, Christi, Sid and I all reported recalling no dreams whatsoever. Scott despondently reported "another fishing dream that didn't seem to have any relevance to the group." (Though one might ask, I suppose, if these fishing dreams had no relevance, why did he keep having them on group dreaming nights?) "We caught a nice Spanish mackerel in a plowed field," Scott exclaimed.

Steve had four dreams. None of them he said, seemed to have any relevance. "I did prove one thing though," Steve noted. "I make terrible notes with the lights out!"

Of the entire group, Ed was the only one aside from Don, whose dream seemed to pertain to the experiment, and even that was probably stretching it. His dream, though all about groups, contained no specific correlations with the project.

Darius commented about the experiment in dream healing in his next letter to the group. "Don should now know what it means when they say, 'a pox on you, sir.' The stuff really works, only we got mixed up."

Darius also said that when he told his wife about the dream healing experiment, her only comment "in between bursts of laughter," was, "Don't ever dream for me!"

Chapter Two - We Meet at the Clock Tower

Two months into the Dreams to the Tenth Power project, several members of the group felt discouraged. People who wanted to dream lucidly were not dreaming lucidly. Some people still had not had a single dream about the group or anyone in it. Sid was without dreams for what was now the second month and Steve remarked one night at Psychic Development class, "I don't know if I like having all these people running around in my dreams." In saying this, he verbalized one of the most common of all complaints I hear from participants in group dreaming experiments.

Dreams are generally believed to be personal and private, relating only symbolically to waking life. They are not perceived, in any general sort of way, to be interactions between the dreamer and the waking world.

No matter how interesting the idea of group dreaming may be at an intellectual level, when the fact of shared dreaming hits home, it tends to induce a kind of culture shock. The dream world suddenly becomes a shared world, one in which other dreamers might participate. In the case of extended group dreaming experiments, a group of dreamers may share dreams repeatedly. An activity previously perceived as intensely private comes to be seen as social. This change in the way dreams are regarded can be transformational.

This first group dreaming experiment, we discovered, was a little like running a marathon. It seemed to stretch on and on while in the meantime the lives of the individual dreamers were changing. Ed was happy with a new job; Darius phoned the office with the jubilant news that he and his wife were expecting their first child; at Reverend Sid's church, the congregation was arguing over whether they could afford repairs to the sacristy. For all of us, the task of writing down every dream plus keeping a waking-life journal in order to pick out the day-residue in our dreams seemed like a heavy chore. Still we persisted, believing that what we were doing might one day enhance the world's understanding of dreaming.

In an effort to lighten the mood of the Dreams[10] dreamers, I encouraged some team work for the fourth dream meeting on March 28. My suggestion was that team members pair up for the meeting, that dreamers who generally dreamed lucidly might go (in dream state) to wake up partners who were having trouble being lucid or remembering a dream.

The idea of partnering brought new energy to the group, and the resultant pairs: Ellen and Byron, Steve and Sid, Scott and Don, Ed and Darius, and Christi and me, were eager to see if this new idea would work.

On the night of the fourth dream meeting, I dozed in and out of sleep, trying to make sure that I contacted Christi. I finally managed to do this while maintaining lucidity, in the early hours of the morning.

I asked Christi whether she had dreamed me. She said that no, she had not dreamed about me, but told me she did have a dream in which three women were trying on party dresses, and another dream in which she worked out the results of a class she was teaching.

The following morning I was disappointed to discover that Christi remembered no dreams at all – neither our dream meeting nor the dreams she told me about in dream state.

The other pairs in the group had no more luck that Christi and I had with our partnering. Steve reported that he had been lucid on experiment night and had in fact reached Sid, though he wasn't sure if he'd awakened him. Sid said he remembered no dreams on the meeting night, though after more than a month of no dream recall, he was excited to have finally begun recalling dreams again. Earlier in the week, Sid reported he'd had a dream in which he helped to load three boxcars full of garbage. His round face lit with a smile when he said, "I guess this dream group thing has brought up a lot of garbage for me."

Although neither Ellen nor Byron remembered their dreams from the night of the fourth meeting, two nights later Steve said he had encountered Byron while he (Steve) was having a lucid dream. Steve said Byron was busy changing the composition of his face and "We had a conversation about whether Byron was really himself or my perception of him."

To anyone who has never experienced the phenomenon of having another dreamer apparently enter a dream and try out different masks or personas, such an idea must seem bizarre. Yet many people who have explored shared dreaming have reported exactly this. Two or three years before this Dreams to the Tenth Power experiment began, while sharing a dream with my friend Noreen, I encountered her rapidly changing faces. Because I was lucid in the dream, I asked Noreen, "Are you, you, or my idea of you?" She laughed and replied, "A little of both."

Dream lucidity is in one sense, like being awake in ordinary reality. Though perceptions may be very vivid, there is a clear awareness that, "This is a dream and I'm awake." At the same time, because dream reality is much more fluid and plastic than waking reality, because the dreamer can do things that are generally considered impossible in waking life, and because dream reality is where we accept that objects or people may masquerade as symbols, the question of identity can easily occur. The practiced lucid dreamer begins to distinguish real from symbolic levels of the lucid dream. Of course in the case of a shared lucid dream, it helps if both dreamers remember the encounter later.

The night of this fourth experiment, Don and Scott made no connection; nor did Darius and Ed. Darius wrote, "Ed, where were you? I had the outside lights and the coffee on. You had to come the farthest. My male Psychic Dog always lets me know when strange things are occurring, by barking if I'm starting to float around. So he should have barked...."

Don's comment was, "If Scott Sparrow came and got me, I was totally incapable of being aware of it." However, Don recorded a dream from March 27, the night before the fourth dream event, which reiterated his concerns about people breaking into his apartment, which he had already identified as being symbolic of his consciousness.

Was lying in bed very comfortably in an apparently new and elegant apartment I have constructed somewhere in the universe.... Everything in the apartment was clean, neat and in order. No disturbance or disarray anywhere. Suddenly an undisciplined and noisy group of partygoers passed my bedroom window and summoned the audacity to bang on my front door, demanding entry. I lay there silently, hoping they'd go away, but no such luck. Got up and went to the door. The moment I opened it, they all poured in (about ten or fifteen of them) and began partying, completely unmindful of waking me up or disturbing the formality of my apartment. They were carrying half-finished champagne bottles and were quite sloshed. I became more and more distraught as they proceeded to lurch about my home, knocking things over and spilling booze on carpets.

I wrote to the Dream Team on April 9:

In my own dreams, either I'm very suggestible or I have been picking up on dream events.... After talking with Don about his March 28 dream, I dreamed both Friday night and Saturday about being at wild parties in Don's apartment. I recognized the people in only one of these, and there were definitely members of the Dreams[10] group there. One of these people was Ed, who was pouring a drink on the carpet.

Of all the members of the Dream Team, Darius had the prize-winner from this fourth meeting night of near hits and total misses. He didn't meet with Ed, but what he did manage to do is not entirely clear either. "I had two dreams that were just rememberable," Darius wrote:

So I put them on the tape recorder. Then I thought I could forget them. Later, I realized that I had <u>dreamed</u> this taping of the two dreams and did not have them on the recorder. Then I had another dream and actually put it on the recorder. Later I wasn't sure if I did that or dreamed it. It was really strange. That's never happened to me before. So somewhere those two dreams are recorded!

In dream literature, we call the type of dream that Darius experienced a false awakening. These are not uncommon. In conversation with people about their dreams, I have heard people tell of as many as two or three false awakenings in one night, where each time they thought they were awake until some bizarre dream event brought to consciousness the fact that they were still dreaming. Dream researcher Curtiss Hoffman has labeled these nesting dreams.

Tantalized by the number of dreams recalled on the target date, and the number of near hits, the group responded enthusiastically to Don's suggestion that we try dreaming on the new and full moon, rather than at the customary interludes. He suggested that the lunar cycles might promote clear dreaming. April 12 was the night of the new moon; it was also Passover. The group agreed to meet that night and following discussion via mail and telephone, we concluded that most people felt more comfortable working in pairs as we had on March 28.

For this meeting, Steve suggested that since many members of the group enjoyed meeting in Seashore State Park, we should meet this time near the clock tower on the cupola roof of the Old Cavalier Hotel, a landmark on the Virginia Beach oceanfront.

This idea really caught on. Fired by enthusiasm for the meeting place and hoping that the moon would enhance dreaming skills, almost every group member recorded a dream on the night of our fifth meeting. Several people had what could only be called direct hits.

Darius detailed a record number of seven dreams on the night of the fifth dream meeting. He wrote in some amazement: "This series of dreams all occurred between 2:05 a.m. and 3:30 a.m. Almost every 10 to 12 minutes I had a dream. Using the recorder allows me not to shuffle for lights, pens, etc, and I don't really wake up." In his third dream of the evening, Darius reported:

There was a long incline of steps that went straight up about a 25-degree angle, a very long incline. And I was sitting at the bottom looking up. I knew these were the steps to get to the Cavalier Hotel. The architecture was the same as the old hotel.

An earlier dream of the series found Darius and his wife Kay on an "outing." "We kept going up and down a large hill," Darius wrote. "There were all types of other people gathered there. Lots of people coming and going." Other dreams of the series involved the now-familiar symbols of television sets and fishing. In one of the dreams, Darius and a friend received a letter from me. Darius concluded his message to the group by saying: "I did not get to the top of the Cavalier, but I don't think I have ever had such an intense period of dreaming as this session. I kept saying over and over, 'Must get to the Cavalier,' or 'Where is Ed?'"

Ed was having his own difficulties. On the morning of April 9 Ed dreamed:

I was with Jean Campbell and a group in a classroom. Each person had written a short paper as an introduction to others in the group. One fellow in a white shirt, maybe Steve, was working on a proper means of breathing.... He wondered why developing something in the physical body was so important when there were so many other realities available. I explained that all realities in which we exist are important and therefore we should learn and grow in each.

On the morning of April 12, the day of the dream experiment, Ed dreamed that he was meeting with a group of people in a "compound" which had a "complex of houses and rooms with bodies of water around." In the dream, he met Randy, a college friend who lived in Richmond – as did Ed's dream partner Darius – and "a couple of other friends." As close as he had come to the goal for the fifth session, Ed concluded his letter with these words:

> The first dream feels like it may have been an actual group meeting, though the comments about breathing were certainly relevant to me as well as to the ones in the group I was talking to.
>
> I did not receive Jean's letter until the day after this second dream. So I did not consciously know what the dream night was all about....

In the days of the Dreams to the Tenth Power research, communicating by mail created unforeseen difficulties. This led us to lengthen the time between target dates in later experiments.

On the fifth meeting date of the Dreams[10] experiment, Scott, Christi, Steve, Don and Sid all recalled non-lucid dreams which had no apparent bearing on the targeted group activity but Ellen's dream inspired a cartoon drawing from Darius, one of many with which he entertained the group.

> I am on a Greyhound bus, taking a tour. Byron, Christi, Ed, Scott, and Don (among others) are on the bus.... It's early in the morning and we are going to visit a city far away. I'm sitting next to Darius. We are in the very front seat on the right side. He is telling me that I don't love people enough. In the dream I am very relaxed, comfortable, don't mind at all what Darius is saying....
>
> The bus stops and we are at a kind of scenic overlook to the city. We all get out and walk up a short, steep hill to the overlook. I walk slowly and carefully since there are lots of small, loose rocks. I am contemplating what Darius said.
>
> Suddenly I know I'm dreaming. I feel <u>exactly</u> as I do when awake. There is no difference in my perceptions. At first I am so delighted to be lucid that I start to play—floating up into the air, looking around, etc. Then I get serious and decide to go visit Jean. I start flying to Virginia Beach, but I am shocked to find myself settling into my body. I fight to stay asleep, but alas....

If Ellen did not reach the Cavalier Hotel in her dream that night, she certainly seemed to meet the group. Her dream also returns us to one of the central questions of dream lucidity. If it is possible to be <u>awake</u> in the dream, and yet fly or travel through space, are those realities we could be awake to all the time? With what sort of training? As we shall see in later chapters, dream lucidity and flying dreams often go hand in hand.

Whereas Ellen managed to reach the group of this fifth meeting night, I did just the opposite. I arrived at the hotel in dream state, but missed the group entirely. Here is what I wrote:

> I fell asleep almost immediately after turning off the television at 2:30 a.m. Almost as soon as I fell asleep, I was aware I was in my room and

dreaming.... I set off to look for Christi (which I did for some time without success.)

By then, feeling hopelessly lost, I ended up wandering, still lucid, in a town at evening. But then I sighted a building down the street which made my heart rise. I was looking at the Old Cavalier. It was evening and there were people coming down the long flight of stairs in evening clothes. I had the feeling of being in the 1920s (the heyday of this magnificent old building). I headed for the hotel and made my way to the cupola, where I met a young man...in evening clothes...a black tux and white shirt. He stood at the front of the copper-domed part of the roof. He had in front of him, on a stand, a guest book. He handed me a pen to write my name down. I looked around me, but no one else was there. I looked at him and said, "They've all gone, haven't they?" (meaning the dream team) He said yes. At that point, I gave up and went on to more ordinary dreaming.

During this first Dreams to the Tenth Power experiment, as people on the dream team began to recognize that in some cases at least, they seemed to actually be dreaming together, a sense of the potential of this type of shared dreaming began to grow.

As we moved into the spring of the year, people in the experiment group talked with others not in the experiment group and there began a sort of cross-pollination process. People who were not in the experiment group, friends, families, staff and students at the Institute, began to dream with the Dreams[10] team. At times it seemed as if the very air we breathed buzzed with the excitement of shared dreaming.

In the middle of April, I walked into the Advanced Psychic Development Class one night to find Steve, Darius and Ed gathered on a sofa in the comfortable house in Norfolk where the class was being held. The three of them stopped their conversation, looking up at me. Steve was at the end of the couch. I touched his arm. "So when are you getting married?" I asked in a bantering tone. All three of the men looked at me as if I'd lost my wits entirely. Steve's eyes opened in astonishment as he shook his head no. Even though he had been dating someone at college, he said, they were far from getting married.

Sitting down on the arm of the couch, I told the three of them what had happened the night before. I'd been half asleep, but still awake enough to be aware that my partner, Leonard, was talking on the phone. He was talking with someone who planned to be married in June. Suddenly I had the clear, strong feeling that it was Steve on the phone saying that he'd be married in June.

Darius, Steve, Ed and I had a good laugh over my apparently off-base precognition.

Ed, looking a little pensive, began to tell us about a series of dreams he'd been having about a woman with long, black hair. "For weeks now," he told us, "I've been dreaming about this fantastically beautiful woman." He looked to see how we were taking this. "She was in the dream I had on Dreams[10] night about the escape from the physical." We nodded our encouragement. "She was sitting there and I said, 'Now that's the one who's been spending nights with me for a while.'"

Ed reminded us of the far_memory book *Eyes of Horus*, written by British psychic Joan Grant. In that book, the main character, RaHab Hotep, meets his future bride several times in dream state prior to their meeting in waking state.

I asked Ed if he'd been feeling like this woman he met in the dream state was someone he might eventually marry. "That's the feeling I've had," he grinned as we all moved toward the center of the room for class to begin.

A recent addition to the Institute's staff, Lola Murrell had been friends with Steve since high school. She and her soon-to-be husband, Barry, often shared dreams with Steve and others.

Love was in the air as well as dreams. Over the weekend following the class, I took a trip to the mountains of western Virginia, where the redbud trees were just beginning to bloom. On Sunday night, not long after I returned, the phone rang in my office. It was Steve.

"I've got something to tell you," he chuckled.

"When are you getting married?" I asked. The words popped out of my mouth with no thought.

"June wedding," he replied, as we both dissolved into laughter. "It's not fair that you knew about it before I did." And truly he had not expected to propose to his future bride that weekend. The person he proposed to was not the girl he'd been dating, but his roommate, Patricia, who was actually engaged to someone else. The two of them had been sharing an off-campus apartment space for over a year, each dating other people, convinced that they were only good friends, until that weekend when they found out otherwise.

The sixth meeting of the Dreams to the Tenth Power experiment was scheduled for May second, but the group had also decided to schedule a physical meeting at the Poseidia Institute office on May fifth. By now, most of the dream team members had met in person, and there was a growing sense of camaraderie. People wanted to get together to discuss some of the issues and questions this experiment had raised for them.

I suggested that we might use the sixth meeting night to see if we could precognitively dream the upcoming physical reality meeting. But apparently the group felt otherwise. Ellen, still living in Florida and unable to attend the physical meeting, was the only person to respond with a dream to the sixth meeting goal.

"The big night was May 2," she wrote, "on which I had (appropriately) two dreams.

1) I am at a farewell party given for me by the PI group. Everyone is giving me presents. Jean gives me a long dress which is pink and brown and

blue all covered with some kind of glittery stuff. My mother is also at the party and she tells me that the dress is horrible and would look awful on me. She says I should give it to Christi, that it would look good on her. Every time I get a present, she tells me what's wrong with it. Finally someone (Darius I think) gives me a scarf that has blue and while flowers on it. I like it and so does Mom.

2) I am at the airport with the Dreams[10] group. Everyone is getting onto a huge airplane. I am riding in some kind of tram that is going along the edge of the runway. I see that I have gotten there too late and the plane will leave without me. I sit in the tram and watch the plane take off. It doesn't get far before it turns around and comes back. There is something wrong with the engine and I am really glad that I wasn't on it, even if it didn't crash. I feel relieved that I can go with the group on the next plane.

She added that these were the first dreams she'd remembered since the last dream meeting; though, "I do feel the presence of the group very strongly all the time and feel very close to everyone except Scott, whom I have never met. If I just got my mail on time to know when the dream nights are *before* they happen, it might help...."

The day of the physical-world meeting dawned, bright and clear, an already-hot Saturday in southern Virginia. Four members of the dream team sent their regrets. In addition to Ellen's expected absence, Scott and Christi both had to work that day. Byron was unexpectedly called away to a funeral. But the rest of us: Sid, Darius, Ed, Don, Steve, and I were all there and eager to talk. Questions about the startling intimacy of group dreaming, the concept of reality creation, how to integrate the awareness we were gaining into daily life, and exercises for lucid dreaming were the topics of the day. We met in my large office, where I turned on the tape recorder for later transcription of the entire session.

Almost as soon as Steve came into the room, he began to regale the group with a dream from the night before:

Patricia (his fiancée) Barry and Lola, Sid, Jean and Leonard and I were together in the dream when I said I was getting married." He looked around the room laughing.

Where upon you all sat down at the table across from me. Everyone else was in the room, Jean, but I was the one you were talking to. And you say, "Don't do it. Move in with her. All of you get married together. Have a group marriage. Individual marriage is out. We all tried it and it didn't work."

I felt as guilty as if I had been in the room with him, telling him just that, though I didn't remember any such dream. On a technical level, it would be easy enough to say that Steve was only having a dream that expressed his anxiety about his upcoming marriage, but given the ongoing banter about me knowing his wedding plans before he did, this position was difficult to maintain. It was only natural that after this, the conversation would turn to the subject of the unexpected effect of shared dreaming with a group—the feeling that suddenly several other people might have access to one's most intimate thoughts and feelings.

"I believed so long and so hard that people appearing in my dreams were parts of me or things I was creating that the other way didn't seem to make any sense," Steve noted. "But as we started working on Dreams[10], I started admitting to myself that other people could be appearing in my dreams as themselves. That was kind of scary. And I also realized that just because I believed the other way so hard, of course I was having trouble with the new way."

"What I'm finding with this project," Ed said, "is that I am making connections with people in an emotional, non-visual, nonverbal way. The experience is just as 'real' as actually seeing people in my dreams, though it doesn't lend itself to description as easily."

"There's a lot going on with Dreams[10]," Darius chimed in. "Things I can't really put into words. I am really experiencing the way it's being set up as being outside of the way we're supposed to do things. There are things going on which I can't quite put my finger on, a rapport with the whole group." Heads nodded around the room.

"Well my way of working with the process over the years," Sid said slowly," has been to look at dreams narrowly, in the spectrum of what's been experienced in my family. Because all of my family are dreamers. In fact, my whole clan is dreamers, and most often when we dream about a particular thing, it comes about."

Sid paused as if deciding whether to express his next thought. "So when you dream about an event and it comes about in the material plane or physical world, that's what you've been calling reality creation?"

In an attempt to soften the blow, Ed pointed out that not all precognitive dreams turned into physical reality. "Some of them are just warnings," he chuckled.

Sid shook his head. "I think the hardest thing for me is that I am creating reality," he said. "Because, well what idiot would create this kind of problem and pain, you know?" We laughed in agreement.

"Like I had a problem in my church," he went on. "And I heard this voice say, 'You can change the whole thing.' And it scared me. You become very leery of knowing you have such power to affect. But in Dreams Ten, I think a lot of us are having problems. I think we're all afraid of this ability to make it happen."

The rest of us were saved the discomfort of a response to Sid's soul-searching questions when Don arrived at the meeting over an hour late. He'd overslept, but apparently for good reason.

Rather than paraphrase the experience Don told us, let me include it here as he recorded it later for the records of the experiment. The astral projection Don describes is another term for the out-of-body experience or OBE:

I had astrally projected and was singing a song with Jean Campbell. Afterward we embraced happily. Then I found myself being pursued back to my body by a man with a shiny bald head. I entered my bedroom through the east wall, which was not solid but appeared more to be made of screening, like a screened in porch. I jumped into my body but nervously watched the bald man pacing up and down outside my bedroom wall.

I began to awake, but was not yet fully integrated with my physical body. It must have been about 5 a.m. The birds were just beginning to chirp. I lay there listening to them begin to pick up the tempo as the light was starting to dawn. I realized that I was experiencing every chirp and warble in a sequence, remarkably slowed down. Each sound was part of a building orchestration of praise. The joy of the birds and of nature at dawn was transmitting itself to me. The first intermittent cheeps and peeps were not unlike listening to an orchestra warm up before a performance. Then gradually the clouds and clusters of bird calls began to form an orchestrated piece, and finally they began to perform the most exquisite, delicate musical score which was suspended above and beamed down upon me from a canopy overhead.

My chest began to expand with happiness; I was hyperventilating with the joy of nature at sunrise. Though it was basically a peaceful feeling, I could hardly contain myself. Then the thought came to me: Each dawn is a creation. Each dawn is THE creation. Anything is possible in each day—renewal, rejuvenation, transformation. There is no past.

Another thought followed as I lay entranced: I am in the Presence. This immediately translated itself into: I am in the Present, the eternal present. The Presence is in the Present Moment. The Noumenon [1] is the Now.

Darius broke the awed silence that followed Don's dream account with a wry chuckle. "Well, I guess that answers our questions about reality creation," he said.

Don agreed. "The way Dreams to the Tenth Power approaches these expanded awarenesses," he said, "is pretty unique."

As the afternoon sun slanted through the windows of my office, the conversation turned to the subject of lucid dreaming. Although several people in the group were accomplished lucid dreamers, others were still trying to attain lucidity. So naturally people were interested in tips and techniques.

To put this conversation into a broader context, it had been less than five years since British dream expert Ann Faraday had claimed to a group of people attending at a party at my house that she had tried lucid dreaming and didn't think much of it. Most of the serious dream researchers she knew, Ann said, believed that if lucid dreaming were possible at all, there were very few people who could do it.

Thus, on the word of this well-traveled scholar, who maintained correspondence with dream researchers around the globe, we concluded that the group gathered for the first Dreams to the Tenth Power experiment must be quite an extraordinary group. At least five out of the ten of us were lucid dreamers.

"You had a tape of Ellen's once which suggested a very efficient method of being lucid in the dream," Darius said to me. Then turning to the others he said, "This method utilizes a round circle of light in the conscious state and taking that, eventually, into the dream state.... I started doing that for three or four days, but then it happened to me when I was in the car, so I stopped doing it. It did happen a couple of times in the dream state."

"Right, Darius," the others chided. "No lucid dreaming while driving."

"What happened to the spot of light after you got used to it?" I asked him.

Animatedly, Darius explained. "Well, if you're not having any lucid dreams, you can visualize a bright, round circle of light in this (waking) state, and then project it into the dream state. Eventually, you'll reach the point where you'll project it into dream state and then you'll start remembering, because what you're doing is bridging the gap between those two circles of light. Instead of separating the two states and saying, 'Here I am conscious; and here I'm unconscious,' or living in such a way that the conscious is separated from the unconscious, this exercise says to combine them."

More stories followed about how people became lucid or maintained lucidity. Finally we agreed that we needed to wrap up the discussion so that some group members could begin long drives home. The last statement of the day came from Steve, who pronounced grumpily:

I'm doing this thing now where I have a dream that's not a lucid dream, and I'm sitting there telling this dream to someone while I'm still asleep. Then I wake up and remember the dream. One dream that I've written about that was on a non-Dreams[10] night, I waked up several times.... I was telling someone in my dreams... I was going through my dreams with Jean Campbell, telling her all the dreams and saying, "And I didn't have any dreams with you." Then at that time (still dreaming) I remembered a dream I'd had with Jean in it. So then I told her the dream. All this while I was dreaming. It's getting very complex.

Complex was what Steve labeled the dream work we were doing and it was an accurate description. In addition to keeping a schedule of predetermined meeting nights and goals, while developing some very distinct dreaming skills, the dreamers faced a number of questions raised by their success in actually performing these tasks. Questions arose like: What is the relationship between waking and dreaming? If I create my dreams, do I create my waking life as well? And is all experience shared experience like group dreaming?

Like other members of the dream team, I was feeling the effects of a structured, long-term program of group dreaming. On the Monday following the physical meeting, I went to sleep with the idea of looking for dream guides. Sid had brought the subject up. I'd never had much luck with dream guides, though others I knew had regular visits from entities such as spirit guides, angels, deceased relatives, or teachers and found them very helpful. I was feeling like I could use any kind of help in understanding the process in which we were involved. The dream I recorded that night was:

> I kept going from ordinary dream state to lucid state. When I would become lucid, I would be confronting some particular type of "guide." The first time it was a snarling dog. I faced him and he turned around. The second time, it was a large, fierce-looking man. I made a sound and faced him. He turned away.
>
> Finally, I was attending a graduation ceremony which was being held in a farm house. The graduation was from a class in lucid dreaming, and the final exam was to either fly or teleport from the house to the barn loft.... The group was, in part, Dreams Ten members and, in part, people with whom I'd gone to grade school. I realized when I got to the barn loft that, even though I knew how to teleport, I still hadn't learned to whistle; and I had to (amid much laughter) get one of my elementary school friends to whistle for everyone's attention.

For our May twenty-third dream event, the dreamers who attended the physical-world meeting had agreed upon something a little less concrete than what we had been doing, as if dreaming is ever concrete. Don and Ed both argued that a nonphysical location might be easier to reach than a physical one. Steve argued that he wanted team members to recognize the entity formed by all of us dreaming together, so the assigned task became to "Meet at Green and Become the Group."

This was the most abstract goal to date, but it netted some unique results. For the first time since the project began, every one of the dream team members responded in writing. This was something of a success all by itself. Most research done with human subjects is short-term. It can be completed within a few hours or a day in a laboratory setting. The members of the Dreams[10] group, living normally fast-paced and high-pressured lives, had taken on a significant commitment by just agreeing to participate in a six-month long experiment.

Steve's response to the seventh meeting date arrived first:

> I remembered. Did you? Here's the dream. I am at a neighbor's house and I notice a large moth on the curtain... I am outside the same house and there is Jean Campbell, disguised as a bush. The bush has been trimmed too closely, has tiny flowers, and is a poor disguise. Jean asks me several times if I am

sure I'll remember seeing her. I repeatedly say yes and am a little put off by Jean's lack of confidence in me. Finally I tell her that this experience is absolutely real, that it is no different from any of the other times we have talked, because the dogwood trees in the woods behind us are upside down....

Well according to Steve we met in green all right—the green of a bush.

Personally, I generated one of those experiences which baffle anyone attempting to collate group dreaming research material. For the first time since the research project began, I totally forgot the dream date. I went to bed exhausted that night after a day of strawberry picking with nothing on my mind but sleep. Here is what I dreamed:

I was in the yard of a farm house.... There was a small shed in the yard. A large, black dog came from the shed, baring his teeth at us. I pointed my forefinger at him saying, "Get thee hence, Satan!" After the second time of this, he turned around and slunk back into the shed.

Then I was in the farm house and Tom (a member of the Psychic Development class) was crushing a plant between his fingers. He gave some of it to me to smell. We looked out the window toward the shed. He told me the plant was vervain or verbena and that it was good for driving away evil spirits.

The remainder of the dream included other members of the psychic development class, but it contained no members of the class who were participating in Dreams[10]. I awoke just in time to dress for an appointment, realizing that I had forgotten the dream project but that it was too late to do anything about it.

Later that day, I had time for a nap. I had been sleepy all day, feeling out of sorts and as if I was half asleep. Almost immediately upon falling asleep for my nap, I found myself in the dream state:

I was in a large, circular auditorium, lecturing to a group of students. The subject was dreaming.... My sister and the psychic who started the Institute came into the room.... It seems that they were going to New York to work with a new Dreams[10] group. It was obvious that the Institute had grown considerably, and that the dreaming project had grown considerably as well.

When I woke up from the nap, I felt as if it was the first time I had been awake all day. I had dreamed "green" but with entirely the wrong group; and then I dreamed about the project without dreaming any of the team members.

When I arrived at the Advanced Psychic Development class later in the week, I discovered some interesting facts. Tom, the student from my dream, told me that he had been thinking about me off and on throughout the day of the dream experiment. He had also been doing some experiments with a friend, using lemon verbena. Two other students from the class also remembered dreaming with each other and with me that night.

Darius said that he'd gone to see the movie *Love at First Bite* the night of the Dreams[10] dream meeting. Although unaware of my dream because it hadn't even happened yet in linear time, Darius was struck by the fact that *verbena* was used to ward off Dracula in the movie.

As his official group dream the night of the project, Darius recorded the following:

I awoke and a typed paper was beside the bed. There were two paragraphs.... I realized this was channeled information that had come through me. As I was reading this, Kay woke up. I said, "Did you see this? When did I do this?" Anyway, right after this I really woke up and realized this was all a dream.

Sid, who had gone for months without a single dream involving another group member, found himself aboard a Navy transport ship with Ellen.

...we started talking about channeling and how it could be used in the U.S. government. This went on for a few minutes and then she (Ellen) says, "I've got to get back to Florida." She got up and did a Southern belle-type walk. She was dressed in a long, pure white gown, embroidered, and she swirled around showing me her gown....

Like Darius, Sid had dreamed about channeling, or transmitting information from one area of the collective unconscious to another.

Ed too dreamed a group activity though like me he had forgotten it was Dreams Ten night. In Ed's dream, he was "in a James River mansion." Possibly this was an echo of Sid's perception of Ellen as a Southern belle, or the fact that the James River is the major waterway between Tidewater, Virginia and Richmond, where Ed's dream partner Darius lived.

...walking along, several old stone structures caught my eye, and I started investigating what now seemed to be a museum. There were many hallways and artifacts around. I then heard a piano playing and followed it to another room. It was played by a young girl who reminded me of Jean. The music was really a full orchestral concerto on one piano, which continued even when she stopped playing. As I came into the room, I danced and twirled for a bit and did one small leap, which surprised me when I was suspended in mid air for about a second.... I wondered if I were really free to leave and mentioned that I had just appeared here and did not know how I had gotten in. She (the pianist) said, "Oh those things are really only a problem during the times you are a person."

Ed gave the following interpretation: "Here I am, looking for the right inner state. I am concerned about my ties to the physical. The concerto that Jean plays is really the music of the group—a concerto featuring one instrument, supported by a great orchestra. And it is this music that I dance to, suspending myself for a moment."

Other members of the dream team responded to the project goal by doing what Steve had requested as a second part of his "become the group" suggestion. Even those who did not recall any dreams responded with their impressions of one another.

Despite this outpouring of responses to the "dream in green," by the end of May the group seemed to automatically shut down. Four months of group dreaming had been enough. On May 28, Scott wrote:

Dear Jean,

Even after you sent your reminder postcard, I forgot the May 23 Dream[10] attempt. I feel that I haven't given the project the attention it deserves, and would therefore prefer to give my place to someone else....

Some team members made an effort to keep the group together. And had events remained stable within the Institute, the dream experiment might have managed to continue. But by the end of May, Poseidia's Board of Trustees erupted in a conflict over a proposed new building site. The Dreams to the Tenth Power team was not spared. Conflicts developed. People took sides. If it was challenging to dream with people who shared a goal, dream team members found that it was nearly impossible to dream with others who took the opposite side on an issue over which all the dreamers felt strongly.

Finally, on June 21, Byron, who had appeared in one person's dream after another, but who recorded no dreams for the entire period of the group dreaming experiment, sounded in. "Actually, I do have a dream," he wrote:

Once upon a time, there were ten little Indians who wanted to become a tribe. They were all brave, but they weren't all braves. They sat down in a circle and decided to dream together about their tribe.

At first they sat with their backs to the center of the circle—looking out at the world. The longer they sat, and the more they dreamed, the crazier the world began to look, and they became frightened and began to argue about whose view was the "real" view. Some of them actually thought about getting up and running away from the tribe.

One day the Great Spirit turned them all around so they were facing each other. They all saw that what each saw was "real"—it just depended on the point of view. They could still see the outside world past the circle of the tribe, but they could all see each other as well.

Then Great Spirit spoke: "The choice is yours. Look through yourselves to the world and become a tribe—or look from yourself at the world and become separate.

They chose the former, and one by one many other braves came to join the circle. They became a large, happy and powerful tribe.

Byron accompanied this little allegory with a line drawing showing the figures of the tribe facing outward, then inward. Darius responded with his usual humor a week later:

Byron, you won't believe this. I took Jean's collected works (photocopied correspondence from the dreamers) out of the envelope backwards, the papers facing me. I saw these crisscrossed lines and I yelled, "What?" About a week ago I was reading about holography and the brain when I "saw" these lines, about three per person, intersecting each and every one of us in the dream group.... And some of you say nothing is happening.

Ellen responded in August to a final questionnaire requesting the group's responses to the project with:

When the project began, I had a lot of hopes about the experiences to come, but I must tell you my enthusiasm died a horrible death about halfway through.... I think the "experiment" was a direct reflection of the group's programmed ideas about dreams and dreaming, not to mention the worst of pop psychology. I think that everyone got so caught up in trying to force their dreams to be like everyday waking reality that nobody had a decent creative event....

In retrospect, there was a wide range of response to the first Dreams to the Tenth Power experiment. Some people in the group never recorded a dream that corresponded precisely with the project's set goals. Some people got frustrated and/or angry. Some, like Scott, dropped out with polite correspondence; and some, like Ellen, simply dropped out. Others maintained their excitement and commitment to the end.

Despite any of this, if one conclusion might be drawn from the first experiment, it is that dreamers, when asked to produce a dream about a particular target on a particular target date, can apparently do so.

Did the dreams of the first dream team contain something more than symbolic representations of other people in the group? Were dreams actually shared? The dreamers in the Dreams[10] project felt they were. Even those who dropped out of the experiment acknowledged their feelings that at one time or another, they were every bit as present with the group or specific members of it in dream state as they might have been in the waking state.

Could any of this be taken as conclusive proof that groups of people can and do dream together or that we are all dreaming together whether or not we remember it? Despite indications of these possibilities, one dream group, one test run of any experiment, could not be taken as proof, particularly when the group being tested included a majority of psychics and would-be psychics who were prone to extraordinary experiences anyway.

The results were interesting but inconclusive.

Chapter Three - Phase Two

For several years after the initial Dreams to the Tenth Power experiment, the work on group dreaming was set aside. The demands of managing the Institute left little time for research.

Still, the thought of group dreaming often tickled at the back of my mind. Within the environment of a consciousness research organization such as ours, group dreams were a fairly common occurrence. During a time of intense work on a building fund for example, staff members and volunteers dreamed aspects of the new building. Some of these dreams were solutions to problems like where to place the filing cabinets in the new office space for maximum advantage.

Because staff members openly shared their dreams, students and others who participated in Poseidia Institute's programs frequently asked when we were going to do a group dreaming experiment again.

Finally in the spring of 1982, with the promise of help from two staff members, June Cooper and Lola Murrell, I agreed that the time might be right to begin phase two of the group dreaming research. Then an interesting thing happened.

At this time, Poseidia Institute was involved in a dispute with the City Council of Virginia Beach over the legality of a large prize raffle we wished to conduct. We saw the raffle as a fund-raiser with a built-in public relations factor; the city didn't like it.

This was prior to legalization of a state lottery in Virginia and public sentiment in this conservative state was running high. Politicians and preachers railed against the corruption of legalized gambling. The City Council, a bastion of conservatism, saw our raffle as gambling's foot in the door. What began for us as a fun idea soon became a political football. Although raffles such as the one we planned were legal in the state of Virginia, the City Council blocked our permit, forcing us to take the case to court. Due to the nature of the test case and the appealing fact that we were David going against the city's Goliath, Poseidia Institute was getting a lot of local publicity.

One day Jeff South, a reporter for the area's major newspaper, came to my office saying he would like to write an article about the work we were doing at Poseidia Institute rather than yet another raffle story. I could not have been more pleased. It often seemed to me that Poseidia's real work was being eclipsed by the public battle. What emerged from the conversation with Jeff South was a story about the Dreams to the Tenth Power research.

Published in the Metro section of the newspaper a few days later, the article ran on the front page of the section accompanied by an eye-catching line drawing. Jeff mentioned in the article that we were selecting members for a new dream team and gave the Poseidia Institute mailing address. Within hours, the story was picked up by the Associated Press wire service.

By the end of the week, we were deluged with letters from across the state of Virginia—and also from throughout the East Coast and Midwest, where newspapers had picked up the wire story. From wondering exactly where we would find the candidates for resumed Dreams[10] research, June, Lola and I went directly to the position of having more volunteers for the dream experiment than we knew what to do with.

Looking at this outpouring of response, I also learned an unexpected fact about group dreaming, something I would see repeated again and again. The idea of shared dreaming fires the imagination of many, many people. Housewives from Ohio, psychologists from local universities, teenagers from Charlottesville, and senior citizens from rural West Virginia all wrote that they were eager to start dreaming together.

Prior to the appearance of the news story, we had already promised two or three local people that they could participate in this new phase of the group dreaming research. In order to keep our word, June, Lola and I quickly decided that, given the influx of potential dreamers, it would be easy enough to create two teams rather than one. Each new ten-member dream team would have a staff member to facilitate it and to coordinate group correspondence.

Since we had a large pool of volunteers to choose from, we aimed for as wide a range of personalities and professions on each team as possible. But before we began the selection process, we created psychological profiles of potential candidates.

Even after eliminating numerous clearly unsuitable correspondents as research participants, we mailed close to one hundred questionnaires to possible candidates. We asked questions about their backgrounds, their interest in dreams, and their families. As a backup to these questionnaires, as soon as we received the photographs from potential participants, psychics who worked for the Institute did readings on each of them. This served to weed out any people who might be unstable or become seriously disturbed by several months of dream work.

The responses we received to our questionnaires, though varied, pointed to some interesting facts about people interested in group dreaming. The majority of the respondents were well educated. Most had at least two years of college, while many held advanced degrees. Overwhelmingly, this group of people loved dreaming. When asked to comment on their dreams, many wrote, "Dreaming is fun!"

Several of the respondents regularly dreamed precognitively, many dreamed lucidly, and quite unexpectedly, over one-third of the people who responded to the questionnaire said they could dream about a particular thing when they wanted to. Many also said they could, if interrupted during an interesting dream, go back to the same dream later in the night or even the next day. Reading these applications, it seemed that maybe the reason we know so little about how the general populace dreams is because we fail to ask.

Even though the selection process sometimes seemed endless to us, within a few months of the original newspaper article, we created two teams of dreamers from a mostly random pool. Members of the teams ranged in age from fourteen to fifty, selected primarily for their ability to recall and record their dreams. We selected teams of mostly women as they applied in the greatest number, however two men were also chosen for each team.

For Team One – Lola's team – we selected a high school senior, a salesman who sold construction tools, a learning disabilities resource teacher, and an array of other professionals. June's team – Team Two – included a high school freshman, two college students, a taxicab driver, a greenhouse worker, and the mother of seven children who worked part time outside the home.

Participants in Phase Two of the Dreams to the Tenth Power Experiments

---

Team One
Lola—Team facilitator, office manager for Poseidia Institute
Annette—Learning disabilities teacher who dreams about cats
John—College mathematics professor
Tom—Construction tools salesman
Catherine—Retired teacher
Caroline—Social worker
Shelly—High school senior
Darlene—Legal secretary
Connie—Stay-at-home mother of two young children
Nora—Owner and operator of a general store

Team Two
June—Team facilitator, composer
Jill—Copy editor for a publishing firm, studies karate
Barbara—College student, studies karate
Jennifer—Secretary
Angela—Mother of seven grown children
Katy—High school freshman
Chet—College freshman, baseball player
Felicia—Case worker, New York Department of Corrections
Carol—Greenhouse worker
Arthur—Entrepreneur and sometime taxi driver

As team coordinators, June and Lola played an active role in the selection of their teams. Both women were in their mid-twenties. In addition to sharing the research responsibilities, they were personal friends.

Lola, a recent graduate of James Madison University, had been active with the Institute in a variety of ways since high school. She was a capable psychic in her own right and had studied with the best teachers the organization had to offer. She was soft-spoken, intelligent and slow to anger. And when she took on the role of Office Manager at Poseidia, she became a cohesive force for the younger members of the organization.

On many afternoons that summer, Lola and June could be found at the long work table in Poseidia's back office, poring over the photographs submitted by applicants for the Dreams Ten research. Together they decided who would fit best on each team.

June, who was a graduate student at Old Dominion University, taught classes at Poseidia in creativity. A brilliant musician, her compositions were performed by theater and dance groups throughout the area. June was, in many ways, the temperamental opposite of Lola. High energy and nervous tension made her quick to speak and act.

Finally by mid-August, the two had selected their teams. The new research experiment would begin on September 24. It would continue for four months, with two dream dates scheduled for each month. We hoped to correct some of the technical difficulties of the first research experiment by shortening the period of research and lengthening the time for mail to travel.

Although most of the dreamers on each dream team were from Virginia, there were also team members from New York, California and Ohio. We deliberately selected people for each team who had never met before. The dreamers knew nothing of each other but the first names of other team members.

As for those of us conducting the research experiment, we knew that group dreaming might not happen at all. These people were not psychics or researchers. They had little in common but an interest in dreams. Could such diverse individuals, thrown together in a group, dream together? We had no idea what would happen.

Once the dream team members were selected, we went to some lengths to help them feel comfortable with the project. We sent them a brief history of the Dreams to the Tenth Power experiment, information about the Institute, and a list of target dates. We suggested that they have a good time with the research, maintain a playful attitude, and try not to have too many preconceptions. Since no one had ever encouraged total strangers to dream together we pointed out, there was no blueprint for what might happen.

We attempted to start the groups off slowly, giving them time to acclimate. The first dream goal was simply to have each team member on both teams "Find a place where you would like to meet other members of your dream team, and might feel comfortable meeting them in the future."

"If you find that expectations are creating pressure and your dream self isn't cooperating," Lola cautioned in an introductory letter to her team, "don't be upset."

Watch all of your dreams, enjoy the possibilities, and if you feel you are dreaming Dreams[10] dreams before or after the assigned date, just record them and send them along with your next letter. My suggestion is that you keep a journal for the duration of the project and include in it any new experiences or feelings as well.... I realize there may be a tendency to edit the information you send, but please resist it. You might edit out something very relevant.

Though our intention was to give these dreamers, all strangers to each other and to dream research, an easy entry into the field, they surprised us. Phase Two of the Dreams to the Tenth Power experiment began with a bang. On the first goal, six members of Team One found a meeting place, and five members of Team Two did the same.

Out of the twenty people on the two teams, two dreamed of meeting a group of people in a class, two dreamed of going to the beach – more on this subject later – several dreamers met people in restaurants, in houses, or at parties. Barbara, who seemed to have a great sense of fun in her dreams at any time, met people riding on a roller coaster in groups of ten.

More in line with our expectations, several of the dreamers had some anxiety. They felt nervous about whether they could meet the goal and also about dreaming with strangers. The procedure in this experiment, as it had been in the earlier version of Dreams[10], was to photocopy each individual's response to the dream goal and send the collected responses out to team members after each meeting night with an announcement of the next target date and goal. In no time at all, this method encouraged comments and responses to responses, becoming a sort of round-robin letter which happened to include dreaming.

In response to the first goal, Learning Disabilities teacher Annette, a member of Team One, wrote of attending a party.

I kept looking around for someone I knew, but there seemed to be no one there I recognized. There was a guy there who had brought his cat... I tried to play with it. The cat, however, was tense, nervous, uptight—not in a playful mood! His claws clung to the carpet when I tried to pick him up.

I think the cat represents the portion of myself that is somewhat afraid of the dream experiment," Annette wrote. "Even as I looked forward to the first meeting during the last week or so, I found myself having some negative thoughts along the lines of: Even though I know it's possible for us all to meet, what if we just can't manage to pull it off? Or, worse yet, what if everybody else in the group is able to find each other except me? I'll feel like a failure, as if I've let the group down.

John, a math professor at a Washington, D.C. university, had a similar experience when he tried to meet the goal. He was one of the Team One members who did not dream of a place. Instead he said:

I was walking down a corridor with a friend. There was a white watch dog who ignored my friend, but looked menacingly at me. I knew well enough to show no fear, but the dog continued to trail me and bark. This reaction struck me as unusual, since my friend was not of any interest to the dog. The dog jumped up and snapped at me a few times, but I kept walking.

The feeling conveyed by the first set of written responses to the Dreams to the Tenth Power experiment was that of anticipation. In their dreams, people either eagerly anticipated group interaction, or felt that the experience might soon be snapping at their heels.

There were several interesting correlations between dreams recorded on this first meeting night which could only be seen if the dream reports were studied side by side. One of the most startling correlations came from the dreams of two members of June's group, Team Two.

Jill, a copy editor for a large publishing firm, wrote that in her dream she met with her advanced karate class. After recording a first dream, in which she met with five or six members of the karate class to talk about a "trip we were planning," Jill went back to sleep. In a second dream:

I am walking alone downtown at night. I am on my way home from a movie. I'm nervous about being out so late by myself. I hear footsteps approaching rapidly from behind. I cross the street and walk faster. Whoever is back there also crosses. It now sounds like two or three people. There's nowhere I can run. I'm starting to panic.

I hear Master Hong saying, "You can retreat three times; on the fourth attack you must stand and fight." I glance over my shoulder. There are three men following me. I turn around and put my purse on the ground, slip off my sandals. My knees are shaking and I'm sweating. The first man comes up and says, "Lookie what we got here!"

Another: "Looks good to me."

I try to keep my voice calm and say, "What do you want?"

The first man says, "You know damn well what I want."

They move up closer. I feel my energy sinking into my <u>hava</u>. I suddenly realize that they can't harm me. I stand there. I don't want to fight, but I'm afraid to turn my back just yet. The leader starts toward me. I extend my <u>ki</u>, looking into his eyes. He stops. He tries again and stops. His friends are teasing him. He gets angry, but still can't touch me. We are both afraid, I realize; I also realize that I don't know what I'm afraid of because he no longer frightens me. I wake up.

Later, after reading Jill's dream, Barbara wrote to the group: "I edited down my first dreams to fit on the front and back of the goal sheet. Mistake. This may be too late for official correlation, but in case Jill is interested (or anyone else) here is the sequence that got condensed into, 'One of the women almost runs into a bit of trouble in the street but gets out of it.'"

One student is walking down a deserted street. It's in an older section of town. There are stone houses on the left side and a tall, gray stone wall on the right... Two young men come up on her quickly from behind and edge her in. They make a few smart-alecky comments. She is worried because the street is deserted and she isn't dressed to cope with this situation. I am about to go down and help her when the men retreat before the situation comes to blows.

Barbara commented that she also studied karate and was very interested in self-defense techniques for women.

As in most cases where the dreams of several people are studied for indications of meeting a specific target or goal, the Dreams to the Tenth Power experiments provided many examples of significant correlations outside the parameters of exactly what we were looking for to prove the existence of group dreaming. Even though similarities between Jill's dream and Barbara's were stunning, Barbara did not submit her actual dream record until after she had read Jill's dream account. Additionally, neither dream related specifically to the given goal of finding a comfortable location for group meetings. Nevertheless, correlations like these seem significant in the more comprehensive evidence of shared dreaming.

This particular bit of shared dreaming between Jill and Barbara produced an even more startling result in late October. In a postscript to her dream report for the third group meeting, Jill commented:

One interesting thought. My dreams from the first Dreams[10] date might have been precognitive. Exactly a week later, I was attacked by two men, who accosted me in much the same manner as the dream. "Reality," I'm afraid, was much more violent than my dream confrontation, in that I was forced to fight, but the ending was the same. I escaped unharmed.

Given this beginning to an experiment we feared might be unsuccessful, June, Lola and I were eager to see what the results might be for the second target date, set for October 7, 1982. This time we made the goal as challenging as anything we could think of. Still without having given team members any photographs or information about each other, we asked them to "get acquainted with Dream Team members. See if you can describe the people on your team."

What we were asking the dream team members to do was an exercise in dream telepathy. And we were not disappointed with the results.

As with any experimental group of this size, earlier commitments kept some of the twenty subjects from responding. However, on Team One, all eight of the team members who responded had group dreams of one form or another.

Annette, whose cat dream on the first target night had shown her anxiety about the experiment, dreamed she was with other people in a swimming pool. "I was floating in the pool with my legs thrown up over the side," she wrote. "Other people were in the pool. I could hear their voices but could not make out what they were saying, and could not see them due to my awkward position."

Later in Annette's dream:

> The other people in the pool had gone to art class, and now it was time for me to go too. The assignment was "portraits," and I had forgotten to do mine! We were sitting around in someone's living room, about eight or ten of us... I'm sure this group represents the Dream Team, but none of the faces were distinct enough for me to remember. We began to take turns around the room, discussing our art work, though no one showed any pictures. I began to wonder what I would do or say when my turn came, since I had no drawings to show. On a sketchpad on my lap, I began to draw a cat with one paw stretched out as if to touch someone or something (slightly more friendly than my last dream cat!), but the class faded before my turn came.

Annette had begun to read my book, *Dreams Beyond Dreaming*, which has a section on shared dreams. She was insightful enough about the current dream goal to remark to the group,

> It occurs to me that most of the stories of "dream meetings" (as told in *Dreams Beyond Dreaming*) involve family members, friends, or people who are fairly well known to the dreamer. I'm guessing that emotional ties, or whatever it is that makes people connect intuitively in these cases, have already been established in waking state. If so, then we've set a tough task for ourselves in the Dreams[10] project.

What she said was true and I felt a little embarrassed to have our cover blown by her perceptive reading. Most mutual dreaming experiences, including those in my earlier book, have been reported by dreamers who have deep emotional ties. Again the question of dream reporting comes to mind. How often do people who don't know one another well ask about each other's dreams? And who would walk up to a perfect stranger and ask if they shared a dream last night? No one had ever asked strangers to deliberately dream together. Maybe we are dreaming together all the time and just don't know it.

John, the mathematics professor who had been menaced by a barking dog in his first target dream recorded this response to the second dream goal:

> I dreamed that I was in my apartment in bed. A friend of mine, Tom, was in the other room getting ready for something. I think to go somewhere. I was supposed to be getting ready too, but I wasn't. Finally he came into my room, stood at the foot of my bed, and said, "Come on, let's go," a few times. He was persistent, but I seemed to be dragging my feet about the whole matter.

I awoke at one a.m. My first thought was, "Well, you weren't concentrating. There you go, dreaming about friends instead of the dream group." With an unbelievable suddenness, I snapped awake, as it occurred to me that I don't have any friends named Tom. I had never seen this person before and there is someone in our group named Tom. So here is a description of the person in my dream: About 5' 10", curly dark hair of medium length, in the neighborhood of

150-160 pounds, and probably has to shave a lot. I specifically remember his being 23 years old.

What John had written was a remarkably accurate physical description of one of his fellow dream team members, with the exception of one detail. Tom was 32, not 23 as John had dreamed.

Even more arresting was the fact that John, after he went back to sleep that night, dreamed that he was

Swimming laps at the pool. At one point, I stopped and exchanged greetings with a lady in her late thirties who had shoulder-length black hair, streaked with gray" (a fairly accurate description of me, although I wasn't officially participating in the experiment). In the early morning, I had another quick encounter with Tom, who said, "Boy, you really missed the boat—I'm 39!

Unlike other members of her team, Lola had seen team member photographs. She knew their vital statistics and had corresponded with all of them. Because of this, both Lola and June were having some anxieties of their own.

"I didn't remember any dreams when I woke up," Lola wrote. "I thought about it off and on all day, but still couldn't remember any dreams. In the evening, my husband said something about flying saucers, and I yelled, 'Oh, my dream team!'"

I dreamed about communicating with beings in flying saucers (not exactly saucers, but non-human space vehicles). I was with other people, but I don't remember exactly who. We were talking, and I was telepathing to the beings in the UFOs. I knew I was dreaming, and I said I'd heard that a lot of well-known psychics have had experiences with UFOs. I asked if it counted when we were in dream state. Someone said they didn't think so because it wasn't real. I said, "But this is real! It's a dream but it's real."

Catherine, an older member of Lola's dream team, responded to the night's goal with great enthusiasm. She was one of several members of Team One who picked up on a flying theme. She also experienced lucidity.

Wow! For the first time that I can remember, I knew I was dreaming. I was in a big shopping mall for some reason. I was there to conduct an AA meeting. Suddenly I said, "Hey, I'm dreaming." The idea that I could really take an active part in the dream experiment delighted me. I decided to have some fun, so I jumped and flew over large objects and wandered over the mall looking at faces.

She did not remember any members of her dream team from looking around the mall though; Catherine said, only "old movie stars."

Another member of Lola's team, Caroline, said she was "taking plane trips" during the night of the experiment. In a room on the plane she saw a woman who

In a room on the plane she saw a woman who seemed to be in her mid-thirties, about 5'5" tall with dark, possibly black, hair above shoulder length. It was in a flip, or at least curly at the ends. She didn't wear glasses, had dark eyes, a pale complexion, and was attractive.

Annette, whose shy cat appeared again in her "portraits" dream seemed to have reached out and touched someone. Caroline's description accurately fit Annette.

Shelly, who at seventeen was Team One's youngest member, said:

I dreamt I was with a large group of people. They were milling around in some sort of room, I think. I only distinctly remember talking to a young man with dark hair. He was very nice, and he had a pleasant voice (and a moustache or beard, I think).

Another team member, Darlene, noted:

I was at a large gathering to hear a speaker of some sort deliver an address.... My father and I were sitting off to ourselves, expecting others to join us. Whether these others were our group or not, I'm not sure, but I think so.

One of my other dreams, details of which I cannot recall, had me talking to a person named Kelly (Shelly?). She was of medium build with dark brown hair, a rather pretty girl, and very pleasant to talk with.

Amid all of these reports from Team One members who apparently connected with each other in dream state on the night of the second target date, Connie brought up an interesting dilemma.

Dear Lola," she wrote. I had lots of dream interference. There were Dreams[10] and others all mixed up. At any rate, I think I can describe two or three team members. I do not know which name goes with the descriptions. One of the two guys is about 5'9'-5'11," medium build, has dark brown hair and a beard and wears glasses.

Connie was the second person on her team, Shelly being the first, to describe a dark haired man of medium build. In waking life, though John fit the general description both Shelly and Connie gave, he had neither a beard nor a moustache.

The second person Connie described in her letter was a young woman, "small, with very long blond hair and blue eyes." This description fit none of the members of her team, but it accurately described Jennifer, a member of Team Two.

One of the unanticipated results of the research we were doing came from the fact that two dream teams were dreaming on the same night. In our enthusiasm to make the most of the abundance of research subjects provided to us by the newspaper article, we had failed to anticipate what might happen if two different dream teams were dreaming about the same goals on the same target dates.

Because both groups were involved in the same project, members of the two teams seemed, on occasion, to mingle with one another in dream state.

When I looked at the overall results from Team One for this second target date, I found them rather amazing. Not only had eight of the team members who responded attained the goal of meeting with a group, over half of them were aware of meeting specifically with members of their dream team. At least three of them also appeared to have scored hits when it came to describing individual team members. As Annette pointed out, the goal we had set for these dreamers was a difficult one; yet the members of Team One seemed to achieve it with ease.

The results from Dream Team Two were no less remarkable.

"I went to bed hoping to meet my Dream Team members," wrote Angela, an attractive, middle-aged mother of seven grown children.

In my first dream, I found myself in a medieval type setting, traveling with a group of people up a red clay road. We were all barefoot, but some of us had large-brimmed, flat hats on, and our clothes were sort of brown, coarse, rustic-looking material (medieval type such as scholars, students, or pilgrims would wear). On our right side was the hill upon whose side the road was built. Below us dropped the village of thickly-clustered buildings. It was late afternoon, and a golden, rosy glow was on everything. We were all laughing and enjoying ourselves. There was the feeling that comes from a warm, loving family group.

"Then I was awakened by my daughter's baby crying to be fed," Angela said. "I went back to bed, still hoping to meet my team members, not realizing, I think, that I had already met them in the first dream."

The youngest member of Team Two, fourteen-year-old Katy, wrote that she had gone to a party where,

Somebody tapped me on the shoulder. I turned around, startled. There was a guy with short, brown hair. He was around 5'11." I remember he had a beautiful smile and white teeth.

In doing this type of experiment, where we asked participants to describe one another without having first been given any photographs or other description, I believe that we hit upon a unique method for verifying the existence of shared dreaming. I have since been urged to set up an experiment in which participants were asked to do only this—identify one another in dream state by means of a ranking scale.

Although this would be useful research, there seem to be many factors involved in any test to validate the group dreaming process. Even though Katy for example, was able to identify someone in her second group dream on the target date and that person may well have been her teammate Chet, there are numerous factors which must be considered before we could unequivocally call something a direct hit by the standards of quantitative research.

One excellent test of shared dreaming is to determine if both people who shared a dream experience – or in this case all ten of the people – recall the same details from their dreams. Needless to say, this does not happen frequently.

And that was the most interesting thing about the dreams Katy and Chet had the night of the second dream meeting. Whereas Katy remembered talking someone in her dream who might have been Chet, Chet's dream of that night was:

> I am only able to recall a small fragment of my dream. I remember that I was eating lunch with a girl who had short, light-brown hair. Her facial aspects were unclear. I also remember that our conversation was on basic things like we were just introduced.... Also I remember that her age was pretty close to mine, maybe a year or two either way.

The members of Dream Team Two were generally more tentative about feeling they had successfully met the goal of finding the members of their group than were the members of Team One. Katy, of course, had short, light brown hair, and her age was within four years of Chet's, since Chet was a college freshman. It is quite possible that they shared a dream, but to what standard should we hold dream accounts before we agree that shared dreaming took place? And what is to be done about dreams which, for example Ed, in the first Dreams[10] experiment might have claimed were happening at the feeling level rather than at the demonstrably graphic level of waking reality?

"I feel like I may have had some success with this goal," wrote Jill, whose karate class dream on the first goal night had so closely correlated with Barbara's. "Although I remember very little in the way of specific details from the dreams, I recall that my dream 'characters' were all people I had never met before, which is unusual for me."

Felicia, a young woman who worked for the Department of Corrections in New York, said, "I don't remember very much about what I dreamed. I was very tired. All I recall is a series of impressions about being in class."

Two members of Dream Team Two were able to identify people in their dreams that night, but Carol and Barbara both pointed up the problem we had created in asking two teams of group dreamers to share the same nights and goals. Each of these two dreamers identified someone from the other team.

> All of a sudden," Carol reported, "I was standing at a blackboard in a school. At the blackboard on the other side of the room was a guy about 5'8" or 5'9." He had light brown hair. He was doing a long math problem that took up the whole board.

Carol was quite probably dreaming about John, the math professor from Team One. And this brings us to another question. Was there something unique about John that might cause two of his own teammates and one dreamer from another team to dream about him?

Clearly John was a powerful dreamer. He was the only person of all twenty dream team members who not only described another member of his team the night of the second dream meeting, but who also connected both the person's name and age with the description. But is dreaming skill enough to connect two dreamers? Possibly it was John's image-producing math-teaching profession or even the fact, since two people dreamed that he had a strong desire for facial hair, which attracted him to the dreams of other dreamers.

These questions may sound far fetched when we are only attempting to ascertain whether or not group dreaming exists; however, they become quite important once the existence of group dreaming is accepted.

Barbara's dream on the night of the second target date was even clearer than Carol's on the subject of two dream teams. She dreamed of coming to a white, wooden house with a large side yard and an "enormous" back yard. The first person she found in the yard was me.

Before going farther with Barbara's dream, I should point out that Barbara was one of the few members of either dream team who was selected prior to the flood of volunteer participants. She was a student at Old Dominion University in Norfolk and had been taking classes at Poseidia Institute for over a year before the second phase of the dreaming experiment began. She was a talented dreamer and thoughtful student. Even though she and the other local dreamers were asked not to discuss the Dreams to the Tenth Power Project with staff, Barbara knew June and Lola well and had adopted me as her special teacher. It was not unusual in the middle of a work day to have Barbara open the door to my office, plop down in the orange leather chair in front of my desk, and ask some question about dreams or metaphysics that would draw me in for an hour's discussion. So when she put me into the Dreams[10] landscape, it was not surprising.

> Jean was with several people from Poseidia Institute I don't recognize, Jean doesn't say anything, but I gather something about a big, new project, and she's checking things out. I am standing near the corner of the side yard. A young, brownette [sic] woman comes out of the house. She has just won an award for teaching small children, and I can see why. She is calm, but vital and cheerful. She asks me why the group has split into hot spots and cold spots, some outside and some inside the house. I tell her it beats me. Tom is trying to figure it out while a couple of people from our group mill around nearby.

In this dream, Barbara has noticed the split between the two groups of Dreams to the Tenth Power dreamers, though her dreaming self doesn't understand why the groups need to be split. Prior to this second target date of the experiment, we had not told members of either team that there were two experimental groups being run at the same time. We did not even see this as necessary. But it was obvious from the dreams on the second target date that we needed to explain to what was happening or risk having some very confused dreamers. The people Barbara saw most clearly in her dream were two members of Team One, Annette and Tom. In Annette's case, Barbara not only picks up her profession as a teacher of young children, but also picked up the fact that in waking life Annette had recently won a teaching award. Annette is the person on Team One whose shy cat reached out as if to touch someone. The other person Barbara named from Team One was Tom, the man whose description John's dream gave so precisely.

The complexity of accurately judging group dreaming events is apparent here. Later in the same dream recorded above, Barbara apparently met some of the members of her own team as well. She met a man named Arthur (one of her team members) and "his children." Barbara's descriptions of Arthur's children matched the waking physical descriptions of Chet and Katy, not Arthur's children but members of Barbara's dream team.

Chapter Four - Meeting at a Restaurant

In their second dream meetings, the new Dreams to the Tenth Power dream teams far exceeded any expectations that Lola, June or I might have had for the experiment. The results from this night pointed us to several important discoveries about group dreaming. We had invited people who were total strangers to one another to dream together, not knowing if they could do it. We had also invited ordinary dreamers, with no particular training, to dream about a specific target or goal. In the dream groups that night, eighty percent of the group members had dreamed about meeting a group of people, while fifty percent of them dreamed of specific group members. Moreover, several people either dreamed lucidly, or had at least been aware they were in a dream.

On October 21, 1982, the dream goal assigned to the dream teams for their third meeting was to: "Meet at a restaurant for a meal. What do people eat or wear?" We had not yet sent dream team members photos of their fellow team members so all the dreamers had to go on was their impressions of one another from dreams and correspondence.

Having performed so exceptionally on their second target date, some of the members of this new experiment began to show the symptoms we first saw in the earlier Dreams to the Tenth Power dream team: a dawning awareness that they might actually be sharing dream space with others and a resultant reluctance to dream.

"Dear Lola," Connie wrote from Team One:

I did not get to the restaurant! I wanted everyone to go to a restaurant called The Eastern Standard. I've never been there, but it looks quite elegant from the outside.... I seemed to be wandering, looking for teammates. The only thing that I really liked was some member of my team, a man, called me from a phone booth (I could see him even as I answered my phone) to tell me that I was late and to come on. I know this was a Dreams[10] part and he was one of my teammates. He was laughing in a friendly fashion because I could not get to the restaurant. I think some of the others were there. I can't wait to find out who they were.

Shelly, the high school student from Lola's Team One, got to the restaurant. But both her dream and the letter she wrote about it showed the feelings she was having about group dreaming. "First of all," she wrote, "I'd like to say that everything's seeming to tie together nicely. Our dreams seem interwoven. It's kind of spooky, but I love it! I only remember vivid, horrible nightmares. I didn't sleep very well. I have been sick for four days."

Despite being sick, Shelly recorded this dream:

I was in a restaurant. I had filet mignon and everyone else (there were about five others) had something different. Then I heard some funny noise, and I saw that the man with the beard from my earlier (Goal 2) dream was choking. He had been poisoned! I couldn't move, and no one else seemed to be able to either. Luckily I woke up.

Later I remember dreaming something else in the same restaurant. It was a combination between The Gaslight and the St. Charles, I think.

John, the math professor, may have appeared in Shelly's second group dream. And if so, he would have been the man in this dream as well. John was not aware of going to a restaurant in dreams that night. Nor did he give any indication of choking. For the third group meeting night in succession, John dreamed about waiting to go somewhere, even being urged to go somewhere, but never going there.

"Not much dream activity," John wrote:

It seems as though I was supposed to be dreaming a restaurant scene, but instead I dreamed about a supermarket. There were three of us, I think, another man and a woman and myself, standing inside the entrance to the grocery store. We had a shopping basket, but were more or less just hanging around waiting for something.

Always cheerful about his connection with the dream team though, John appended a "Miss Peach" cartoon to his letter. In the cartoon, Miss Peach is asking Ira why he has decided to live only in his dreams from now on. Ira's response is, "You meet a better class of people that way."

Both June and Lola had been away in school when the first Dreams to the Tenth Power research had been done, but had closely followed the results of that experiment. In fact, they were two of the people who had ultimately dreamed along with that initial group of dreamers. So they were more than casually interested in seeing what would happen with Phase Two. As team facilitators as well as participants in this second round of group dreaming experiments, they were also feeling the pressure to dream.

After the third target night, Lola wrote to her team: "Both Tuesday and Wednesday nights I woke up in the middle of the night saying to myself that I needed to do my dream team dream. So Thursday, the actual target night, I was sleeping very lightly and not comfortably at all."

Lola was hesitant to share her dream, which she said seemed "very personal, not like the dream team at all." But since the group had agreed to record and share all dreams from the target date, she reluctantly sent it on.

In the dream, Lola is elected president of a group of people in a large auditorium. The group is very rowdy, so Lola tells them that if they don't want to participate, they should leave. Many people get up to go. Lola later discovers that this has been a test of her authority.

In light of Lola's protest, the dream which one of her team members sent from that date is particularly interesting. Darlene wrote, "I was not successful in meeting the group at a restaurant. The entire night was a very restless one for me. I had difficulty in sleeping at all. I did have another dream early this morning, seemingly unrelated to the assignment, but I'll list it anyway."

I was a political aide of some sort to the President of the United States, and we were in a crisis situation. Somehow the President was a woman, and I remember seeing her hands, very slim, pretty hands, well manicured, with bright red nail polish (a color which Lola often wore). She said that within nine hours we (the country) would be at war.

"Frankly," Darlene ended her letter, "I was very glad to get out of bed this morning. I overslept and have been disoriented ever since."

As we had seen in other cases, the dreams that Lola and Darlene recorded for the night of the target date related to one another but dealt only indirectly with the target goal. Several people on Team One dreamed about food, but not in restaurants.

"For some reason," Catherine wrote, "I couldn't get a dream on the dream night. However, the following night I dreamed I was in a drug store and then a hamburger stand.

Then (for the third target date in a row) I realize I am dreaming, so I look for team members. One woman had on a suit with a red collar, dark hair, mid length. There was a man in a blue suit, thirty I think, with a beard.

"I'm sorry to say I didn't remember my dreams this night," said Caroline. "I got very little sleep and just didn't remember anything.... I have one question though. Isn't it possible we might appear different in our dreams than we look? I know I don't look the same in my own dreams!"

It was gratifying to have a question such as this one surface from within the group of dreamers. Because of the diverse population of research subjects participating in the experiment, we had not wanted to give them preconceived notions of either the potentials or the pitfalls of group dreaming before the experiment began. But questions such as the one Caroline asked seem natural once one acknowledges that group dreaming might exist. We also had not wanted to startle the dreamers in advance with the very real possibility that they might appear in each other's dreams as eggplants, unicorns, or something even more fanciful.

But Caroline's question was right on target. By the time she asked it, participants in this experiment had already dreamed the typical-to-group-dreaming symbols of a class or large meeting to represent the project, along with a variety of other, fairly easy to penetrate symbols such as flying machines and swimming pools.

Despite the concerns that several people on the team had mentioned, Team One managed a total of five food dreams for the target date. Although Shelly was the only team member to actually recall arriving at a restaurant, this along with the correlation between Lola's and Darlene's presidential dreams and

Connie's and Catherine's dream-state awareness that they needed to meet the goal proved that Team One was still achieving quite a lot.

As with Team One, several members of Team Two managed to reach the goal, or some close approximation of it, on the third target date with apparently many of the same difficulties.

Felicia, whose work for the city Corrections Department involved long hours and a fair amount of stress, finally reached the goal for the third target date through a long series of dreams. First she dreamed about her father feeding the neighbor's dog. Her second dream was "something about E.T. I don't remember what. It couldn't have been much, since I've never seen the movie." (As another team member later pointed out, apparently Felicia missed the play on words, since E.T. resembles the word eat.)

Felicia then dreamed about being asked to play softball for her office team and about weight loss followed by a dream about a conference at which she sat down at a table where there were two glasses of water and some cookies.

"In the last dream," she wrote, "I remember being in a restaurant. I remember plants and a spinach salad. Then suddenly I was awake and dying for a glass of orange juice."

Felicia's dreams from this target date exhibit another type of dreaming that I have come to see as common in group dreaming experiments. In many cases the dreamer will record a series of dreams which seem to represent feelings about the target goal from many perspectives, almost as if the dreamer were regarding the goal through a prism.

On the night of the third target date, Angela was suffering from a bout of the flu. She dreamed of driving to the beach with two of her daughters. It was cold and snowing. They stopped the car at one point in the dream to pick up "several people wearing dark clothing, long scarves and hats." One of these people, a boy around nineteen or twenty, said he knew of a good place to eat.

Arthur dreamed that "Mrs. Jimmy Kreticos" a local Greek woman, went to her restaurant in another city, Syracuse. "I went later in the evening," said Arthur.

On the third target date, June did not dream about either her team or a restaurant. She dreamed that Lola's husband Barry, and Jill, a member of Team Two, were laying out cloth for sets or a stage project. Even though she had only dreamed one member of her team and the husband of the other team facilitator, June was happy. "They cut out a purple and red clown for me," she said.

For this target date, three members of June's team, Carol, Chet and Arthur, all reported that they had received their packages after the target date. Unfortunately, even with the change in experiment design, we were now encountering the same problem that had plagued the first phase of the Dreams[10] experiment and we knew it might get worse as the holiday mailing season approached. We urged members of both teams to try a group dream as soon as they knew the goal, and return reports to us as soon as possible. Fortunately for the experiment, it was already clear to us that group dreamers paid far less attention to time in the dream state than in the waking state. On the November fourth target date, both Arthur and June from Team Two dreamed they were in restaurants.

We set the actual goal for November fourth out of a great curiosity to see what might happen. We asked people to: "Come visit Poseidia Institute. Who's there? What does it look like?" On each team, aside from the team facilitators who worked at Poseidia, only one or two people had at least visited the premises. The remaining seven or eight members of each team were as unfamiliar with Poseidia Institute as they were with one another.

We had enough hits on this target to make us aware of just how skilled many of the new dream team members were. We had asked people to perform a type of dream telepathy or remote viewing.

Over the years, several other dream experiments of this type have been performed. Researchers Alan Vaughn, Montague Ullman and Stanley Krippner at the Maimonides Dream Laboratory had conducted some of the seminal work in dream telepathy during the 1960s. Later, during the 1970s, the U.S. government conducted a series of remote viewing experiments called Stargate. These experiments are discussed by Dr. Dale Graff in his books on the Stargate experiment. Ullman and Krippner's work is detailed in one of the classic texts of dream research, *Dream Telepathy.*

To our knowledge though, when we invited the Dreams[10] teams to visit Poseidia Institute, no one had yet asked a whole group of people to visit an unknown place in dream state and report back what they saw. "I was with several other people, walking along in the dark," Annette reported to her team, Team One, after her dream visit to Poseidia.

We came to a house where we were greeted at the door by a heavyset, pleasant woman. I don't remember her features clearly, but I do distinctly recall her clothing. She wore dark brown slacks and a flowing blue blouse, under a loose-fitting, matching, blue knit top. She took us up some stairs and opened another door to show us a room which was a sort of aviary—There were many colorful birds of all kinds, a sort of jungle-like, hothouse atmosphere. But the birds were watching TV and listing to radios!!! The room seemed to be vibrating with energy. I wondered if the birds liked all the "technology" that surrounded them and what they learned from it. It all seemed to be a grand experiment, conceived and carried out by the woman in brown and blue. I was intrigued, but the door began to shut before I had a chance to go into the room, and the dream faded.

What Annette could not have realized, never having met her, was that she had accurately described her team's facilitator, Lola, right down to Lola's favorite color, blue, and an outfit she frequently wore. I'm sure that, to Annette, we were pretty strange birds there at Poseidia, including the others on her dream team. But she also thought it was a "grand experiment."

Nora, another member of Lola's team who only responded when she had something specific to report, owned and ran a general store in the western part of Virginia. Her response to the fourth target goal was brief and to the point.

"I dreamed of a white clapboard building," she said. "Later the same night, I dreamed of a modern building, something to do with a second floor."

Without fuller description it is difficult to tell whether or not Nora saw Poseidia Institute buildings or some other. What is true is that the Institute began its existence in the downstairs of a white clapboard house in Virginia Beach near Lake Holly and that the location where the organization was later housed was the second floor of an office building.

The second statement Nora made in her letter echoed Annette's earlier description of Team One's facilitator, Lola. "In every dream since this experiment began," Nora said, "I have dreamed of a medium-height woman in her mid-thirties. Keep seeing a peculiar shade of blue slacks, maybe periwinkle blue, with a blue plaid (large) blouse and light blue sweater or jacket. Have seen this person in several dreams."

Lola, from the age of sixteen when she first began classes at Poseidia Institute, had worked hard to develop her intuitive abilities and dreaming skills. As a result, she may have been a strong focal point for group dreams. There is no way we will be able to tell if this is true however, or speculate as to whether one or two strong dreamers might be able to focus an entire group of dreamers until we understand much more than we do today about the nature of consciousness.

Not everyone on Lola's team dreamed about her on the night of the fourth target date, or at least not in any recognizable form.

"I remember a tall, pale building and a woman with short brown hair and a bright pink outfit," Shelly wrote. Not much else though."

That night Lola had a dream, which she described as, "It wasn't a lucid dream, and I'm not sure it was a dream team dream, but it was a Poseidia dream." Somewhat apologetically she added, "Since I work at Poseidia, I have Poseidia dreams a lot." In her dream, Lola had a discussion with a man about a "theory of learning I had developed through a research project at Poseidia."

Of all the dreams on both teams, Connie's probably came closest to an actual description of the Poseidia Institute building.

Poseidia seems to be located in a building that has more than one story or level. I think the building is made of light brick or stone. I saw rooms that looked like dorm rooms or motel rooms.

At the time the experiment began, Poseidia Institute was housed in a one story, brick house on a large lot, surrounded by trees. This building may have inspired many of the dreams group members to dream about a big house surrounded by lots of land. However, shortly after the beginning of the experiment, we moved to the second floor of a modern office building faced with light brick. Connie was not the first person to note that the office building looked like a motel, though she was the first to do so from dream state.

In final analysis, four out of ten people on each of the dream teams dreamed of buildings which, in some way, could describe Poseidia Institute. Several people gave possible team member descriptions; and Caroline, from Team One, dreamed that she was in a classroom with "twenty or thirty others." As June pointed out in her notes on the experiment, both Team One and Team Two came to Poseidia that night.

"If the team went to Poseidia Institute, I missed them," Barbara commented in her dream report for the fourth goal. Despite her heavy college course load, Barbara was becoming more and more fascinated by the potentials of human consciousness and had been spending all her spare time reading and asking questions of anyone who would listen. Barbara was occupied on the night of the fourth target date with a lucid dream experience she later described to the group:

The floor under the bed starts to quake. The quaking is so forceful that it feels like a series of physical shocks. When everything quiets down, I rise up on one elbow and look out of the door, which is wide open. A golden light suffuses the hall, which is empty. I am startled but not frightened.

Lucidity was not the goal of the Dreams[10] experiment, but we discovered that this format of group dreaming tended to develop lucidity. Why this is true, can only be imagined. There are many hints though, in the dream records of other cultures, that intent and attention promote lucidity. And Dreams to the Tenth Power dreaming required both intent and attention.

By month two of the second Dreams to the Tenth Power project, even though neither group had again achieved the spectacular results seen early in the experiment, the twenty members of the research project were beginning to treat each other like old friends. In their weekly letters, they began to not just tell their dreams but to dialog with one another. Though they had never met, they were beginning to form friendships. Around this time several interesting threads of conversation began.

About the November 4 target date goal, "Come to Poseidia," Team One's math professor, John, wrote:

I didn't make it. My Dreams[10] dream occurred on Wednesday night, and it was horrible. Wednesday was the day I got the latest letters, and I guess I was excited about the whole thing. I dreamed my best friend was somehow similarly involved in some sort of dream research/telepathy, etc. There was one woman with whom he was regularly communicating in this way. One day the "transmission" brought across a message about someone being killed in an automobile accident. Who, it was not clear, but the whole thing was very disturbing. When I awoke, the message that remained in my mind was very clearly that I shouldn't be messing around with this project. I felt ill all day.

But that didn't stop me. I tried again on Thursday, with little success. Although I dreamed a lot, I kept waking and realizing I wasn't doing Dreams[10] dreams. In one dream though, I talked with a woman with long, dark hair, who also seemed to be part of our project. I think we were sitting at a table, drinking a soda. We realized we were "skipping class," but didn't feel much like attending.

Once she read John's dream, Shelly, who had, on two separate target nights dreamed about a character who may have been John, fired off an immediate reply: "I remember that dream. I also had it in my dream journal! We were in the teacher's lounge at my school. We were drinking sodas from the machine and discussing the fact that I was, at that moment, skipping class. Wow!"

Shelly's response contains the "ah ha!" so common among dreamers when they recognize, at the gut level, that they have been dreaming together. On the other hand, her response was another of those that are so frustrating to the dream researcher. Because the dream she had was not reported immediately after the target date, because she waited until she had already read John's dream, Shelly's dream report could not be seen as hard evidence of group dreaming.

We found it amusing to see how John, who had repeatedly shown his reluctance to dream with the group, was still one of the first to attain such a clear connection with another member of his dream team. In spite of his reluctance, John was a very talented dreamer. He appeared repeatedly in the dreams of the others on Team One. He was the first to succeed in identifying one of his team members in a dream, even to the point of knowing the other person's name. And John was repeatedly aware, while in dream state, of what he should be doing, even if he didn't always do it.

It appears that for some individuals who are particularly sensitive or intuitive, group dreaming is a difficult challenge. Our culture offers little in the way of training people to erect boundaries against the emotions and feelings of others while in waking state, let alone at the dream level.

Caroline had just the opposite problem from John's. Even though she was a volunteer at the Institute, and generally had excellent dream recall, she had not had any luck during the weeks of the dream experiment. "To tell the truth," she wrote to her group after the November fourth date, "I'm feeling frustrated by not being able to join in the dream team! I thought for sure I could do this one. I thought I had been too tense about it, and I tried to relax this time."

Earlier in her letter, Caroline had raised the question, "Isn't it possible we might appear different in our dreams than we look?"

Of course this question, which made sense to anyone familiar with dreams, raised a flurry of comments. Darlene replied, "I agree with Caroline that it's very possible for us to appear different in our dreams than we are day-to-day. Perhaps it's a desire to be different than we are."

In response to Caroline's question, John raised the issue that those of us facilitating the experiment had discussed only among ourselves. "I also wondered like Caroline did about what we would expect to look like in other's dreams," John said. "Would it be the same as we look right now? I wouldn't necessarily expect that to be the case.... I wonder also about the appearance, in a few people's dreams, of a (roughly) 5'10", 170 pound, bearded man. Apart from the beard, the description is close to me, though a little smaller."

The question of what people looked like in dream state would become even more important for the next goal. On November eighteenth we asked the dreamers to: "Pick someone in the group that you would like to get acquainted with and go visit them." Once we were sure that the team members had completed this goal, we finally sent photographs to each of the team members to all members of their teams so they could determine whether they had met one another. On this date, the fifth of seven target dates planned for the dream teams, Team Two actually had the greater number of hits but the comments from Team One were especially interesting in light of their earlier discussion.

"I decided to try to visit Caroline," Annette wrote:

I read over all her Dreams[10] goal sheets on both Wednesday and Thursday night before I went to bed. On Thursday I saw lots of strangers in my dreams, both male and female, but there were no clues from any of them that could lead me to recognize Caroline. I dreamed I went to my parents' house for Thanksgiving. They had lots of company, including several strangers. Then I dreamed I was in church. The priest went and stood in the back and let a woman take over and lead the services. But I still didn't recognize Caroline!

Still undaunted, Annette continued, "Oh well, I've decided to think of our group as pioneer scientist-experimenters in the early days of psi-science. How many times did Wilbur and Orville sputter out before they got off the ground? Let's keep trying."

Shelly was closer to the target that night. "I chose Annette," she said, "but I just had bad dreams all night. I do remember about a woman, maybe thirty, with short to medium length light brown hair. The only distinct detail I can remember is that she had on a pair of stout, English walking shoes but then I think she took one off and hit a little old lady on the head with it. (Nothing personal, Annette.)"

To this amusing dream sequence Shelly told, Annette replied a week later:

I got quite excited about Shelly's dream because she had planned to meet me, and the person she described sounds very much like me. I don't specifically recall participating in the events of the dream she described, but there are some interesting parallels with some waking experiences I had. Around that time, my husband told me that he had invited to our home for

Thanksgiving an English couple. I had met the husband once, but I had not met the wife. My husband described her to me as the sort of person who "wears sensible shoes...."

I think the connection between Shelly's dream and my waking experience illustrates how important it is for us to include as much of our dream content with as many details as possible, especially on the night we do Dreams[10].

Annette added, "Now that I've seen everyone's picture, I think the woman I saw leading the religious service in my last dream looked a lot like Caroline."

"Someone came to see me," Connie wrote, "but I don't know who! I tried on successive nights to identify the team member, but they would not let me go to meet them." Despite this failed attempt Connie said, "I feel encouraged and excited about this project. It is frustrating to feel like I am so close to specific goals and details and just miss. The good part is being able to ascertain that I am experiencing Dreams[10] dreams. The people on this team seem to be influencing my dreams. I just can't seem to get a picture of how! I think we need a long time—or maybe a little more information about each other."

"I'm really frustrated with this now," wrote Darlene, "because I <u>know</u> I'm dreaming <u>when</u> I'm dreaming, but details fade immediately on waking. I had chosen to meet Lola, and unfortunately don't know if I succeeded."

Since Lola dreamed that she was at a convention at an oceanfront hotel where she met several team members, there is some possibility that Darlene dreamed the event but didn't recall it. "Darlene was there," Lola wrote, "but after just saying hello, she went into another room.... There was a lunch buffet. There were several people there. There was one woman that I focused on. She was standing by a window with a drink in her hand. I think it was Annette."

Catherine, who also appeared in Lola's dream, wrote that she had gone to a party where, "There were a few people milling around. Some were old friends; others were strangers. All were urging me to try the homemade cider."

Again from the two teams, fewer than fifty percent of the participants achieved direct hits on the night of November eighteenth. However, compared with what we had earlier asked people to do, later goals were increasingly complex and more specific.

From Team Two, Felicia wrote. "I decided to visit Chet because of the softball dreams we have both been having." Unfortunately, she said, she met no one in her dreams that looked like Chet, nor did she have any softball dreams.

Chet on the other hand, wrote:

After reading the packet of dreams, I decided to try to concentrate on Felicia. I started to dream about my softball team here at school. (This isn't surprising since I live with four other team members) I was dreaming that we were practicing for the season. Then I remember seeing a girl, someone I didn't know but felt I should. She was about 5'10"-5'11", with dark, shoulder-length hair. Her hair was parted in the middle and kind of feathered back. I woke up as she was walking toward me.

In Chet's case, the girl he dreamed about looked nothing like Felicia, who in waking life was a young African-American woman with a nicely shaped afro. The problem of course, is that given the discussion of dream selves resembling waking selves, who is to say that the young woman Chet dreamed was not some dreamland version of the person he intended to meet?

Barbara, continuing her string of rather impressive dreams, gave an exact description of Chet, with whom she met and talked. But she did this in such a dismissive manner that it must have been terribly frustrating to others on her team who were having difficulty even remembering their dreams.

"I eventually spoke to someone associated with the dream team," reported Barbara, who had been dreaming about skiing in the mountains.

I was still in snow gear, complete with down mittens, but he was dressed in a simple sweater and cords. Since the conversation took place in a black/white area, the context was probably not important. He was between 19 and 25, had light brown hair with a golden cast, parted on the far left—short, collar length or less. I think he also had brown eyes. His skin was pale. I don't remember what we talked about.

Notice Barbara's use of the words "black/white area" to describe the dream region in which she met Chet. Although there has been research done on dreaming in black and white, such research is limited. However, evidence points to the possibility that people sometimes use "black and white" dreams to describe a mood or feeling. For Barbara, her dream of Chet appeared in a more neutral area than appeared in her earlier dreams, which were in full color. The Dreams to the Tenth Power experiment, with its wealth of recorded dreams, allowed us to take an unparalleled look into people's dreaming psyches.

Arthur, for example, seldom sent verbal descriptions of his dreams. He most frequently sent drawings sometimes accompanied by words. For this particular goal, he sent a drawing of a man with lots of long, curly hair and a full, bushy beard. Aside from the bearded man, possibly John, who so frequently turned up in Team One dreams, none of the members of either team wore a beard. Dream team members often complained about the difficulty of writing down everything that happened in one dream, let alone recording all of their dreams in detail as we had asked them to do. Even though his drawing did not resemble any of his teammates, Arthur's solution at least provided an alternative to writing.

Angela from Team Two, was in Japan for two weeks during the time of this goal and the previous one. Through a clerical error, since she needed to have a package prepared for her before her trip, Angela received two copies of the fifth goal to meet someone on the team and no copy of the fourth goal to meet at Poseidia. In spite of the error, she valiantly aimed herself at the task of meeting team members two weeks in a row from a distance of several thousand miles.

Her dreams were full of oriental art objects and oriental people, no doubt the result of her travels. Yet on the night of the fourth target date, she attended a business convention in her dreams, where she met a man who looked very much like Arthur, the only businessman on her team.

> One particular gentleman in a black suit and black bow tie sat by himself at the table I was struggling to get by. He was balding on top and had gold-rimmed eye glasses. He seemed <u>very important</u>....

The night of the fifth goal, when Angela attempted to meet either Arthur or Chet in the dream state, she dreamed instead of Friedrich Chopin. "I was eating breakfast with Chopin," she commented, "the <u>composer!</u> He looked just like his pictures!"

June, like Lola and Angela among others, dreamed on the fifth target date of being at a convention:

> I was talking with a girl of medium height with brownish hair. I think it was Carol. She was laughing and saying how surprised she was (that we met.)

Arthur also tried to meet Carol in the dream state with no success. Carol, a greenhouse manager in the western part of Virginia, wrote that she dreamed "something very vague, something about boxes of stuffed animals."

At the end of her letter, almost as an afterthought, Carol added a line which led us to one of the most interesting events in the entire Dreams to the Tenth Power experiment. "I'm getting married on Saturday," she said. "Maybe next dream date everyone could visit my wedding and say who was there."

Chapter Five - Team Two Goes to a Wedding

As the holidays approached, a number of people in each group, particularly the students, began to miss deadlines. This was understandable, given the length of the project and student schedules at the end of the semester. But June, Lola and I regretted the loss of momentum. We began to think and talk about how to bring some renewed energy into the research.

We worried that we had given the dream teams goals which were too difficult or too unclear. Maybe we should never have given both teams the same goals. It had seemed like a good idea initially, since we hoped to compare performance between the two teams; but maybe it had led both teams into confusion. We were especially concerned about the next goal, number six.

As we had designed it, the goal was: "Meet your dream team at Poseidia, and all travel together to the beach." Not a very exciting goal, we said to each other, too much like goal four, the come to Poseidia Institute goal. Boring.

When she read Carol's note about her wedding, June began to laugh. She looked at Lola and me with eyes full of mischief. "Why not ask Team One (Lola's team) to go to the beach," June said, "and ask Team Two to go to the wedding, just like Carol suggested?"

Why not? No rule that said both dream teams had to attempt the same goals. As no one had ever done this type of research before, there were no models to follow. We had emphasized to the dream teams the need to have fun with the experiment. This divergence from our original plan seemed exactly the type of spontaneous event that could fan the flames of interest, making the experiment seem more like fun and less like work. For the December second goal, we instructed Team One to go to the beach, Team Two to Carol's wedding.

As we had feared, the instructions to go to the beach seemed to prove less than interesting to Team One. Only five people from the team bothered to respond and for the first time since the experiment began, no one on Team One achieved the goal. Not that they didn't come up with some interesting commentary, as this team was inclined to do. Of the two teams, they were generally more chatty in the responses they wrote to each dream goal.

"As for the goal of traveling to the beach together," Annette wrote, "I was enthusiastic about trying it:"

I had visualized us all holding hands and flying (astrally) through the air to the beach like Peter Pan and Wendy, then frolicking and having a wonderful time in the waves and the sand. Unfortunately, I have no recall of such a dream that night, or of seeing any Dream Team members. Although I dreamed frequently throughout the night, most of the dreams I can recall seem to be of a personal nature and tinged with anxiety. In the dream state I kept looking at my watch and seeing that I was late to meet my carpool to drive to work.

However, there was <u>one</u> element I recall that I know had Dreams[10] significance. Several times during the night, I heard Tchaikovsky's "Sleeping Beauty" theme playing far off. I was aware when I would hear it that it was symbolizing the Dreams[10] experience.

One of the more interesting aspects of Annette's dream record is her mention of Tchaikovsky's "Sleeping Beauty," because it reminds us of a seldom-explored fact of dreaming. Although most sighted individuals tend to focus most closely on the visual aspects of dreams, there are many dreams which involve primarily sound, taste, smell or touch. These dreams tend to be largely ignored by researchers though there have been a number of articles written about dreams of the blind. Questions of perceptions and the symbols into which perceptions are translated are highly pertinent to any study of shared dreaming.

"Sorry group, I couldn't manage anything," Shelly responded to Team One, "maybe because I've been sick for a couple of days. I tried again for a week. Nothing."

John, with his usual resistance to dreaming with the group, reported that "The CIA needed me to carry out a project for them." His dream was a cloak and dagger adventure involving neither team members nor the sixth goal. However he had a lot to say about the Dreams[10] experiment in his letter. "I was very interested in Connie's comments concerning some of the parallels in her dreams and mine," John said. "I have also noticed striking similarities with Annette's dreams at times."

He closed his letter with the following comment: "Thank you for the pictures. I was bowled over when I saw the picture of Shelly, because she is a perfect likeness of the girl I met in a dream a few weeks back—a dream where we sat at a table, sipping sodas and talking about 'skipping class.'"

"I felt very sad when I read that we only had two more dream goals," Caroline said in her letter. "I feel like I'm just getting into the swing of this. I would suggest that the next experiment be a month or even two longer." She added, "Darlene looks like the lady I've seen in a couple of dreams, the airplane dream for sure."

Even for Lola, who frequently dreamed the goals clearly and lucidly, the trip to the beach was a bust. "I think I did this one last time [in her convention at the beach]," she lamented. "I couldn't get anything this time. I didn't remember any dreams from Wednesday through Sunday."

Although Team One had no luck with their goal at all, what we discovered was that for Team Two, the challenge of going to Carol's wedding created quite a different picture. On the sixth target date, not only did nine members of the team respond, but six out of the nine dreamed about weddings or wedding-related activities.

Reading the responses from Team Two for this date however, provides a clear picture of one major flaw in the type of experiment we had set up. Presented with the idea that they could dream mutually, lucidly, and with clear focus, people tended to believe they should do just that. The Team Two dreamers appeared to believe that success, in the case of Carol's wedding, could be achieved by nothing less than attending the actual wedding in the dream state.

Said Felicia:

> I had very little luck with this goal, perhaps because I was up so early on Friday morning. At any rate, the bride I dreamed of was not wearing white but a gown of red velvet. And I can remember only one of the people present—a blonde man in a dark grey tux.

"I didn't achieve the goal," Chet said. "The only dream I had involved an old girlfriend. When we split, it wasn't under very good terms, and we haven't spoken since. In this dream we met and became friends again." Apparently it had not occurred to Chet, as it did to the rest of us, that making up with an old girlfriend in dream state might have been a response to Carol's wedding.

"I dreamed several weddings this week," Barbara said, "but none of them was the right one. Thursday's dream was of a couple from a nearby karate dojo getting married. There were several people there, and we were all helping set up for the wedding reception afterwards."

Angela responded,

"Although I recall doing a lot of dreaming, I have difficulty remembering them. One thing that does stand out though is being with a small group of people."

> We all stood in more or less the dark shade of a forest, and in front of us was a clearing around which, in a half circle on either side, were straight, white birch trees (an altar with candles on each side?). The clearing had golden-green grass covered with small, white flowers. It seemed almost like a medieval painting, especially since a little to the right, in a clearing, was a knight in blue armor on a white horse (How's that for symbolism?). His visor was open, and he was obviously waiting for someone. Though there were spring-like flowers in the grass, the valley and hills behind the clearing were covered with "autumn colored" trees.

Angela added as an afterthought, "I hope the knight didn't wait in vain. Did Carol have second thoughts?"

Team Two's facilitator, June, almost made it to Carol's wedding, though in a somewhat "fuzzy" form:

> On Friday I thought about the goal before I went to sleep. The dream I had was fuzzy, but when I awoke I knew it had been about the wedding, and that the wedding was outside and/or in the country.

> I was at a building where there was a gathering. We were all organizing to go someplace. I left the group and started driving on a road away from the

building. As I drove farther down, there was a house or a river station on a peninsula which jutted out into the river. For some reason, I had to get across the river. I think that's where the wedding was going to be.

There was much more to the dream, but I don't remember it.

Arthur was also driving to Carol's wedding in his dream but got sidetracked in a rather interesting way. "I awoke about nine a.m.," he wrote, "after having this dream."

I was driving a taxi (which I actually do) and stopped to pick up two passengers, Angela (from the dream team) and possibly her daughter. I drove southward on a city street, and as I got into the country I noticed that the overcast sky was dramatically broken in the distance by bright sunshine.

The excitement of seeing the illuminated countryside that I was approaching caused the dream to become lucid, and I began to fly. I extended my arms forward, which surprised me because I did it automatically. I decided to gain some altitude to take in as much as possible, but as I started the ascent I noticed an electrical wire which connected a well-kept country house to a white and partly-stone, barn like building. I began to feel an electrical tingling which told me I was too close to the wire, so I decided to land.

I was then standing in my driveway next to a step ladder that my father was using to repair a wire he uses as a short wave radio antenna. The wire runs between the house and the garage. He was holding a notebook and asked me something specifically about the Dreams[10] project so that he could write it down. I thought about the question but didn't feel obligated to answer because I knew I was dreaming. I walked toward my house and woke up.

Dream team members who did not make it to the wedding were unanimously apologetic. "Sorry to miss the wedding," Jennifer wrote. "Restless nights have been consistent. I don't remember any dreams, good, bad, or indifferent."

Carol, the bride, said, "It wasn't until Sunday that I had a dream about a wedding." In her letter, she sent a brief description of the celebration, which was, of course "in the country." She also mentioned that, on the night of the dream experiment, she had concentrated on the faces of dream team members before going to sleep, as well as sending out "dream waves." Notice some of the details Carol sent in comparison with the dream team's dreams.

It was a candlelight wedding," she wrote, "with brass candelabra and candles in the windows. My two brothers were ushers, and there was a maid of honor and a best man. The maid of honor had a long, burgundy velvet skirt with an off-white, Victorian type shirt. My husband and the best man had gray, pin-stripe tuxes, and I had a long, eggshell colored skirt with a Victorian shirt also. (It was really beautiful.)

At Poseidia, we discovered that Carol had participated in the sixth dream target date in a way we could never have imagined.

"I didn't dream of my wedding," Carol said of her target night dream, "but of going instead to a beach with a group of both gals and guys:

> Nobody was really clear but one person. He had dark hair, was slender, and had a long nose. It was almost actually like Chet's picture. We all went to an apartment to take showers and then to a <u>restaurant</u> to eat pizza. I was about to see others in my beach group (might have been my dream team) when I woke up.

Prior to the target date no one had mentioned to Carol or to any of her team members our original plan to ask the dreamers to meet at the beach. Nor had anyone clued her in to the fact that Dream Team One was still being asked to go there.

The magnitude of Carol's response left June, Lola, and me wide-eyed and doubled over with laughter. Not a single person on Lola's team recalled being anywhere near the beach in dream state on the target date, although several had made the attempt. But Carol, who was probably tired of dealing with wedding preparations by then anyway had effortlessly arrived at the beach in the company of a dream team she did not recognize and then topped the evening off with a trip to a restaurant.

The next week Carol sent the group a drawing of her wedding dress and noted a few of the correlations between the dreams of her team members of the target date and the actual wedding. "Felicia mentioned red velvet," she noted. "My maid of honor had on a burgundy velvet skirt. And my husband has sandy blonde hair and wore a dark grey tux."

At this point, the four months scheduled for the second phase of the Dreams to the Tenth Power experiment were almost over. The time had passed quickly. We had barely become accustomed to the Dreams[10] rhythm of goals sent out, dreams sent in, before it was time to stop. For the dream teams, there would be a party in the dream state.

The target date was set for December 18, 1982. The message we sent to the dream teams was: "Come to a Christmas party, and bring a present for _____."

We explained to them that at the office, we would put the names of all team members from one team and then the other into a bowl, randomly selecting who would bring a present to which of their teammates. Then we would notify them of this selection individually so that the others would not know. Part of the fun of the evening would be to see if anyone remembered the gift someone gave them.

From Team One, Caroline, who had repeatedly tried and repeatedly been unsuccessful in matching her dreams with those of others on her team, was bursting with excitement after the final target date. At last she had achieved success. She wrote:

> As I was falling asleep, I started thinking about the gift I wanted to give Annette. I was thinking about the gift and, half asleep, I began talking to

Annette. I wasn't dreaming a picture yet. I couldn't remember completely what I told her the next morning, but it was something like this: "Annette, you are a perfect soul, perfect in every way. That is how God sees you and how you really are." I don't remember the rest, but I'm sure I would have ended with a blessing: "God loves you, Annette, and thank you for sharing so much with all of us." I think I would have given you something. It might have been an evergreen or possibly a plant as a symbol of life. I love cats too (have five), but hope I didn't give any of them away.

I then saw Poseidia, and the room where the couches usually are had a table with a punch bowl and food on it. I saw John by the punch bowl and introduced myself. I was very happy to see him and looking forward to seeing everyone else, but I fell completely asleep here. I don't know if I was really dreaming or not, but I can't wait to see what dreams all of you had.

As usual for the project, Caroline tended to discount her dream experiences. This time she wondered if she was really asleep. The state of consciousness she was in, called the hypnogogic state, does qualify as part of the sleep spectrum though generally dreams do not come from this state. We can see the transition Caroline makes from wakefulness, where she was simply lying in bed thinking about Annette to the point where she begins to dream about a party at Poseidia.

Team One facilitator Lola's goal for the seventh target date was to take a present to Shelly. In her dream, she gave herself a gift as well.

"Saturday night I dreamed I was going to the meeting of a group," she wrote:
I was taking a dream journal with me. It was like the one I use now, a 9"x 6" spiral-bound notebook, but the pages were yellowed. I couldn't understand, because my journal isn't very old. I was riding in a car with my husband Barry. We stopped off at some friends' house. I don't really remember being at the meeting, but I do remember a new dream journal and the "old" one being there.

"When I first remembered this dream," Lola wrote, "I knew it was the dream team dream, but I thought I didn't get to the party. Then, when I wrote the dream in my dream journal, I remembered that Shelly is a high school student."

This was the key to understanding the dream, she explained. The friend she had been visiting in her dream was Steve, from the first Dreams[10] experiment. Steve and Lola met each other when they were in high school. I was their teacher.

"At the 'real' Poseidia Christmas party Saturday evening," Lola explained, "Jean gave me a joke gift of corridor passes that she found when she was looking for Christmas wrappings."

The dream journal I used in high school was the same size as the one I use now, but the pages had a slightly yellow-green tint. I would say that when I was in high school, the most wonderful 'present' Jean gave me was my introduction to journals and dreams, and therefore the introduction to a new area of myself. Throughout my development and my work at Poseidia, I've wanted to work with high school students because I remember how open I was, and how anxious I was to learn about symbolism, dreams and everything like that. So I guess the present I wanted to give you, Shelly, was my experience with Jean at that point in my life. What someone had given me was a new journal and a new experience.

Shelly's response to Lola, once she read this interpretation of Lola's dream was:

The relationship that you and Jean had is very much like the relationship I feel I have with the group. The experiment introduced me to the world of DREAMS. I had some previous garbage on the subject, but no science, nothing with a purpose or meaning. Since you are our conductor, I guess I feel that you are my Jean, more so than the rest of the group. I'd like to thank you all for my gift: the gift of friendship, dreams and wonderful new friends.

Concerning her own dreams on the last night of the experiment, Shelly's response was ecstatic. "I did it!" she said. She had been asked to bring a gift for Darlene. She wrote:

Darlene, I remember in my dream I went shopping for you, and realized I knew absolutely nothing about you. So I decided to get you a gift that reflected me. I got you a <u>huge</u> Snoopy, a red-striped night shirt for him, and a holiday Garfield. You seemed shocked, but surprisingly happy with it. The party was in the building, in the Poseidia office. There was eggnog and mistletoe, and plenty of yuletide spirit. I had a great time, and apparently I brought a couple of friends, because my closest friends were there too. I got so excited that I had to remind myself not to wake myself up! I'll never forget all of us getting around a piano (appeared out of nowhere) and singing, "May old acquaintance be forgot, and never brought to mind..." Then I woke up. I must have cried for an hour! It made the whole experience for me.

Even though the only dreamers on Team One who reported remembering dreams specific to the Christmas Party goal that night were Shelly, Caroline and Lola, all three of them had gone a step beyond what was actually requested by the goal. In addition to bringing a gift, they had each gone to (or been planning to go to) a party at the Poseidia Institute office.

As the youngest member of her team, Shelly had been an inspiration to the other team members through her unwavering enthusiasm and the fact that she almost without exception, dreamed precisely on target. In their letters containing their final dreams, most members of Team One expressed the desire to stay in touch with each other or even continue dreaming together.

Team Two had a similar experience. From Team Two Arthur reported:

I was walking through a large corridor like a subway or airport, when next to me appeared a friend who lives in Boston. "Nat," I asked, "What are you doing here?" We went through a double door and ended up in a room where everyone was seated in upholstered green booths having drinks. It was a room lit by candlelight. My gift items are a bit unusual. I found some large turnips, which I didn't think were especially fresh, so I asked for a reduction in price, half price to be exact. Gold and silver have I none, but I give you what I have, Jill. Hope you like and found a use for some very large turnips!

Chet, who was to bring a gift to Angela, first appended a note to Katy: "You described being at a party in the last dream package. The male you described fits a description of me: 5'10", brown eyes, brown hair. Also I live 'out in the sticks' although my house is smaller. I have an open field out in the back yard that is surrounded by trees, and I live at the foot of a mountain." Concerning the Christmas party, he wrote:

Before I went to sleep, I studied the packet. When I started dreaming, I was in a bookstore trying to decide on a gift for Angela. I found a book called *The Flowering Plants of Virginia*. It was beautifully illustrated, and I thought it would make an adequate gift. As I was getting ready to leave, I dreamed that I hadn't bought my father a gift. I went back in the store and bought a book on the Civil War (Dad's a history buff). I was awakened by my cat at this point, and do not remember any more dreams.

By chance, Angela had also drawn Chet's name for the party. "My first dream was quite vague," she wrote. "It had something to do with people going in and out of a cave in which something 'occult' was happening. I woke up remembering I still hadn't gotten Chet a Christmas present."

In my next dream, I found myself in a small, private school. I went into another room and saw my oldest daughter. She had to get a gift from herself and her schoolmates for a male teacher who was leaving in mid-year (Christmas) and didn't know what to do. So I suggested a large, collage-type card listing his attributes and what he meant to his students.

June had drawn Felicia's name. Like other members of her team who had attempted to bring presents, she said sadly,

I had a really long and detailed dream, but most of it faded when I awoke, and all I was left with was a feeling about it. During part of the dream we (a group) were in a department store. I think we were Christmas shopping. I awoke with the feeling of having given Felicia a song, but I couldn't remember anything specific.

And finally Carol, who was still recovering from the shock of having dreamed about going to the beach while the rest of her group attended her wedding, wrote:

Sorry, Arthur, I didn't bring you a present because I went to some wedding instead (a little behind in my goal). It was very vague, but I did see a group of people talking together with drinks in their hands.

The second phase of the Dreams to the Tenth Power experiment drew to a close at the end of 1982. June, Lola, and I completed this second segment of the research feeling as if we had accomplished more with the experiment than we ever thought possible. With the help of the dream teams we had proved, to our own satisfaction at least, that it was possible for ordinary dreamers of any age to control their dreams, to dream about specific targets or goals, to visit another person in the dream state and remember it when awake, and to do much of this lucidly.

We had seen people accomplish some rather amazing feats of dream telepathy and precognition. These experiences, though not really expected by our research participants, had been accepted and taken in stride.

During the five months we worked on this segment of the Dreams to the Tenth Power research, a number of articles about the experiments had been published. *Brain/Mind Bulletin, The Dream Network Bulletin,* and *The National Enquirer* published features along with other magazines and daily newspapers throughout Virginia.

The research illuminated a number of questions, which naturally follow if group dreaming is a proven fact: Given that individuals can dream together on command, do people do this all the time, spontaneously? If we are dreaming together and also dream precognitively, doesn't that mean that "time" is something other than linear? And what happens to "space" if a dreamer in New York City can share simultaneous experiences with a dreamer in Virginia?

These are not easy questions. The existence of group dreaming implies the need for all of us to reexamine our beliefs about time, space, reality, and the nature of consciousness.

Chapter Six - Some Unexpected Results of Dreams[10]

Although the dream team responses to the Dreams to the Tenth Power experiment went far beyond my expectations, there was another set of responses to the experiment which were equally interesting, sometimes amusing, and often astounding. The pull of group dreaming was evident from the stacks of mail we received whenever the group dreaming research was mentioned in the media.

In these days before dialup connection, the person who heard about our work had to sit down and write a letter, add postage, and send it through the mail. The sheer variety of the letters we received demonstrated the appeal that group dreaming seemed to have for young and old alike.

Keeping in mind that most dream researchers at the time believed that "paranormal" dreamers were few and far between, we were a bit surprised at what we received. We informed correspondents that, although Poseidia Institute had no immediate plans for further research, they should experiment on their own. We encouraged people to try sharing dreams with friends, to write things down, and continue exploring.

Most of the people who wrote to us wanted to know how they could participate in the project. A fifty year old mother of two daughters, whose husband worked in the Middle East, asked if she could participate even though she traveled frequently between the U.S. and Iran. A twenty-seven year old U.S. Air Force Recruiter talked about how he always recorded his dreams.

We had letters from a Virginia housewife who was a lucid dreamer, from the retired head of an engineering firm, from a psychologist living in Paris, from a biologist from Leningrad. One letter, which came in the form of an inter-office memo from a defense-logistics agency said, "To Whom It May Concern. I am interested in joining the Dream Team."

Like many others, one high school student from Pittsburgh was eager to join the research effort. She wrote in rounded letters: "I don't know what you would want to know about me as a prospective team member. I'm sure I would be considered a lucid dreamer."

Some correspondents felt they needed to put forth their credentials by telling us what they had already achieved in their dreams. One woman wrote on official Girl Scouts of America letterhead: "I have had many a dream that has become the real happening within days or weeks, and many out-of-body travels."

A Navy wife from Massachusetts commented that: "On several occasions I have experienced clairvoyant warning in dreams. Also," she said, "I believe I have traveled to another plane in my dreams and communicated with my grandparents who are deceased."

A clinical psychologist from Texas reported: "I am a lucid dreamer and have conducted experiments in transpersonal communication for many years."

However, the prize for uniqueness among people offering their credentials for possible dream team membership would have been awarded, had we been giving such prizes, to a correspondent from a jail in Ohio. "My dreams are extraordinary," he said. "I once dreamed I'd go to two Ohio prisons, and sure enough I did." He made us an offer that was hard to refuse. "There's no doubt I could be of help to you," he wrote. "And it might even be interesting to see if other members of the team can determine if I'm a prisoner now."

Some people got right into the spirit of group dreaming in their introductory letters. One elderly man from West Virginia stated in crabbed script: "Just recently, shortly after dozing off in a chair, I was able to attain a metaphysical second body (if you can follow me) and crawled down a long, dark pipe. At the end of this pipe, I arrived at an opening where I encountered a small group of people. I know these people were real people somewhere."

A student of religious studies in Washington, D.C. wrote that she'd had recurring "rendezvous" dreams with friends with whom she was working on a spiritual project.

A woman from Florida wrote: "I've had dreams where I've been in groups of people that I've felt very familiar with, although they were not known to me in everyday life." Another woman wrote from Chicago: "Many of my dreams take place at conferences, in hotel cafeterias, etc. I would love to know who I'm conferring with!"

The most difficult request to refuse came after an article, "¿Nos Soñamos Esta Noche?" was published in the Spanish language journal, *Integral*. We were unaware that the article, drawn from U.S. publications, was in print until suddenly the Poseidia office was deluged with letters from Spain. An entire group of students at the University of Madrid wanted to become part of the Dreams to the Tenth Power experiment. Sadly, given the distance, the language barrier, and the unreliability of the mail, this request would have been impossible to reply to affirmatively, even if we could have been talked into starting a new phase of the experiment.

In order to comprehend the excitement about group dreaming, a brief look at what was happening in the entire field of dreams and consciousness studies during the seventies and eighties might be useful. It is hard for us to imagine now the excitement about dreams and other altered states of consciousness then being generated. After a decade of flower power and experiments with mind-altering drugs, young people the world over had discovered the importance of dreams. They were participating in what became known as a revolution in consciousness.

These young people, including many recent college graduates such as Stephen LaBerge, Jayne Gackenbach, Henry Reed and others, were out to prove that dreams were viable, exciting and creative and could be used to make a difference both in the lives of individuals and in the life of the community.

Books like Herman Hesse's *Steppenwolf*, with its dreamlike quality, and Aldous Huxley's *Island* were found everywhere. Huxley's essay, "The Doors of Perception," became an underground best seller.

Into this milieu came a young professor from the California Institute of Asian Studies in San Francisco, James Donahoe, who began to explore group dreaming in a parapsychology class he taught at the Institute.

"The discovery that you and a friend have awakened from the same dream might seem incredible," Donahoe said in a 1975 article written for *Psychic Magazine*. "But my own study of such events, mutual dreams, suggests they may be more common than people realize."

In this ground-breaking article, Donahoe noted that psychologist Hernial Hart identified the mutual dream as a special category of psychic experience as early as 1933, discussing his findings in an article written for the Society for Psychical Research. Donahoe noted, however, that among the thousands of dreams collected by Louisa Rhine at the Foundation for Research on the Nature of Man (FRNM), there had been so few reports of mutual dreaming that these dreams had not even warranted a separate file. And the handful of accounts which had been filed, Rhine told Donahoe, were hardly impressive enough to be called shared dreams. Louisa Rhine was the wife of Duke University's Parapsychology Chair, Dr. J.B. Rhine. Her research, along with her husband's, made FRNM one of the world's leading parapsychology research centers.

Not to be daunted, Donahoe had suggested a series of dream meetings to his parapsychology class. "If mutual dreams are so rare," he inquires in the *Psychic Magazine* article, "why did they occur so readily to members of my class?"[1]

During the 1970s and into the 1980s there developed in the area of dream studies what has been called a "grassroots dream movement." Dream workers who were not psychotherapists began to reclaim dreams and dream interpretation from what they saw as a monopoly by classically-trained, primarily Freudian psychologists and psychoanalysts. As exciting and chaotic as a real revolution, there was a groundswell of opinion that dream work could be helpful, even transformative, for anyone—not just those with the patience and financial wherewithal to afford long years of therapy.

Dr. Henry Reed, mentioned earlier in reference to the Dream Helper Ceremony which sparked the Dreams to the Tenth Power experiments, has sometimes been called the father of the dream work movement. Henry was editor of the *Sundance Community Dream Journal*, published by the ARE Press between 1976 and 1978. This journal, with its readership of approximately one thousand people, was the first magazine ever published specifically for dream work and, as such, contained articles by some of the foremost dream workers in the country. Truly unique was the fact that it also invited communal participation in understanding and working with dreams. Grassroots dream workers flocked to the publication.

Henry Reed first began to work with dreams in the classroom setting in 1970 when he was an Assistant Professor of Psychology at Princeton University. When asked to comment on his importance to the history of dream work, Henry modestly attributes fatherhood to yet another famous therapist, Fritz Perls. "About the time I began teaching at Princeton," Reed said in an interview for the *Dream Network Bulletin*, "Fritz Perls was doing dream symbol dialogues at Esalen. His work would ultimately open dream interpretation technology to the masses because he was the first person to produce a specific dream interpretation technique in public for all to see. We could experiment with his method and learn from it."[2]

With the *Sundance Community Dream Journal,* Henry Reed created a forum through which readers could speculate on such subjects as the relevance of dreams to daily life, the importance of dream lucidity, and whether dreams might influence or predict the future. The journal inspired many future leaders of the dream work movement such as Gayle Delaney, Alan Siegel, and Robert Van de Castle, as well as the man whose name would be linked with the next stage of the community dream work movement, Bill Stimson.

Stimson, a New Yorker who was active in much of the dream work that went on in the city, was so enthusiastic about the work begun by Henry Reed that, in 1978, when the journal did not receive continued funding from ARE's Atlantic University, he decided to pull on the combined resources of people he knew in order to produce a newsletter called *The Dream Network Bulletin*. This publication, which Stimson ran from his cramped apartment in Manhattan, linked dream workers from coast to coast. And because more and more people wanted to understand their dreams, this little bulletin generated so much public interest that it inspired articles in prestigious national publications such as *Omni* and *Business Weekly*. In one such article, "A Hitchhiker's Guide to Dreamland," written for *New Age Journal* by editor Mark Barasch, Robert Van de Castle, then head of the sleep laboratory at the University of Virginia, is quoted as saying that Sigmund Freud had cast "a cold, paralyzing, 50-year shadow over dreamwork."[3]

At about this time people began to discuss the idea of forming a new organization, one which would include people with a variety of perspectives on dream work: psychotherapists, sleep researchers, dream group leaders, and those who used their dreams to produce art. Quite naturally there were many points of view on how such an organization should be modeled, who should be involved. In some cases, the discussion dissolved into conflict, and any attempt to merge disparate points of view about dreaming seemed destined to fail.

That was when June, Lola, and I, along with one or two others at Poseidia Institute, such as Suzanne Keyes who had participated in the Dreams to the Tenth Power experiments and eventually took a turn at editing the *Dream*

Network Bulletin, came up with the idea of inviting dream researchers and dream workers to join in a Dreams[10] group dreaming process.

This could not actually be called research in the same sense that other Dreams to the Tenth Power experiments had been, since the idea behind this aspect of the work was to see if people who were in conflict in waking state might be able to work out the conflicts in dreams. But there were many parts of the Dreams[10] idea which could be used, such as dreaming in groups of ten, and submitting a record of dreams.

The Poseidia Institute group was feeling a little cocky about the potentials of group dreaming, having so recently seen people who were strangers to one another successfully meet in dream state. But we soon discovered that dream research participants of the ordinary kind were not nearly so difficult to deal with as dream researchers.

The first thing we learned was that a number of the primary adversaries in the conflicts around dream work were not the least bit interested in an experiment that might have them dreaming together. Once we had sent out invitations, we received several polite refusals to participate—and a couple that were not so polite.

Still there was enough interest in the idea, primarily from the grassroots dream workers that we decided to move ahead. In April of 1984, we began another round of group dream work with two teams of ten dreamers. Since this was not really research as we defined it, we made several changes in the group dreaming format.

The goals we set for the dream workers were aimed at exploring the nature of dreams, some of them asking people to dream lucidly, others geared toward group interaction. Goals such as "Construct a Dream Platform" came straight from Jane Roberts' Seth material, since several of the dream team members were interested in Seth. Jane Roberts and Seth, the entity she channeled, had by then produced a number of popular books, including information on dreams in general and group dreaming in particular. The goals we created were designed to inspire dialogue, rather than to prove that team members could dream in a particular manner.

The geographical range of the project was greater than in earlier Dreams to the Tenth Power work. At least two members of each team lived in Europe, and others planned to be traveling during the process. Thus it became important to allow more time between stages of the research for mail to cross the ocean. We agreed to set dream dates at one month intervals for seven months.

Despite any effort on our part to create a good working environment for the project, each team lost a member early in the program, so that around the office we began to call this new project Dreams to the Ninth.

As might be expected, the results from these dream groups were different too. Even though there was some evidence of shared dreaming within each group, and also cross-dreaming between the groups, the dream workers were, with few exceptions, less diligent about sending in their dreams than earlier dream teams had been, and were also more prone to talk about their waking ideas and experiences when they wrote to the group.

Still, there were some rather impressive dream-related events,which happened during this project, events which contribute to our overall understanding of group dreaming.

One of the people on the new dream teams who first wrote to me after the publication of my book *Dreams Beyond Dreaming* in 1980 was a California woman by the name of Linda Magallón. Linda and I began a correspondence then which continued for several years. Her avid interest in dream work led her to helping Stephen LaBerge collate data from his lucid dreaming experiments and then to creating experiments of her own. She was a natural choice for the group-dreaming project.

Linda was not the only one of the eighteen members of the new dream teams who was proficient in lucidity but when in July of 1984 we assigned the teams a goal to "Explore Dream Lucidity," she took lucid dreaming a step beyond what we had seen before in other lucid dream reports.

"I awoke around five a.m. after trying all night to dream about the goal," Linda wrote in her dream summary to the group. There followed a long period of struggling in which I attempted to go back to sleep and incubate a lucid dream, a period of hypnogogic activity intermingled with wakeful intervals. Finally success! At 8 a.m. a lucid dream:"

I am looking at a postcard stuck in the bottom, right-hand corner of a picture frame, which is a pen-and-ink drawing of a woman's face, primary colors on a white background. A dark, diagonal shadow obscures the picture itself. "June, June Cooper!" I exclaim. [facilitator of Linda's team.]

Then "Lenore?" [another team member] The dark shadow moves back, revealing an oil painting of a shoreline water area that waterfowl might inhabit, overhung by trees. The colors are brown and green, the picture frame ornate.

The picture frame disappears and it seems as if I am looking at wall paper. The painting melts into a vivid apple green background with a gold design. "It must be Sam!" (Note: Later I realized the color was the same as that of the latest issue of *Reality Change*, which contains Sam's name.)

The background becomes less upright, more horizontal, like gift wrap. The design changes to silver foil flowers or stars on a blue background. Who is it? "Jean Campbell."

Now I am in the living/dining room of a house. Looking about, I say, "Thank you, lucid dream state for inviting ego, I mean waking consciousness into your world."

I walk toward the front door. The entry way is shaped like a bay window. I decide to go outside, but I don't open the door—I walk through the wall.

There's not much of a sensation. Shall I do it again? I'd better strengthen my focus first.

To have more space, I move away from the house and start to spin, arms outstretched. The view begins to fade as I think, "I go where Stephen (LaBerge) is."

I twist again, saying, "Jean Campbell...Poseidia."

Notice that although Linda worked through incubation to achieve lucidity, her awareness of the lucid state came in the dream itself, the "Ah ha!" realization that one is dreaming while still in the dream. She also did two other things which, to me at least, were new aspects of lucid dream activity. The first is that while the dream was going on, she affirmed her lucid self for inviting her waking awareness into the dream. In doing this, she recognized even in the dream state that waking consciousness and dreaming consciousness are different things though possibly points on the same spectrum.

The other thing that Linda did was to practice a technique devised by Stephen LaBerge to maintain lucidity while in the dream state, that of whirling. This is probably a good place to mention that many of the people then involved in lucid dreaming shared an interest in a particular author, Carlos Castaneda.

Castaneda, who attained instant popularity in the 1970s for his book, *The Teachings of Don Juan: A Yaqui Way of Knowledge*, purported to be an anthropologist working out of the California university system. Later examination revealed that Castaneda may have done questionable research for this first book about a Yaqui Indian sorcerer, Don Juan, and the many books that followed it but that did not stop the many young people who read his book from believing that Don Juan had very real things to teach people about lucid dreaming.

In this first book, Don Juan tells Carlos to look at his hands while dreaming in order to maintain dream awareness, or "focus" as Linda calls it in the above dream. Years later, while I was sitting at a table with several of the early explorers of dream lucidity, someone mentioned that they had learned about lucidity from Carlos Castaneda. Immediately, all around the table, a dozen individuals raised their palms before their faces, laughing and saying they'd done that too.

But the whirling technique which Linda practiced in this dream and several others seems to work as well for maintaining lucidity. Quite possibly it is the focus of consciousness on maintaining awareness, no matter how it is done, that is important to lucid dreaming. At any rate, not only did Linda recognize graphic symbols for several of her fellow dream team members in her lucid dream, but she also made a conscious effort to reach them and to reach Poseidia Institute.

On that particular target date, team facilitator June Cooper took another approach to lucidity. "When I awoke in the early morning," June said, "I was annoyed that I hadn't dreamed, especially lucid dreamed; so, quite determined to achieve lucidity, I did something I have not done before:

As I started to go to sleep, I remember maintaining a strong focus on my conscious self, so I would be able to remember my dream. I started to slip into the in-between state, but it felt very different because I maintained such a strong focus. I remember seeing various images float by, and I just watched them pass, making a mental note about how I was feeling and the clarity of it all. Usually when I go through this state I am aware that I am sort of awake, and I am aware of my physical surroundings at the time, but I sort of let go and allow myself to stay suspended in between. This time my focus was very intent, and much more for the purpose of really observing the quality of that state than allowing myself to slide into it. Although I was still a participant and not just an observer.

I then went through that state into lucidity, at which point I was in a room in front of a table with many objects in front of me. I was suddenly struck by what I had done. I had consciously taken myself from the awake state into the dream state, and maintained my awake observer self involvement the entire time. I was very excited and woke up.

Two other members of this dream team were mentioned in Linda's dream. Lenore Jackson and Sam Menahem shared with Linda participation in the Seth Dream Network, an informal group sponsored by the Austin Seth Center in Austin, Texas.

Lenore was the Seth Dream Network coordinator and in 1984 she agreed to facilitate The Lucidity Project, involving those members of the Network who had experienced lucid dreaming. The Lucidity Project ran from 1984 to 1987 with dreamers sharing dream goals once a month. More than once, members of the Dreams to the Tenth Power group and the Lucidity Project dreamed overlapping dreams.

On the night of the Dreams[10] lucidity goal, Lenore wrote that she had dreamed, but not lucidly, of crocodiles in a series of muddy canals. "My crocodile dream was the result of forcing myself to return to sleep and so occurred at approximately the same time as Linda's (8 a.m.)." Commenting later on Linda's dream, Lenore noted: "In her dream, "shoreline water area" "overhung by trees" and "brown and green" all apply to my dream. "That waterfowl might inhabit" makes me think of all the shore birds I have photographed this summer."

Linda later wrote to the group:

I had just begun writing to Lenore Jackson when the Dreams[10] project was organized, and was delighted to discover that she was on my team. Fortunately, on her goal sheet, she had included some extra dreams from before the target date. I was amazed to find out that my dream of her on the day before the goal date (4/20/84) had correlations with her dreams, not of

4/20, but of 4/22 and 4/18. This was my first major experience of the sort and underlined for me the following lesson: because dreams are loose in time, correspondences can come from days other than the target date. From that point on, I made it habit to look at all my dreams in the chronological vicinity of the target.

The goal to explore dream lucidity was probably the most evocative of the seven goals presented to the group of dream researchers. British author Tony Crisp responded with:

I dreamt I was looking through rooms for a group of people. I walked through one room in which people were talking to each other. They were not the ones I was searching for, but I spoke to them and they directed me to the next room. I walked through, and there were the people I was looking for. There were maybe six or more people. They were asleep on mattresses except for two, maybe three. These latter were awake and waiting for me, sitting on their mattresses. The awake ones wore small, pointed hats such as Tibetan lamas wear. In the dream I realized this meant they had achieved sufficient inner growth to wake up in their sleep. We started to communicate with each other, and we were going to help wake the others up.

At the end of the group dreaming project in October, 1984, Tony's summary of the work reflected the statements of others who had seen the project through "The group experiment has been highly successful for me," he wrote.

Not that I have satisfyingly reached the set goals, but in that it has created an environment in which many issues have been clarified for me in regard to trust and inner meeting. I have been confronted by some of the powerful feelings and reactions I have about this, and have been able to share these with you. These were not always comfortable for me—maybe not even for you—but perhaps real growth has some discomfort in it?

In the meantime, while the dream workers met in the dream state with their dream teams, the dream organization that had been discussed was taking shape. In the summer of 1984 the first conference of the International Association for the Study of Dreams (IASD) was held in San Francisco. Although none of us from Poseidia Institute attended that first conference, the fledgling organization's second conference was scheduled for June of 1985 on the East coast, in Charlottesville at the University of Virginia.

The campus that Thomas Jefferson built, with its stately quad surrounded by brick arched walkways, seemed the perfect place for a dream conference as many of America's founding fathers had been strong dreamers. There were many people attending that conference who would later gain fame for their work with dreams, from conference host and that year's IASD president, Robert Van de Castle, to Patricia Garfield, Gayle Delaney, and other West Coast founders of the organization.

But most exciting for June Cooper and me, attending the conference together from Poseidia Institute, was the fact that many of the dream workers who had participated in the previous year's group dreaming project would be there at the conference. After months of correspondence and shared dreams, the final task for the group would be to see whether we could recognize one another in person. Linda Magallón was easy to spot. As IASD Treasurer, she was the person in charge of registration. Other members of the dream worker dream teams arrived throughout the afternoon of registration day. Suzanne Keyes, June, and I were scheduled on the first day of conference programming to present a panel on the topic of the Dreams to the Tenth Power research. When the time came to present the panel, we simply invited all of the Dreams to the Tenth Power participants up on the stage. The event was a little like a family reunion, though some family members had met only in dreams.

It was plain to see that, for at least some members of the conference audience, the idea of people dreaming together was not quite believable particularly when presented by a group of people laughing so uproariously. Still there was much interest, and many questions. It was not until the next day though, on a panel called "Mental Health Applications of Dreams" facilitated by Patricia Garfield, that I had the chance to describe what for me had been the single most unexpected result of the Dreams to the Tenth Power research. The story I told that day was about Gail Ward, a member of the Poseidia Institute counseling staff, and how she had dreamed with one of her clients.

Gail was new to the staff when we began working with phase two of the Dreams to the Tenth Power experiment. And though she sometimes socialized or took classes with other staff members, she was too busy with her therapy practice to become much involved in the dream research.

One day she came to my office, as she often did, to talk about what was happening with one of her clients. This woman, who had received a medical reading a few months earlier, had been plagued since childhood by a terrible nightmare from which she would awake screaming but unable to remember anything except fragmented images.

What Gail had devised as a treatment for the problem took my breath away. She told the client she would dream with her – that she would accompany her in dream state to the place of the nightmare's origin.

She did exactly that and more. What she did, Gail told me, was go into the nightmare with her client and observe the dream from start to finish. Then still asleep, she had left the dream and worked out its meaning before waking up, remembering the dream and writing down both the dream and its meaning. At the next therapy session, the client said she had remembered the dream for the first time ever. The dream she told Gail was the dream Gail had observed. Together the two of them worked on the meaning of the nightmare, which after that never recurred.

When she finally noticed my open-mouthed astonishment, Gail had paused in her narrative. "What?" she asked. "Did I do something wrong?"

I hastened to reassure her that, as far as I could tell she had done something impossible but exactly right but by then she was looking at me with almost the same degree of amazement I had been showing her moments before.

"Isn't that what you do?" she asked.

"No, I've never done that. What do you mean?"

Gail said, "Isn't that what you do in those Dreams to the Tenth Power experiments? I always thought it was."

The solution for working with a client's dreams that Gail had discovered, I had to acknowledge, was a fine therapy technique—for those who could manage it.

Part Two
What is Group Dreaming?

Chapter Seven - The Language of Group Dreaming

The reason June and I traveled to the International Association for the Study of Dreams conference together was that even before the conference ended, the two of us were leaving for Switzerland to attend a seminar on Jung and Creativity taught by Dr. Marian Pauson through Old Dominion University. Marian was the head of one of the few graduate Jungian Studies certificate programs in the United States and had become my good friend during the many courses I took with her.

The rapid change from the Piedmont area of Virginia to the snow-covered peaks of the Alps was like a dream in itself. June and I laughed and chatted on the drive from Geneva, around Lake Geneva to Montreux, then up a winding mountain road to the village of Caux. The evening sun was dropping shadows amid the trees of the surrounding forest by the time we pulled into the drive of Hotel Les Rosiers. We found the students from our class eating dinner in the glassed-in dining room of the small hotel with its breathtaking view of the lake far below.

We were already a day late for the seminar. The other students gathered around us while we ate and then hurried us off to the chateau behind the main lodge where the seminar was being taught.

When the others learned why June and I had been detained and what our topic had been at the dreams conference, they asked if it would be all right for the class to try dreaming together. So once again that night, after hours of transatlantic flight, June and I found ourselves in the midst of a group dreaming project.

Whether it was the long trip, the wine I had with dinner, or the altitude which left me feeling giddy, going into dreams was easy for me that night. Unfortunately, I found myself in the apartment of the couple in the group who had recently married and were using this class as their honeymoon trip. They noticed me too in my dream. And in dream state, Charlie the bridegroom offered me a toast from a silver goblet.

To my embarrassment, they both remembered the dream in the morning as well, proving once again how many people take easily to group dreaming. But I was happy and relieved to hear that Charlie only recalled offering me a toast, and his wife Judith had dreamed of a "chalice of enchantment."

This was a group with a natural interest in dreams, which went beyond studying Carl Jung. The seminar itself had been prompted by a dream. For at least two years, Marian had resisted the University's request that she teach a class in Switzerland, where she'd lived for many years and raised a family. But then she dreamed of a table with a vase holding three white roses and saw this as a sign that it was time to teach a class at Les Rosiers.

As part of the course requirement, Marian requested a paper on the hermenutics, or mythic underpinning of a dream each student selected from personal dreaming, an exercise which opened new vistas for me in dream work. The dream I selected was a precognitive one, in which Marian had told me I would be going to Switzerland before I consciously knew it and a huge bronze sunburst on the wall of her office in my dream had chimed a deep, pleasant sound at her pronouncement. Researching the history and symbolism of bells and chimes had caused me to remark to June that I should take a tape recorder to Europe with me in order to record the sounds of bells, rather than a camera, a somewhat prescient comment itself in light of what happened before our trip concluded.

The week of the class seemed far too short with mornings dedicated to discussion and afternoons filled with painting or modeling in clay. And on the last morning, we found ourselves seated around the big, circular table on the hotel patio, sun warming our faces, the bright red geraniums which filled hotel window boxes and planters giving off the pungent odor of freshly-watered flowers.

"I wish I could remember the words to the hymn I was singing in my sleep last night," Marian said. "I kept hearing it over and over." Of course we asked her to hum a few bars, and before long all of us were singing: "Praise to the Lord, the Almighty, the King of Creation," an apt ending for a course on creativity. Each evening of the seminar we held a brief ritual in the tiny chapel built at the turn of the century by the British located just a few steps down the road from the hotel. The walls of the chapel were filled with magnificent German woodcarvings. That night, after each person lit a candle with a prayer for the group, we made a candlelight procession three times around the little church singing, "Praise to the Lord, the Almighty, the King of Creation."

Early the next morning, June and I were among the first to leave the hotel in our bright red rental car. We planned to drive across Switzerland, through southern Germany to Austria, where we would spend a few days before leaving from Vienna to return home.

In Salzburg we visited the apartment near the center of the old city where Mozart was born and spent his early years. Not far away was the square that housed the Salzburg Carillon. The chiming of the bells from this carillon was said to have influenced the musical theme of Mozart's most famous opera, *The Magic Flute.*

Both June and I wanted to hear a concert played on the famous old set of bells so the designated hour found us sitting on the edge of the fountain in the square which faced the carillon tower. The hands of the clock in the bell tower pointed to the hour; the carillon began to play: "Praise to the Lord, the Almighty, the King of Creation." June and I looked at each other in amazement. How odd that it should play the very hymn Marian had heard in her dream. At the end of the hymn there was a slight pause. Then the carillon began again. Once more it played the same tune.

By then, June and I were laughing and elbowing one another, despite the looks from other people in the crowd who'd begun staring at us. It played the hymn twice! This ancient carillon, which plays such a variety of music that CDs and tapes of its concerts have made it famous the world over, had just played the same song twice in a row. Again the pause. Then one more time the carillon began to play: "Praise to the Lord, the Almighty, the King of Creation." Then it stopped. Concert over.

June and I finished laughing, shook our heads in amazement, and hurried off to buy a postcard to send to Marian. She wouldn't believe it. Nobody would believe this one. What was that, we asked ourselves? What was it called when dreams jumped into physical reality, played around a little bit, and then jumped back into dreams again? Carl Jung had defined synchronicity, the juxtaposition of unlikely events in waking reality, as an "acausal" principle. What if there was really causality in synchronistic events? And what if that cause came from the area of the human unconscious sometimes illuminated in dreams?

There was no name for the phenomenon we had just witnessed, at least not one that we knew of, but I knew that group dreaming opened the door to further understanding. Maybe there would be a name one day for the type of event produced by Marian's dream and the carillon concert. The answer lay in more research, more study of group dreaming and greater understanding of the implications of group dreaming.

Sadly, those of us at Poseidia would not be doing the research. In December of 1985, after thirteen years of operation, we closed the doors of Poseidia Institute. It was a difficult decision. Our dedicated staff of underpaid and volunteer employees agreed that it was time to stop. One person was having a baby; two others had plans for graduate study outside of Virginia. People needed to develop other aspects of their lives.

At the same time, particularly among people who had worked with the Dreams to the Tenth Power research, the attempt to understand group dreaming went on. Interest was growing. The language of dreaming together was becoming more precise; more people were becoming conscious of the social aspects of dreaming.

For the next ten years, I had little time to think about dreams. I moved to Washington, D.C. to pursue graduate studies, then back to Tidewater for work at teaching and as a senior editor for a local publishing firm. Before long the research in shared dreaming had gone well beyond me.

More and more, researchers were beginning to look at dreams in a new way through the perspective of the new physics of relativity and through another science, linguistics. As in any scientific endeavor, in order for communication to take place, a shared language is essential. Dream researchers were developing the language of group dreaming.

Though we are not prone to think of it this way, the telling of a dream, even prior to understanding a dream, requires that the dream be translated into language. Customarily, people also tend to believe that the language of dreams is the language of their native tongue. Studies have shown, however, that people who are bilingual often dream quite different types of dreams when dreaming in one language or the other.

What created the discovery of group dreaming in the 1970s? Was it that dreams were doing something different from what they had done before or was it that evidence of group dreaming was only then being seen?

In the field of linguistics, probably the most controversial theory of the past fifty years is one introduced early in the past century by Benjamin Whorf. This hypothesis, known as the Sapir-Whorf Hypothesis, is a theory of linguistic relativity. In Whorf's own words, from his essay, "Language, Myth and Reality:"

Actually thinking is most mysterious, and by far the greatest light thrown upon it that we have is thrown by the study of language. This study shows the form of a person's thoughts are [sic] controlled by inexorable laws or patterns of which he is unconscious.... And every language is a vast pattern-system, different from others, in which are culturally ordained the forms and categories by which the person not only communicates, but also analyzes nature, notices or neglects types of relationship and phenomena, channels his reasoning and builds the house of his consciousness.[1]

Clearly Whorf saw language, which he did not equate with thinking, as a filter through which communication, analysis, and reasoning are sifted.

Whorf goes on to say in the same essay:

Thinking also follows a network of tracks laid down in the given language, an organization which may concentrate systematically upon certain phases of reality, certain aspects of intelligence, and may systematically discard others featured by other languages. The individual is utterly unaware of this organization and is constrained completely within its bonds.

At the far end of this linguistic hypothesis is the idea that people can perceive only what learned language allows them to perceive. Suzette Hayden Elgin, a formidable linguist herself, developed an award-winning science fiction novel, *Native Tongue*, around just this hypothesis.

However, we do not have to go that far to see the importance of language in conceptualization. We have only to look at the many words for snow in the language of the Inuit tribes, or to see the word *koosigaan*, which in certain dialects of the Algonquin language means, "the fire makes visions of the future," to understand that perceptions clearly labeled and understood in one language may have no place at all in another.

A more recent demonstration of this strange connection between perception and language was pointed out by neurologist Oliver Sacks when he wrote about his discovery of Tourette's syndrome, a neurological illness that subjects those who have it to outbreaks of sound or words. Sacks, who has discussed his discovery in many books and articles, said that the day he saw his first Tourette's patient and understood that he was seeing the symptoms of a previously-undiagnosed illness, went out for a walk immediately afterward. While walking down the street Sacks said, he saw people with Tourette's syndrome everywhere, whereas the previous day he had seen none. Something similar to this may be happening to scientists who are studying dreams and the nature of consciousness.

In his book *Uncommon Wisdom*, Fritjof Capra interviews experts in several fields of science concerning the impact of an ongoing paradigm shift toward a relativistic view of the universe. "Throughout the history of Western science and philosophy, there has always been the belief that any body of knowledge had to be based on firm foundations," Capra states.

Accordingly scientists and philosophers throughout the ages have used architectural metaphors to describe knowledge. Physicists looked for the "building blocks" of matter and expressed their theories in terms of "basic principles" and "fundamental constants." Whenever major scientific revolutions occurred it was felt that the foundations of science were moving.... It appears that the science of the future will no longer need any firm foundations, that the metaphor of the building will be replaced by that of the web, or network, in which no part is more fundamental than any other part.[2]

Because the world of science and philosophy is shifting, however imperceptibly, toward a new, relativistic paradigm, it becomes important that dream researchers keep pace with the shift. The language with which we describe dreams may need to move away from the rather simplistic definition of a dream as being something which happens to a particular individual while asleep, and expand to contain explanations for phenomena such as group dreaming and mutual lucidity without resort to such confining and pejorative labels as psi, paranormal, and anomalous.

The word for what June and I experienced was coined in 1998, twelve years after the trip to Switzerland, by researcher Cynthia Pearson, who presented a paper at the International Association for the Study of Dreams conference entitled, "Earwigs and Arabesques: Dreaming in the Multiverse."

In this paper, Pearson talks about the dream group she had been meeting with for the past several years and the events surrounding a dream she had. Not all of the events happened in the sleep state and some of the events were shared by other members of her dream group.

What do we call events which bounce from dreamer to dreamer both in and out of sleep state? Pearson names them arabesques, a complex pattern of intertwined lines, which is also the name for a dance form.

"Perhaps all of us who live in this confining space-time continuum are traveling every night, to and through other universes," Pearson writes.

However, the more I think about it, the more I like the classic simplicity of the arabesque. It can depict not only the intertwining of our waking and dreaming lives; of our past, present, and future; and of our connections with others. It can also suggest the endlessly complex and ornate branching of the multiverse.[3]

After Poseidia Institute closed, Linda Magallón continued to explore group dreaming and eventually convinced several others, including Cynthia Pearson, of the value of group dreaming research. Between 1986 and the publication of her book *Mutual Dreaming* in 1997, Linda conducted a series of group dreaming experiments loosely modeled after the Dreams to the Tenth Power experiments. "True to the name of the prototype," she says in the *Psychic Creative Dreaming* course she designed for online use, "there was an average of 10 people in each group."[4]

As part of the design for her online course, Linda further clarified her thoughts about shared dreaming and identified and named some aspects of mutual dreaming which had not heretofore been clarified.

For example, she states in the "Social Dimensions of Dreaming" section of her course, "There are two classic types of mutual dreams, 'meeting' and 'meshing.'" And then goes on to define them:

> In meeting dreams, two or more people dream of encountering one another. Ruby Carrol lived in Parksville, Kentucky. One spring night she dreamed that she was seated alone at a table in a crowded café. When a handsome man approached, searching for a seat, Ruby invited him to join her. "I'm a school teacher," she told him. Surprised, he replied, "Teaching is my job too." After discussing their professional challenges and problems, the two exchanged names and addresses. Because the dream contained specific information, Ruby decided to write St. Paul, Arkansas, to see if there was a Hershel Hughes.
>
> At the same time Hershel was writing from St. Paul to say that he had met a Ruby Carroll from Parksville, Kentucky in a dream. He wondered if such a person really existed. Their letters crossed in the mail. After corresponding with one another for a time, Hershel and Ruby finally met in physical reality. They fell in love and were married. Then they moved to Florida.
>
> In a meshing situation, you have the same or similar dream as that of another person.

This distinction between types of shared dream experiences was also pointed out by James Donahoe, the person whose course at the California Institute for Asian Studies resulted in one of the first accounts of mutual dreaming. Donahoe, who eventually published his findings in a book called *Dream Reality,* says:

There are two kinds of mutual dreams; in one, two or more people experience being in a dream together and later can compare enough memory details to show that indeed was the case. In the other type of mutual dream, two or more people simply have the same dream. They do not experience being in the same dream together.[5]

Some of the people with whom Linda Magallón worked in her dream experiments had also been part of the teams of researchers brought together for the Dreams to the Tenth Power experiments. Suzanne Keyes, who facilitated one of the Dreams[10] teams, took a turn at editing *The Dream Network Bulletin* before the editing job passed on to Linda and she later wrote about shared dreaming in her newsletter, *Dreamcraft.*

Linda and another Poseidia dream team member, New York dream researcher Barbara Shor, collaborated on a chapter "Shared Dreaming: Joining Together in Dreamtime," for the 1990 volume *Dreamtime and Dreamwork,* edited by Dr. Stanley Krippner.

Still, Linda was by far the most active proponent of shared dreaming to continue the work on group dreaming research, making numerous discoveries along the way. In her book, *Mutual Dreaming,* she points out something we had noticed during the first Dreams to the Tenth Power experiment but which Linda, after moderating nearly a dozen different shared dreaming groups, could cite from experience. "The classic meeting dreams were (often) taking place outside the intended circle of strangers—with friends and family. So when dreamers in the shared dreaming projects planned to dream with stranger-colleagues, we might be having...other nonclassic meeting dreams instead."[6]

The question of who or what dreamers might be meeting or meshing with in their dreams has remained a troublesome one to many researchers, particularly those most interested in lucid dreaming. There is quite a divergence of opinion about whether characters in people's dreams might be products of the unconscious with no reality apart from the dreamer or if they might be individuals with autonomy; and if they are individuals with autonomy, whether that means they are individuals with any connection to waking life.

At the 1989 IASD conference in London, lucid dream researchers Stephen LaBerge and Paul Tholey met in person for the first time though each was familiar with the other's work. They discussed the question of whether a polygraph record might show that dream figures other than the "dream-ego" might be capable of signaling lucidly in the sleep laboratory, as individuals involved in LaBerge's research have demonstrated they can.

The conversation between these two giants of lucid dream research was recorded at the conference, transcribed and later published in the Tenth Anniversary Edition of *The Lucidity Letter*. It can be found on *Lucidity Letter* editor, Jayne Gackenbach's web site at www.sawka.com.

The conversation proves frustratingly inconclusive though for anyone interested in the question of who or what we might dream with. At the end of the discussion, LaBerge asks, "So how can we conclude that dream characters have consciousness?"

And Tholey replies, "I have never claimed that! I only claim that you will never be able to prove it, as you will never be able to prove that another person in waking life has consciousness!"[7]

Clearly this perplexing question of who is the dreamer dreaming leads us deep into the philosophy of consciousness—territory there is no need to tread as long as one believes that dreams are only nighttime reflections of waking life issues, or messages from the unconscious to be decoded.

In the same Tenth Anniversary Edition of the *Lucidity Letter*, there is a letter from Scott Sparrow, the person who so accurately perceived the beginning of the Dreams to the Tenth Power experiments in a precognitive lucid dream. Scott's own research in dream lucidity had led him to issue a controversial warning to lucid dreamers, which also involved the question of who might inhabit the dream state.

"One reason I haven't participated much in the lucid dreaming field in the past few years," Sparrow says, "is that I ran into some unpleasant experiences in the late 70s following a period of almost nightly lucid dreaming." He goes on to say:

> Although I don't think we should try to prevent healthy individuals from discovering their repressed complexes and other personal issues through lucid dreaming (after all, what's therapy if it isn't, in part, awakening to these issues), I strongly believe that we need to inform and prepare individuals for the possible ordeal of meeting autonomous, repressed aspects of the unconscious through the widened aperture of the lucid dreamer's awareness…. I'm concerned that many individuals, who do not have someone to urge them onward, may get caught up in the power of the lucid dream and provoke the "retaliation" of largely autonomous, repressed unconscious content.[8]

The question raised by Scott's letter, at least for anyone interested in shared dreaming, is what he means by largely autonomous repressed unconscious content. Where does one draw the line between largely autonomous unconscious content and entirely autonomous other individuals? On the surface of things, this may sound like an irrelevant question but it quickly gains relevance when, for example, one dreams of a dead grandmother or a friend in another city. More than once I have had conversations with dreamers about "scary dead people."

The question of whom or what is being dreamed is one of the frontiers of dreaming research.

Although not active in dream study between the years of 1986 and 1996, I maintained a correspondence with some of the people who were doing dream research, particularly Linda Magallón, who wrote to me in early 1996 with the enticing suggestion that I should attend the IASD conference being held that year in Berkeley, California.

She insisted to me that the dream study organization, which ten years earlier had been quite unreceptive to the idea of group dreaming, was changing and I should come see for myself. I was hesitant. One reason I had left dream research to pursue other interests was that I was tired of being regarded by even my peers as an oddball person doing oddball work of relatively little merit or value.

Since I was planning a trip to California that year anyway to visit a niece who had recently moved there, I somewhat reluctantly agreed to come to the conference and present a paper about the Dreams to the Tenth Power research. I told Linda I would come for two days, stay overnight and then leave.

The conference that year was in the Claremont Hotel. A Victorian wedding cake of 1920s vintage, the luxurious hotel and spa sits nestled in the Berkeley foothills. I was immediately struck by the contrast in venue to the last International Association for the Study of Dreams (IASD) conference I had attended in Charlottesville and by the organization's growth in membership, which now filled a room four or five times larger than the small auditorium we had used at the University of Virginia.

The morning of my paper presentation, I was nervous. I knew almost no one at the conference, although Linda did her best to make me feel at home. She introduced me to some of the people she had invited into her group dreaming experiments over the years and invited me to the slumber party she and other members of the Bay Area Dreamworkers Group had organized in a huge room in the hotel basement. The slumber party was fun, made even more interesting by some of the better known members of the organization dropping by in their jammies. But I still felt nervous as early in the morning before conference programming began, I rode the elevator up to the conference center to locate the room in which I'd be speaking.

To me, the empty room with its rows of lined up chairs looked huge. There had to be seating here for a hundred people or more. Wryly I thought to myself that I'd be lucky to fill more than a few of those seats.

People here didn't know me. I hadn't been active in dream research in years. I'd certainly attended my share of conferences where an audience of half a dozen people showed up for less-popular or less well-known speakers. Oh well, I shrugged, I could at least just deliver my paper and get on with my vacation.

Later, when I returned to the room for the panel presentation, I was surprised to see that most of the seats in the room were full. As the panelists found one another and took seats in the front of the room, the rest of the room filled up. There were people standing in the aisles and lining the hallway outside the door. Linda was sitting near the center aisle midway of the room with a huge grin on her face. She informed me later that she'd been telling people, "This is the one presentation of the conference that you won't want to miss."

Once the paper was delivered, it seemed as if the questions would never stop. Linda was right; things had changed. Group dreaming, though still not part of mainstream thinking about dreams, had at least made its way to the edge of the stream.

Another interesting thing happened that day at the Dreams to the Tenth Power presentation, but I did not learn about until some years later.

The 1999 IASD conference was held in California once again, this time at the University of California campus at Santa Cruz. Again I was part of a panel of speakers including Linda Magallón, Robert Waggoner and Ed Kellogg. I was surprised to hear Ed Kellogg say that his work on a process he calls Mutual Lucid Dreaming began with my 1996 presentation. Later I asked if I'd heard him correctly and he replied, "While I was sitting in your presentation next to Linda, she challenged me to have a mutual lucid dream if I thought I could do it."

The result of this challenge was a dream Ed recounted in an article for the Spring 1997 issue of the IASD magazine, *Dream Time*:

> In a sort of archeological dig—in Mexico—I see people digging for gold, peasants, in a sandy Sonoran type desert. We find huge old wagons on the side of the road, from a circus or something, which had bones of elephants and/or lions, etc. I go with the group—realize that I dream, but don't know if they realize it—a sort of virtual reality field trip. I talk with the leaders and they respond. I see [Harvey Grady] and tell him to give me a collect call on waking up to WPR (waking physical reality), if he recalls this dream, and to let me know if he really does participate in a WPR tour at this time. [Harvey] looks like he just shaved off his beard. He shows me some old airplanes in a museum, and I look forward to virtually flying them, although I wonder what would happen to my physical body if I crash.... [9]

Ed holds a Ph.D. in biochemistry, though he tends to modestly downplay the fact. He met Harvey years earlier while working on a scientific project. Although the two shared an interest in dreams, they were not in regular contact. In fact, they had not been in touch with each other for over two years at the time of Ed's dream.

Harvey did not phone Ed the next day, nor did he even write anything down until prompted by Ed to do so, but the dream he recalled from the night of Ed's dream bears some remarkable similarities to Ed's. The two men agree that they seldom dream of one another, so the fact that Ed was in his dream helped

Harvey recall his dream from that night. Here is Harvey Grady's dream. Harvey was also lucid.

I remember Ed and three or four other men, whom I knew in the dream, but not in daytime, talking about an expedition to explore for probable archeological records, then traveling to an arid desert area...where we split up to search the surface for possible artifacts.

The land in the dream was similar to Israel hill country, or arid portions of Arizona, Nevada or New Mexico. We were searching for ancient artifacts like from Atlantis or Mu. I recognized that the dream dealt only with one part of an ongoing series of the search for evidence of ancient civilizations.

In the dream, I felt that we were going through the motions of the search in the astral plane in order to establish energetic templates for the person who would conduct the search on the physical plane. The energetic templates created from our experiences would guide the search of some physical explorers. Therefore we went through the motions of the search like actors playing our roles, in order to generate thoughts, emotions and desires for the template.

In the role of explorers, we acted as though we were ignorant and blindly searching for something we had only slight reason to expect might be there. On a higher level, as actors outside the role, we knew what would eventually be found. We were well aware of the ancient civilizations and their contributions to history and had accepted tasks in helping recall them to the physical plane. This double level of awareness made the dream more interesting to me.[10]

At the end of his *Dream Time* article, Ed Kellogg makes this observation about shared dreaming:

To upgrade the phenomenon of "mutual" dreaming from an unlikely possibility to a probable reality requires more than anecdotal evidence; it requires a formal and controlled study in which informed participants make use of specific procedures and documentation. Evidential cases of mutual dreaming have significant implications not only to the nature of the dream, but also to that of human nature as well. I look forward to the results of future research in this area.

Ed, who considers phenomenology to be his primary area of study, has continued to promote rigorous research. As creator of the highly successful annual PsiberDreaming Online Conference for the International Association for the Study of Dreams, he has developed a dream description form that has been utilized in several different projects, including the Dream Telepathy Contest hosted annually at the IASD conference by Dr. Robert Van de Castle and Rita Dwyer.

Ed insists, and rightly so, that it is much easier to see parallels between people's dreams if the descriptions are clear and precise. Rather than saying, "I dreamed about my Aunt Sally," the dreamer reports, "I dreamed about my Aunt Sally and she looks like this."

There is still much work to be done with creating precise language around all areas of dreaming, but mutual dreams and shared group dreams provide an area which is fertile ground for this type of study.

Chapter Eight - Spontaneously Shared Dreaming

Two things hastened my return to the world of dream research. One was the advent of the Internet, the other was an invitation from Richard Wilkerson, who created and managed the International Association for the Study of Dreams web site, to host the organization's online Bulletin Board.

My first encounter with the Internet in the early 90s had opened my eyes to a world of possibilities. At the time, the Rev. Jeremy Taylor and his friend John Herbert were hosting a morning dream group on America Online (AOL). What a great place to do research, I said to myself as I looked at the brand new concept of web pages. "Think what you could do with all those people," my mind chattered as I watched the hundreds of people who flocked to the AOL cyber-auditorium to discuss their dreams. For anyone who had slogged through years of research via postal carrier, the idea of being able to instantly communicate with dreamers around the world seemed nothing short of a miracle.

In fact, a major difficulty for dreamers and dream researchers alike, living in a culture that does not particularly value dreams, had always been a sense of isolation. How were people to know that there was even one other dreamer in the world if no one ever talked about dreaming except under very special circumstances? And here I was being offered the opportunity to invite people from every corner of the world to talk to one another about dreams on the IASD Bulletin Board.

One of the nicest things I discovered, about working with Richard Wilkerson was that he shared my enthusiasm for what the Internet could accomplish for dream research. "One of the main reasons that I was attracted to the Net as a vehicle to promote dream awareness," he says in the Winter 2000 issue of *Dream Time* in his column "Dream Cyberphile, "was the appeal of the mass transformation it offers contemporary culture."

He concludes this same column with the words: "With the rise of the Internet, information and education about psi dreaming has become much more available, though dream researchers are slow to use the Net to collect data. Still, the opportunity to time stamp dreams, have large surveys and questionnaires, draw upon potentially millions of subjects, and communicate with interested researchers around the world, will eventually be irresistible."[1]

Through his own website, www.dreamgate.com, Richard had already created one of the first online magazines or e-zines, *Electric Dreams*, which became the locus of publication for much innovative work on dreams.

Although I was interested in dream research, I was even more interested in just watching to see who would come to the bulletin board. I felt much like I did one winter in West Virginia, when a bird feeder attached to my kitchen windowsill allowed me to watch a flow of rare birds passing through on their way south. I was intensely curious about what other dreamers might show up at the Board, and what kinds of questions they might have.

True to my expectations, the IASD Bulletin Board provided an amazingly diverse group of dreamers. People from all over the world plugged the word dream into their search engines and ended up on my virtual doorstep. There were researchers interested in esoteric aspects of consciousness research; there were young people from junior high school classes asking questions for science projects; and there were people of all ages, many of them with interesting stories to tell.

After a while, people began to return to the Board for frequent visits because the conversation was good and, as happens on many online bulletin boards, a community was beginning to form. I started to think of the Bulletin Board as a big boarding house and began calling the board regulars "boarders."

We were having fun, and in many cases sharing a feeling of relief that we had found one another. Many of the Board visitors were teenagers in high school with lots of questions about dreams and consciousness.

One of the most common questions asked on the Board was, "What does it mean if you dream something and your sister/mother/friend has the same dream?"

"I don't know how to describe it," one young woman wrote to the Bulletin Board, "but I often have the EXACT same dream as someone I know. These are people that I either live very far away from, or people that I haven't seen in months or years." She then described four dreams in which this sharing had happened.

"I myself am not very experienced yet at mutual dreaming," wrote another dreamer from the Netherlands. "My best friend and I seem to tune in to each other's dreams regularly, though we live in different countries."

It was heartwarming for me to see evidence providing the answer to a question I was frequently asked when I talked about group dreaming: "Do you think that maybe people dream together all the time?"

Of course, having had my first spontaneous lucid mutual dream many years ago, I could answer that from my own perspective there seemed to be shared dreaming happening regularly, naturally, and often outside the waking awareness of the dreamers. But the leap from subjective experience to convincing, objective evidence is a long one and requires evidentiary data.

As the director of a consciousness research organization, my career with Poseidia Institute allowed me to collect innumerable anecdotes about shared dreaming, many of them quite unique. For example, one story I heard from a student was how she had once dreamed about an empty theater stage. Bright lights shined on the stage. As the dreamer watched, one of the lights fell and crashed to the stage.

The day after this dream, the woman said, she was involved in a rear end collision on a busy downtown street. The fender bender disabled her car and broke out the headlight on the car driven by the man who had rear-ended her.

Late for an appointment, and totally exasperated, the woman got out of her car to wait for the police to arrive and while waiting, began a conversation with the man who had hit her. They found that they had a mutual interest in theater and of all things, dreams.

"I should have known something was going to happen," the woman said.

The other driver it turned out was a theater stagehand who worked with lighting. This was enough to encourage the woman to tell her dream. The man was excited. He'd had exactly the same dream the night before, he said, except that in his dream the stage lights were not turned on.

These two people, who met in a most unlikely manner, were now engaged to be married.

An even more bizarre story of spontaneous shared dreaming came from the weekly radio show that Poseidia Institute was asked to host on a local news/talk station, WNIS, in 1985. The show started at eight p.m. on Saturday nights and ran until midnight. And though we did live interviews and weekly features such as the "Psychic Lost and Found" during which callers were instructed to tell about lost objects while other callers figured out where the lost items were located – with a remarkably high success rate – the last hour of each week's show was devoted exclusively to dreams.

There were many callers who, under the guise of anonymity created by talk radio, felt free to tell about their more unusual dream experiences—such as the woman who said that throughout their childhoods, she and her sister met in dream space almost every night to continue the games they played while awake. But the real show stopper came from a woman who told the following story. She had dreamed for years about a particular house in the country, set back from the road, an old farmhouse. The dreams had been recurrent, our caller said, though they were not troubling. In fact, she was very attracted to the house.

One day, the caller went on, she and her husband went for a drive in the country. Suddenly, looking out the car window, the woman saw an old farmhouse, the house from her dreams.

"I've got to stop and look at that house," she excitedly told her husband. Despite his concerns that the house was occupied and that the owners would not welcome strangers onto their property to look around, he stopped the car and they got out.

Eventually the couple knocked at the front door of the farmhouse, hoping to take a peek inside. The woman who answered the door registered shock. "You're the woman I've been dreaming about!" she exclaimed.

Needless to say, her visitors got a look around the inside of the house.

Still, stories like these, as interesting as they might be, are easily called anomalies. That is, they can be seen as nothing more than significant deviations from a set norm, that norm being a population that dreams in a manner primarily devoid of shared dreams.

We could continue to believe this point of view, as Western dream science has for the past several decades, if it were not for the evidence presented in online forums such as the IASD Bulletin Board where the number of reported shared dream events is significant.

The Internet provides evidence of another type of shared dreaming as well. Simultaneous with the increase in numbers of personal computers during the last years of the final decade of the century, a number of tragedies were reported which riveted the attention of not just the United States but the entire world: the brutal murder of child beauty queen Jon Benet Ramsey, the O.J. Simpson trial, the death of Britain's Princess Di. In each of these cases, Internet message boards available to dreamers overflowed with dreams of these popular icons.

After requesting comments and opinions about the O.J. Simpson trial for his column "Dream Line," which appeared monthly in *Electric Dreams*, Chris Hicks wrote:

> In addition to comments and opinions, I requested dreams about OJ and the trial. What did our dream selves have to offer? And how did these offerings differ from conscious comments? The main difference was in the area of positive focus, as opposed to a negative focus. The comments and opinions almost exclusively dealt with perceived racism, whereas our dreams are filled with mysterious attempts at understanding the tragedy, and symbols of reconciliation.[2]

"In addition to these dreams of reconciliation," Chris went on, "there were several dreams that accurately predicted not only the verdict, but the circumstances surrounding it."

Months later, the tragic death of Britain's Princess Diana produced not only an unprecedented entire book of dreams, Rita Frances' *Dreaming of Diana*, but also resulted in a flood of dream reports online.

I was surprised to see dreams of Diana popping up even in online groups where dreams were never discussed. A woman in one of my writing groups wrote:

> Last night (the night before Princess Di's funeral), I barely slept, and the brief times I did fall under, it was fitfully at best, and full of dreams of her, and of being part of the crowd lining the street outside the cathedral. I don't think it was dreams really. I think I was there with them. A psychic connection links us all. It seems to me that, after all, if you can know in advance that some one individual is going to give you a call or drop in for a visit, that the kind of emotion generated by so many people all around the world would find a spot

in your own psyche. Like being part of a psychic chain, the collective unconscious in action.

The degree to which Princess Di's impact was felt was also reflected in a number of online dream articles. Jungian therapist, Maureen Roberts, wrote in an article, "Dreams, Death and Diana: Lessons in Personal and Collective Healing," for the September 1997 issue of *Electric Dreams*:

Like many others, I have been drawn deeply and with powerful emotion into the tragedy of Diana's death. On the night I heard about it (Sunday), I felt an overwhelming desire to be of some help to her. The same night, I was devastated after falling asleep—I ended up spending the entire night with Diana, in a long and complex dream ritual....

I can't describe the kind of closeness this all involved; it wasn't what you'd call friendship, or sisterliness, or motherliness; it was (for want of a better word) an indefinable sense of oneness, patience and compassion.[3]

In another article for the same issue of *Electric Dreams*, dream researcher Jayne Gackenbach, who had not a dream but an intuitive experience at the time of Princess Di's death, calls the event "a ripple in the collective field of consciousness."

By the summer of 1999, I had moderated the IASD Bulletin Board for over two years. The crowd of Boarders had grown. There was the usual rowdy discussion of shared dreaming going on with people vigorously arguing both sides of the question of whether people could really share dreams when a message posted to the Board set off buzzers in my brain. The subject line of this message read: "Dream Sharing Without Knowing It?"

Not so extraordinary, I thought. Why am I feeling the need to read this post immediately? The story the author told brought to mind other tales that I'd heard and set my thoughts racing off in a new direction. Maybe the person who wrote to Poseidia Institute that she always dreamed about strangers and would like to know who they were was not so far off the mark.

"I feel I have experienced a somewhat different situation from the others discussed here," the Bulletin Board visitor wrote.

For many years I have had very vivid dreams, almost every night. The strange thing is the people and places in the dreams were completely strange to me, as in I would wake up and never have been to the place or seen those people before. But the dreams are very familiar to me, like I know the people and places.

Last year, two very close friends of mine and I finally discovered that all three of us were not only sharing the same dreams, but all three were dreaming about the SAME strangers and unfamiliar places. This is when the three of us started writing them all down.

And it has been just recently that the three of us have seemed to find the strangers in our dreams, the three of us, and three of them, all six of us had been dreaming about each other all along. We found them by a simple twist of fate.

Was it possible that many people, dreaming of strangers, were really dreaming of friends from another area of time and space, possibly even people they were working with or learning from in dreams? Yes, theories of reincarnation speak of continuous linear lifetimes, lives lived one after another in which the soul overcomes karma and grows in grace. But here we were talking about simultaneous lifetimes in what might be called parallel universes.

My first encounter with such an idea came during the second phase of the Dreams to the Tenth Power experiment when Barbara, the college student who dreamed of the late-night attack on her teammate Jennifer, came into my office to talk.

With her usual headlong energy, Barbara threw herself down on the sofa at the side of my office, stuck sneakered feet up on the coffee table, and leaned her head back, blonde curls haloing a face that was still childishly rounded.

"What would you do," she began, looking at me through half-closed eyes, "if you kept dreaming about the same people over and over again?"

"Ummm…" I was still engrossed in the mail I was sorting.

"I mean, what if you kept dreaming these people and you'd never met them?" Now she had my complete attention.

"It started when I was in high school," she told me. Barbara had been an only child, an Army brat. Due to her father's military career, her family moved from one country to another every few years throughout her childhood. "I guess I was lonely," she said, "but I started dreaming about this group of kids my own age. I'd go down to the end of the pasture, (The family lived on a farm in Germany) step over the fence, and I'd be in this place with all these kids my own age, like a real gang. We'd do things together and everything."

For Barbara, high school had been not so long before this. "And you still dream about them?" I asked.

"Not so often as I used to, but yeah." She was quiet for a few minutes, staring at her shoes.

"About a month ago," she finally said, "I went across the fence, but there were a bunch of other kids who said they were coming back with me. I thought it sounded great, but as soon as they did, wham! I woke right up. I haven't dreamed about them since."

Many children have what adults disparagingly call imaginary playmates. It might have been easy enough for me to dismiss this experience of Barbara's as the imaginative creation of a lonely child's mind except for an experience told to me at about this same time by my friend Henry.

Henry was an actor who taught at a children's drama camp in the Berkshires during the summer. His first summer at the job, he worked with the five- to eight- year olds. When the class began, in order to put the kids at ease, he asked who had an imaginary playmate. Several hands went up in the audience. So Henry picked one of the kids and had him come up on stage and just talk with his imaginary playmate. Then he asked a second child and a third to do the same thing.

On the third kid's turn, Henry noticed something. One little girl in the audience seemed to be tracking the moves of the "imaginary" playmate with her eyes.

"Can you see the person Sammy is talking with?" he asked her.

She told him yes.

Then Henry decided to ask if anyone else could see this imaginary being he could not see at all. When he asked them, Henry told me, almost every hand in the audience of twelve or thirteen children went up. Maybe Henry couldn't see the playmates but everyone else could.

Hearing Barbara's story planted a question in my mind. No wonder this girl was interested in group dreaming. She'd had her own gang of dream friends for years.

I wondered if there were other people who dreamed like that and if anyone ever met the people they dreamed about. A few years later, while working for a publishing house as a science fiction editor, I met someone who could answer both of these questions of mine in the affirmative.

Robyn Wood is well known in Science Fiction/Fantasy circles as a top-flight artist and illustrator who has created numerous magazine and book covers as well as a popular tarot deck.

In 1989, Robyn was co-authoring a book *The People of Pern* with award-winning author Anne McCaffrey. As the book's editor, I met with Robyn at the American Library Association convention in Washington. We enjoyed each other's company and spent several hours over the course of the convention talking with each other about many things other than the book.

On the last day of the convention, as I rode behind her up the interminable escalator from the Metro station at Woodley Park, Robyn turned to me and began telling me about a dream she'd had since she was a little girl.

"This dream takes place somewhere else," Robyn told me. "But it's the same place all the time, just like this is." She gestured to the walls around us.

Robyn said when she first began having this dream, she shared a room with her two sisters. The dream was so vivid and continuous that she got confused about whether she was asleep or awake. "Am I awake?" she would ask her sisters when she woke up in the morning.

"Of course you are," they would assure her.

The problem with this, Robyn said, was that when she awoke in the other reality, the dream reality, she would ask people there the same question. Was she awake?

"Of course you are," they would assure her.

This was highly distressing for the little girl, until she began to devise ways to tell the two states of consciousness apart, noting the subtle distinction between abilities she had while <u>asleep</u> from those she claimed while <u>awake</u>. What happened later was a surprise even to Robyn. Once she began to work professionally, she began to encounter other people, mostly artists, who dreamed of this same place she had dreamed for years. Not only that, but these people recognized her from the dreams, just as she recognized them.

In this case, the dream characters had crossed the boundary into waking reality. Robyn believes that part of her work involves delving deep into the imagery of this alternative dream space, and bringing the images of that world into this one via her paintings.

Although there are still not many anecdotal accounts of spontaneously shared dreaming with such dramatic results, the idea that spontaneously shared dreams do exist must be accepted. In recent years there has even been confirmation of this from scientific sources.

Fred Allen Wolf, a physicist who is also a science writer by trade, has gained popularity recently from his appearance in two surprise-hit movies: *What the Bleep*, and its sequel, *Down the Rabbit Hole*, where he plays—well, himself.

In his 1994 book, *Dreaming the Universe*, Wolf says:

> Recently I have interviewed people who not only have lucid dreams but are also apparently capable of waking up night after night in a parallel world where they have a continuous life in a different body. (I myself have had this experience as well as the experience of other ordinary lucid dreams unrelated to other lucid dreams).[4]

And Wolf is not the only scientist to hold such an opinion. By the time the second edition of his classic work, *Dream Telepathy*, written with Stanley Krippner and Alan Vaughn, was published in 1989, Dr. Montague Ullman had been meeting with Experimental Dream Groups for several years. Ullman's article, "A Group Approach to the Anomalous Dream" appears in an appendix to the second edition.

"Experimental dream work generates emotional closeness among the participants," Ullman says. "It is expected that this developing rapport in combination with the natural psi facilitating effect of the dream itself, would result in an increasing number of identifiable psi occurrences among the members of the group."

"What I am suggesting," he says,

> ...is that our dream self is organized along a different principle (than our waking self). Our dreaming self is more concerned with the nature of our connections with *all* others. There is some part of our being that has never forgotten a basic truth.... The history of the human race, while awake, is a history of fragmentation. Our sleeping self, I am proposing, is connected with the basic truth that we are all members of a single species and that while

dreaming our concerns have to do with [whatever]...damages, impedes, obstructs, or enhances these connections.[5]

Before leaving the subject of spontaneously shared dreams, I would like to mention one or two other types of spontaneously shared dreaming that seem to produce quite practical results.

Probably anyone who has ever conducted a dream group over a period of weeks or months has noticed what I've come to call migrating symbols. That is, one person in the group will share a dream containing a particular symbol, and the next week one or two other dreamers in the group will report dreams involving the same symbol, until sometimes, as happened in one of my recent dream groups, every dreamer in the group will be dreaming the same symbol.

I believe that this is a type of spontaneously shared dreaming that can have immediate practical applications, as dreamers begin to talk about the meaning of the particular symbol to their waking-life issues.

A variation on this theme was part of an early Internet user group, alt.dreams. However, this one had the advantage of providing objective proof of shared dreaming, while at the same time being a lot of fun.

In the game as it was played, the dreamer who started the process dreamed that he left something at the base of a tree in a mutually-agreed-upon dream location. The next visitor to the tree got to pick up whatever the first dreamer had left under the tree and replace it with an object of her own. The discovered object would then be described to the group, to verify whether the dreamer had picked up the right thing. Some found this game to be extremely frustrating, while others were quite adept at locating what was left under the tree.

The second practical application of spontaneously shared dreaming that I've seen was pointed out to me by a student in one of the classes I taught at Poseidia Institute.

The woman was an artist who had been taking lessons from a very fine art teacher who also happened to be connected with the Institute. When the teacher moved to take a job in New England, at first his student was devastated by the loss.

But a few weeks later, when I talked to the woman after class, she seemed cheerful as ever. How was her artwork coming along, I asked her? And had she heard from Bob, her former teacher?

Her smile was radiant. Oh yes, she said, her artwork was coming along just fine. Bob had decided to come back to town once a month to give a few private lessons and in between sessions, they were sharing art lessons in the dream state. "He's even better in dreams than he is when we're awake," she told me. "You should see my new paintings."

I might not have believed this type of precision to be possible in spontaneous mutual dreaming except for what happened to me a few years later when I began training in Energetic Metatherapy, a type of bioenergetic psychotherapy created by Dr. Hector Kuri-Cano of Guadalajara, Mexico.

Hector conducted his training workshops at three-week intervals over a period of several years. He would come to the Tidewater area, do a workshop for the general public one weekend, a training session the following weekend, and see clients privately during the week in between. He was undoubtedly the finest psychotherapist I have ever met.

But I soon discovered that he had another, unexpected skill.

Even my first meeting with Hector was a little strange. I had been urged to go to the weekend workshop he was conducting, but declined. That weekend, as I was sitting at the dining room table completing a watercolor I'd been working on, even though I was alone in the house, I heard the word *brujo* spoken beside my right ear.

Now, even though I have worked with dozens of psychics in my life, I have never had any particular experience with what some would call auditory hallucinations. So I did what most people would do. I pretended to myself that I hadn't heard anything, and went on painting.

The next time the voice was louder, "*Brujo*," it said with gentle insistence.

This time I got the message. *Brujo* is the Spanish word for sorcerer. I knew that the voice was talking about this man Hector and telling me that here was a teacher I needed to meet.

So the next weekend, when the first local training session began, I found myself there even though the training was for psychotherapists and mental health professionals. When I told Hector my story, he graciously opened the group to me. And I soon found out why.

Between the first training workshop and the next time Hector was in town, I had a dream. In the dream, which took place in my childhood home, I discovered that there was a black cord, like a thick electrical wire, running down my back just to the left of my spine.

As the dream progressed, Hector, who had been in the kitchen talking with my father, came into the living room with me, asked me to bend over the back of the sofa with my back to him, and proceeded to pull the cord until it released the pain from my neck and shoulder. In waking life, the pain I had actually been having in my left shoulder was alleviated.

The next time Hector was in town to do a training workshop, I scheduled a private session with him. Somewhat hesitantly, as I barely knew the man, I asked if he remembered the dream we had in which he worked on my back.

At first I thought he was not going to answer me. He stood, looking down at the rug. Then his eyes met mine and they were full of sparkling laughter. "I work with many of my clients in dreams," he said. "Most times they don't know."

This was only the first of many times I worked with Hector in the dream state. Later, in waking state we would go over the same process, and then talk about it. For those unfamiliar with bioenergetic psychotherapy, this body-oriented approach to therapy was created by Wilhelm Reich, fine-tuned by Reich's student, Alexander Lowen, M.D., and then taught to a number of therapists around the world, including Hector.

The work with dreams and with the transpersonal and spiritual realms was Hector's own addition to the Bioenergetics process. I found it so effective that I have continued to utilize it in my own practice of DreamWork/BodyWork.

What are the implications then of the idea that we may all be dreaming together on a frequent and regular basis, whether we are aware of doing it or not?

Like Cynthia Pearson, the person who so aptly named the dance between dreams and waking life an arabesque, I find a statement made by Seth in the book *Dreams, Evolution and Value Fulfillment* to be one of my favorite quotes.

"There is an entire global dreaming network," says Seth through Jane Roberts, "that goes quite unrecognized—one of spectacular organization in which exchanges of information occur that give you the basis for the formation of recognized physical events."[6]

Chapter Nine - The Family That Dreams Together

As members of the Dreams to the Tenth Power groups noticed, and Linda Magallón remarked upon as well, when groups of people purposely come together to share dreams, often the people who spontaneously join in are family members and other intimates. In fact, as Linda Magallón reports in *Mutual Dreaming*, well over fifty percent of all spontaneous dream reports involve family members because we most naturally seem to be able to dream mutually with those who are closest to us.

Looking at the patterns of dreams shared in families and looking at the pattern of how families deal with dreams, can give us great insight into some of the issues to be faced by anyone convinced of the efficacy of group dreaming because the issues that arise in family relationships are key psychological issues.

As an educator, I have always been interested in the impact of dreams on children but my interest in family dreaming was given a serious boost in 1993 when I found myself sharing a deeply compelling dream theme with members of my own family.

In December that year, my mother was in a nursing home in Michigan recovering from a broken hip. I was planning to visit her. Not long before my visit, I had the following dream:

There is going to be a workshop. Hector is conducting a workshop at 2 a.m. in my mother's bedroom. I want very much to attend the workshop, but I am told by Bob Friedman that I must address a group of people in an auditorium. He has set up a lecture for me, and people are waiting. Reluctantly, I agree. Attending the lecture is a famous writer by the name of Sheena. I strike up a conversation with her, and we travel together to California. It turns out later that Sheena is a shape changer, and not such a nice person.

Hector was the psychotherapist from Guadalajara, Mexico with whom I had been training in Energetic Metatherapy for the past several years. Bob Friedman had been Chairman of the Poseidia Institute Board of Directors. Sheena? I thought to myself. Sheena is me as author of course—tricky, shape-shifting author. The meaning of the dream seemed clear. I was making some choices about what to do with my life and several of them were represented in the dream. But I had the slightly uncomfortable feeling that comes with some dreams. I wondered if I was missing something.

The day after the dream, I phoned my niece Carol, in California. She and I have always been close and we share a mutual interest in dreams.

When I told Carol the Sheena dream, there was a long pause on the other end of the line. "Ummm..," she finally said, "I think I dreamed about Sheena this week too. She's got red hair, hasn't she?"

I could feel the goose bumps rising on my arms. "Uh huh." As accustomed as I was to sharing dreams with my friends, I had never to my knowledge dreamed with a family member. How strange. After comparing descriptions of the mysterious, red-haired shape changer, Carol and I laughed about how I had traveled to California with Sheena in my dream. Maybe I'd been visiting Carol in dream state too.

All in all we both found it interesting, though a little puzzling. Why were we sharing this particular dream when we'd never shared dreams before?

Then came my trip to Michigan. At the nursing home, my mother had been having an adverse reaction to some pain medication and was suffering from what the doctor called drug-induced hallucinations. She seemed edgy and startled and talked about having nightmares. She said, in answer to my question about the nightmares, that she couldn't tell anyone what she was dreaming about. Although her medication had been changed, she was still disoriented and somewhat confused.

The second day of my visit, I arrived at her room before she awoke in the morning. As I came to her bed, she opened her eyes.

"They're going to get me."

I took her hand, "Who's going to get you, Mom? Who are these people?" I knew she'd been dreaming and was not quite awake yet.

"Sheena and Jennifer Freed," she said in a clear voice. "They live in the basement and set fires. They write the scripts for the next day." Her voice carried a note of rebellion, since I knew she had been afraid to tell anyone this.

I tried to hide my shock. Sheena the Shape Changer was in my mother's dreams as well and writing the scripts for our lives? Why should I have been surprised?

Years of working with shared dreams had convinced me that every dream contains valuable meaning for the dreamer and that shared dreams are not excepted. It was important for me to look at the information Sheena had brought me despite the titillating fact that other family members were dreaming her too.

In this case, and I believe in other cases of shared dreaming, there was an additional context for me to explore. In the case of all three dreamers: my mother, my niece and myself, Sheena seemed to be conveying a message about creativity, about writing. Yet what caused her to appear at this time, and so dramatically? In my mother's dreams, Sheena was "writing the script for the next day." The shared meaning of Sheena, the family meaning of Sheena, seemed to be about how the women in my family responded to life, how the message of appropriate behavior is carried from one generation to the next.

This episode of family dreaming rekindled my interest in the connection between group dreaming and family dreams. My mother died not long after the first Sheena dreams, but Sheena has appeared in both my dreams and Carol's since that time. She has also shown up in the dreams of Carol's young daughter, a sort of family spirit passed along through the female line. All of this has caused me to question the role that family plays in attitudes toward dreaming and how the attitudes play out in dreams. As soon as I returned home from my trip to Michigan, I began to look for books on the subject of family dreams. I was sure that I would find a lot of them. Thinking about how family-oriented therapy was becoming increasingly popular, and recalling the many family dreams I had heard over the years, I expected shelves of new, exciting reading. What I found shocked me.

Yes, there had been books written about family dreaming, I discovered – exactly two books, both by the same man, Edward Bruce Bynum. A clinical psychologist and Director of the Behavioral Medicine Program at the University of Massachusetts Health Services, Bynum wrote *The Family Unconscious* in 1984 and followed that with *Family and the Interpretation of Dreams: Awakening the Intimate Web* in 1993. He also created the Family Dream Research Project, which he still conducts. I had known Bruce since the early days of dream work and looked forward to reading his books.

But where were the rest? I wondered why dream researchers were paying so little attention to the most logical of all groups in which to study dreams, the family. Thinking about possible explanations for this, one idea came immediately to my mind: Senoi Dreaming.

Now this may seem an odd leap of thought to anyone unfamiliar with the history of the subject of Senoi dreaming, but the effect of this concept on the dream research community has been profound.

According to anthropologist Kilton Stewart, the Senoi, a nomadic tribe from the foothills of the Central Range of mountains of the Malay Peninsula, produced an amazingly sophisticated form of family dreaming. Stewart reported in a 1954 article for the magazine *Mental Hygiene*, "The Senoi have not made the mistake of Western civilization, of thinking that the images of things and people that appear in sleep are unimportant."

I remembered being handed a copy of this article by Dr. Herb Puryear, then Director of The Association for Research and Enlightenment's (ARE) Education Program when I first came to Virginia Beach. He told me that this was the most important article about dreams that had been written in the past twenty years. He explained that Stewart presented proof of the value of dreams for families. That if families could sit down together each morning like the Senoi and discuss their dreams, even young children could be taught to create something from their dreams or make amends to someone they'd injured in the dream state.

The effect of these ideas about dreaming, presented by Stewart as regular practice among the Senoi, had an immediate and dramatic effect on dream researchers in England and the United States. Researchers such as Patricia Garfield, Ann Faraday, John Van Damm and Herb Puryear began to promote the

Senoi approach to dream work in their books, firing the popular imagination. Entire groups were created based on this remarkable approach to family health.

Then it was discovered that although Stewart had traveled in Malaysia, members of the Senoi tribe denied all knowledge of the kinds of dream teachings ascribed to them by Stewart. In fact, they laughed openly at some of his ideas.

Reaction within the dream community was swift. Dream workers who had begun to use Senoi techniques backed off from using them. The controversy that developed was so hot that Ann Faraday traveled to Malaysia herself to converse with the Senoi.

Ann and I had been regular correspondents for several years when she made this trip. In a letter to me from India, dated December 1981, she wrote:

I have almost definite "proof" now that Kilton Stewart more or less made up (or grossly exaggerated) the Senoi story…and like the more modern Peter Bloch in 1977, my informants were quite sure the Senoi used dreams in the same old superstitious way for prophecy and healing—by the shamans, of course, who don't let you do your own dreams. When Peter's article came out, some people insisted that the real Senoi had gone away to the forest, leaving the remnants of a tribe, which was now being ruined by civilization. Apparently that's rubbish.

She concluded this letter in scathing tones. "Somebody should write an article on The Wish to Believe in the Noble Savage. It is obviously a very powerful image—also a myth."

Not too long after this letter, in fact someone did write such a book about Stewart and the popularity of Senoi dreaming. Published in 1990, G. William Domhoff's book, *The Mystique of Dreams: A Search for Utopia Through Senoi Dream Theory*, addresses the subject of Senoi dreaming in a manner that upset more than one of Domhoff's peers. Even today the argument goes on about whether or not Kilton Stewart mistakenly represented the Senoi, and about the value of Senoi dream work.

Probably the most interesting thing about this ongoing argument is the intensity with which it has continued for over thirty years. In this, we would have to say that Kilton Stewart and the Senoi hold a position similar to that held by Carlos Castaneda and his teacher, Don Juan. Whether or not the historical narrative told by either of the anthropologists is true, the material they present has an unmistakable impact on the group psyche. Unfortunately arguments about the validity of Stewart's work have also served to divert attention from the primary subject – family dreams.

The other reason for the lack of attention to family dreaming might be found in the subtitle of Bruce Bynum's second book, *"Awakening the Intimate Web."* What could be more intimate than sharing our dreams with the people closest to us? And what could be more daunting?

As the Rev. Jeremy Taylor says in his book *Where People Fly and Water Runs Uphill*, "Sharing dreams and searching cooperatively for their meaning regularly creates deeper intimacy and understanding between and among people participating in the process. Dreams reveal the projections and self deceptions that so often interfere with honest, intimate, successful relating."[1]

In reviewing the few articles and papers that had been written about family dreaming, I discovered an interesting fact. Some dreams from the family setting seemed more acceptable to discuss than others. Dreams that did not threaten the power relationships between parents and children were more frequently discussed than those that did.

Here are some examples. One quite commonly reported family dream was the subject of Theresa Danna's February 1997 article for *Electric Dreams*. She wrote about parents who dream with their children before the children are born. In "The Children of Our Dreams," Danna reports that when she first told her own parents that she'd dreamed about the baby she was carrying, they considered it a little strange but accepted that it was true. Eventually she met several other parents who'd had the same experience.

Chilean author Isabelle Allende, when interviewed by Naomi Epel for the book *Writers Dreaming* said: "One dream that is always prophetic for me is pregnancy. I knew with my two children when I was pregnant before there was any sign. And I knew what the sex of the child would be.... I never had to think of a name because they already had names in the dream. Names that I never would have chosen...."[2]

I have found that a discussion of this type of pre-birth dream can often be elicited from expectant parents, whether or not they are interested in dreams, by simply asking, "Have you dreamed with the baby yet?" Although the question may startle them, the answer is generally firmly and directly in the affirmative.

Not long ago, four people I knew were pregnant at the same time. It seemed like a good opportunity for research. When I asked if they'd been dreaming about the babies, one expectant mom told me the baby had given her name in dream state. Another parent said that she dreamed regularly of the baby and kept in close contact, as he was experiencing some difficulty during the pregnancy; and a third, the prospective father in this couple, said he'd been dreaming about the baby for months—as a Tibetan monk. These three out of the four couples I talked with accurately predicted the sex of their expected child as well. The fourth couple told me they had no recall of pre-birth dreams.

If there is any area of family dreaming that holds no hint of family power conflicts, dreams of the unborn must fill the spot. Another family relationship mentioned frequently in dream literature is that between mothers and their children, especially children in danger. For some, this type of dream is easily explained away as part of the natural sensitivity between parent and child, yet what is this sensitivity if not a form of telepathy? Many of these dreams would have to be considered dreams about someone rather than with someone. Yet they seem significant because of the high level of connectedness shown between the waking individuals.

One mother, for example, told me she dreamed her little boy was standing on a high ledge, in danger of falling, only to discover once the dream woke her, that somehow her three-year old had gone outside while she was still asleep and was making his way to the top bar of the swing set.

Many mothers will tell you they can unerringly pick their own child's cry from a crowd of crying children. To dream when a child is in trouble may certainly be an extension of that faculty. But there is still the question of what this type of bond might imply. Does it simply go away as children grow up? Or does it remain?

Berthold Schwarz, M.D recorded an interesting example of parent/child connectedness in his 1971 book, *Parent-Child Telepathy*. Schwarz relates a dream event that took place between him and his then four-year-old daughter.

June 29, 1960, Wednesday: In my dream a General deGaulle-like figure had reluctantly ordered a General Masseau-like figure before the firing squad for being desultory in squashing a rebellion. Just as he was shot, I dreamed within a dream that Lisa would awaken startled. Indeed this happened.

In the dream report immediately following this one, Schwarz notes:

Then the scene shifted to where Lisa appeared, walked away, and screamed as she stumbled down the hill. I ran frantically after her.... I entered a lighter sleep in which I was aware it was a dream and it was but a question of waiting for Lisa to scream. Lisa complied by screaming—as she fell out of bed.[3]

Clearly, father and daughter in this case had a remarkable degree of telepathy.

Another type of telepathic sharing between family members was mentioned to me in the audience of a lecture I gave several years ago at the College of William and Mary. Looking timid but determined in front of a good-sized audience, the young student said that a few months earlier she was dreaming one night about her twin sister. She and her twin were very close. In the dream, the twin was riding in a car with her boyfriend. The car hit a patch of black ice, spun out of control, and smashed into an embankment. "It was almost like I was in the car with them," the girl said. "I could feel the crash and everything."

She was awakened from the dream by a phone call. Her mother, who had also dreamed that night of a car crash, was calling to say that the girl's twin was in the hospital after a car accident, but would be all right.

Dreams between twins, particularly dreams between identical twins, are another commonly accepted area of family dream discussion. Part of the mythology of twin-ness, in fact, is that they, like mothers and their children, are so close as to make mutual dreaming a given.

Novelist John Barth, author of *The Sot Weed Factor*, is the Jack of a Jack and Jill set of twins (identical, but of opposite sex). Interviewed by Naomi Epel for *Writers Dreaming*, Barth noted:

I happen to have a twin sister, and when we were little we were very close indeed.... Even before we could speak, we were enormously close. We valued that closeness. Its touchstone for me was a morning we began to compare our dreams, as we used to do. We will both swear to this day that there was a night when we dreamt the same dream.[4]

For Michelle Lusson, the psychic who started Poseidia Institute, this type of dream connectedness was commonplace. Mikey was one of a pair of identical twin girls. She often told stories of telepathic communications between her and her sister Dottie. One of the more dramatic episodes between these two is recounted in their book, *The Beginning or the End* published in 1975.

After leaving school, the twins went their separate ways. Mikey was married to a student architect in Philadelphia, while Dottie was the wife of a young physician serving military duty overseas in Naples, Italy. Communication between the two was limited to occasional letters or phone calls.

When Mikey was pregnant with her third child, the baby arrived prematurely. During the birth Mikey developed a lung embolism. As the doctors struggled to save the baby, she stopped breathing, and was given up for dead.

At the same moment, on the other side of the world, Dottie woke from a dream about her sister and went into anaphylactic shock, with severe breathing difficulties and a feeling of doom. She was taken to the hospital for treatment, still worrying about the dream she had wakened from.

Fortunately for everyone involved, Mikey's doctors soon realized that their adult patient was not dead, though she had temporarily stopped breathing. Sister Dottie recovered completely, as soon as her twin was revived.

Thus far, the areas of family dreaming we have mentioned are reasonably comfortable for most dreamers. But that seems to be the end of the comfort zone. When we return to Kilton Stewart's model for Senoi family dreaming, we have reached the dreams that challenge family security. What if families really did begin each day with a discussion of dreams? What if families were to become like dream groups that as Jeremy Taylor points out, create deeper intimacy and understanding? What if parents were to interact with children as if children were capable of both coming to grips with dream material and being useful parts of a dream circle? These ideas challenge the very foundation of family structure.

Let me illustrate with an example.

A few months ago, I was invited to visit friends in North Carolina. This couple introduced me to their five-year old son as "the dream lady." "She's someone who knows all about dreams," the father boomed. "Why don't you tell

Jean about the dream you had this morning?" With a great deal of trepidation, the boy began to tell his dream about "Mommy Island and Daddy Mountain."

In his dream, he had been enjoying himself on a lovely island (Mommy Island) surrounded by bright, sunny waters. But when it came time for him to ascend Daddy Mountain, he was afraid. Daddy Mountain's peaks were stormy, and there was loud thunder, lightning and rain. It was fairly clear to all of us what the boy was feeling. Dad grumbled something about Oedipal dreams, and the conversation moved on to another subject.

As I watched the little boy turn away from us, head down, dejected, I wondered what might have happened if the family had dealt with his dream in the Senoi manner. What if this boy had been encouraged to talk about the feelings his dream brought up for him? The level of openness and respect required by such an approach to dreams is enormous.

The practice of honest and open dream work in the family setting is a challenge that makes most people shudder even before any thought is given to group dreaming because dreams expose our deepest vulnerabilities. Here is another example of the type of issue that can come up in any family. This one was presented by a young Navy doctor in one of my classes at Poseidia Institute.

This doctor, Joe, was very close to his four-year old daughter and obviously loved her very much. One evening in class, when the discussion turned to shared dreaming, he announced that he often dreamed with his little girl.

"I'll be lucid," he said, "and she'll come to my bedroom door, asking me to come out and play with her. She knows she's dreaming too." He smiled at his daughter's precociousness.

Well, did he go out and play with her, the class asked? Did he play in the dream state with his little girl? Did he discuss dreams with her when they were both awake? I could see on the faces of the class members the looks of longing. What would it be like to play in mutually lucid dream state with dad?

No, Joe answered. There were tears in his eyes. He never went out to play with his little girl in dreams and he seldom discussed dreams with her at all. He was afraid of his sexual feelings toward his daughter Joe said, and he wanted to make sure he never acted on them.

There is a term for what this father did in order to avoid dealing with his incestuous feelings. It is called repression. But we also might want to consider the degree of integrity and bravery it took for Joe's admission to the class that he had sexual feelings toward his daughter.

Dreams break taboos. In all cultures, whatever the cultural mores, dreamers are regularly and consistently breaking taboos in their sleep. They are sleeping with movie stars rather than partners, killing their bosses, tasting forbidden pleasures. In families, dreamers also break taboos, both family taboos and societal ones.

Interviewed for the Fall 1994 issue of *Dream Time*, Jeremy Taylor said:

I think my daughter has finally forgiven us for not warning her about cultural taboos against dream sharing. She grew up steeped in dream sharing and assuming that families and people sharing dreams was normal. When she began to go to public school, it never occurred to us to warn her that her teachers and other kids wouldn't be interested in dreams. She arrived in kindergarten and started asking all the kids about their dreams and created a minor riot.[5]

Personally, I believe that most people are interested in dreams. I have been in too many situations to believe differently. Such as the minute the word dream is mentioned, every person in the room wants to share a dream with me—often in a low whisper, not wanting to be overheard. There are many reasons why adults share in society's taboo against dream discussion but few of them have to do with lack of interest. One reason adults find the idea of family dream sharing so daunting is the children themselves. Children often exhibit abilities that do not fit into the usual categories.

Author Madeline L'Engle, famous for her Newberry Award winning young adult novel, *A Wrinkle in Time*, describes her own childhood talent in her memoir *Walking on Water*. "Small children," L'Engle writes, "do things which to adults living in the grown-up world are impossible."

They see things which grown-up eyes cannot see. They hear things which fall on deaf ears with their parents, and they believe the things they do see and hear. And when, eager and unprepared, they describe these marvelous things, they are told, by kindly and reasonable, and well-meaning parents that they have vivid imaginations. Less understanding adults tell the children that whatever it is they think they have done, seen, or heard, is impossible. Some children are told to stop telling lies. Some are even punished....

When I was a small child, visiting my grandmother at her beach cottage, I used to go down the winding stairs without touching them. This was a special joy to me. I think I went up the regular way, but I came down without touching...

When I was twelve, we went to Europe to live.... I was fourteen when we returned, and went to stay with my grandmother at the beach. The first thing I did when I found myself alone was to go to the top of the stairs. And I could no longer go down them without touching. I had forgotten how.[6]

This poignant tale was echoed with more humor in one of my dream classes at the Institute, when a class member came in with mud-caked shoes.

"You should have walked light," one student said.

Conversation stopped. Seeing her classmates' blank stares, the woman laughed. "You mean you never walked light when you were kids?"

The story she told was that, growing up on a farm in central Virginia, she and her brothers figured out how to keep from getting muddy and upsetting their mother by skimming across the top of the mud, or walking light. She said they had once played a trick on their least-favorite cousins by inviting them to come play in the muddy fields, then coming away clean, so to speak, while the cousins got punished for getting their clothes and shoes dirty. As Madeline L'Engle points out, many adults cannot or will not believe the abilities children possess and are quick to belittle them.

In 1984, I did an eight-week seminar for students in the Lighthouse Program of the Norfolk, Virginia Public Schools. The dream groups met in the relaxed comfort of a student lounge, sprawled on couches or seated on pillows on the shag rug that covered the floor. One day an attractive ninth grader stayed after class, supported by a friend who moved her in my direction with a sharp poke in the ribs. The girl's hair was long, russet and shiny, her laughter nervous. She looked away as she spoke to me, saying almost too softly for me to hear: "When I was little...I mean, well it was only a couple of years ago...." Relaxing as she talked, she went on to say how, when she began junior high school she had been sick for several months and spent a lot of time in bed.

"There was a tiny little village on my bedspread, you know? Little people. Could that have happened? I mean I used to play with them. My mother said it was just a dream. Four months of dream?" She laughed.

Anyone familiar with the work of Robert Louis Stevenson knows that at least one other child had this experience. His poem, "The Land of Counterpane," records the experiences Stevenson had as a child, with another miniature village.

Certainly not all children have experiences like the ones described here, but enough children do that it must be seen as a factor in why dreams in the family setting have been so neglected. The fact that children are likely to be frank and open in their assessment of dreams can be a factor as well.

What would you do, for example, if you were the distraught mother who told me this tale? For years, ever since she was a child, this woman had experienced recurring nightmares. She dreamed of a house. The downstairs of the house was dark and old. There was construction. A stairway led up past a kitchen where "something bad had happened." Upstairs was a large, empty room full of sunlight. A breeze blew a curtain at an open window.

One evening this woman told her dream to her youngest son, who was still in high school. It was the first time she had ever told the dream to anyone.

"Hey, I've had that dream," was his response. And he went on to describe aspects of the house she had dreamed but not mentioned to him in the conversation.

A while later, the woman's daughter came home from a date, pausing in the kitchen doorway to ask her mother and brother what they were doing up so late. "Oh <u>that</u> dream," was her response when they told her. Both of the children had dreamed of the house for years.

Of course the group dream researcher in me wanted to begin asking questions immediately when I heard about this experience. How frequently did the dreams occur? Did the three dream of the house on the same night? What were their ideas about why they would share this dream?

But this dream was a nightmare, and a recurring nightmare at that. Particularly when it comes to nightmares, with their heavy emotional freight, it is important that the dreamer feel safe in the environment of dream work in order to deal with emotional issues. The mother, shaken by this evidence of family dream sharing, chose not to work with the dream.

According to Bruce Bynum, who has collected shared family dreams for many years in his Family Dreams Research Project, one hundred percent of the shared family dreams reported to him involve crises. He says in his book *Families and the Interpretation of Dreams* that these dreams, "...all involved crises, the high motivation or need to communicate information, and a certain apparent *coordination* of psychological and physiological states."[7]

My own assumption, based solely on the stories I have heard during a lifetime of dream work, is that there may be far more incidents of dream sharing in the family setting than are ever reported and probably many more which pass totally unnoticed, due to the family dynamics involved.

For example, years after working through the nightmares that had plagued her childhood, when Linda Magallón was preparing the manuscript for her book *Mutual Dreaming*, she had a visit from her sister Cynthia.

I handed her the manuscript to read and walked into the kitchen to get us both something to drink," Linda reports in her book. "'Oh my God!' I heard her groan. I ran back into the living room.

"What's the matter," I asked anxiously.

"I had the same dream!'[8]

In all, Linda discovered that three out of four of her siblings had shared the same dream or dream elements, which involved flying to escape Mafia-like figures (Men in Black) who grabbed at her ankles as she flew above their heads.

For Linda and her family, knowing that dreams were being shared might have helped the children to feel supported and to cope with the cause of the nightmares, but this can happen only in families where each family member is willing to be open to the magic of dreams.

It would be misleading to say here that no dream researcher ever looks at family dreams or that there are no families operating within dreaming traditions. I have met members of many families who have told me about the dreaming traditions which operate in their own families. It has been interesting to me to notice that the families that most often follow a practice of emphasizing dreams seem almost entirely to be families that are marginalized by race or ethnicity, who come from what Western science might call a "primitive" tradition – Native Americans from both North and South America, central Europeans, African-Americans, and others.

In many African-American families, there is a strong foundation of predictive dreaming and it is not uncommon for several people in the family to share the same foretelling dream. Reverend Sid, who participated in the first Dreams to the Tenth Power experiment, recalled how members of his family, when they gathered for funerals or baptisms or other family events, would exchange reminisces of who had dreamed about what events.

This same custom of strong predictive dreaming often holds true for families of middle European descent, though in the case of these families, there is often one particular patriarch or matriarch to whose dreams everyone in the family gives the most attention.

At a recent conference of the International Association for the Study of Dreams, a woman came up after my presentation to inform me that her large, Italian family dreamed together all the time. The story she told me was about a set of dreams that she, her husband-to-be, and her father all shared. I was particularly struck when she ended this narrative of shared dreaming with the words, "And when my father dreams, you'd better listen!" This custom in some families of having a designated dreamer must surely remove the pressure of shared responsibility.

Native American family dream reports, in comparison, tend to grow out of a tradition that believes all individuals can and should develop an understanding of dreams. Two of the most interesting recent accounts of Native American traditions of family dreaming come from non-tribal people who have become close to tribal elders. One is from Robert Moss, who found himself dreaming in the ancient Iroquois language. Moss, an Australian native who received a firm grounding in Aboriginal dreaming traditions as a child, set out to find the source of his Iroquois dreams. He talks about this search and where it has led him in one of his recent books, *Dreamways of the Iroquois*.

Another account comes from Jayne Gackenbach, who has spent considerable time with the Cree tribe of central Alberta in Canada. In 1996 her essay, "Thoughts About Dreamwork With Central Alberta Cree" was published in the book *Among All These Dreams*, edited by Kelly Bulkeley. The original, longer version of this essay is also available on Gackenbach's web site.

Writing about the final days of Crowwoman, the sister of the tribal member with whom she worked most closely, Gackenbach brings up an element of strong tribal belief:

> She wasn't always "here." This 49-year old Cree woman was in and out. Her family felt she went to the spirit world and then came back time and again. Crowwoman would say something when she woke/"returned".... This Native woman knew things. She knew somebody was coming. She brought messages from the dead. Near the end, Crowwoman had a powerful vision.
>
> Since her death many family members and friends have had dreams of Crowwoman.... The dreams and visions vary from person to person, but what

all seem to hold constant (white and Native) is the reality of these dreams and visitations by Crowwoman with specific messages.[9]

Let me briefly mention that the Native American family dreamers are not the only people who apparently have very real dreams of the deceased, and that this fact in and of itself may impact why many families do not share dreams. The role of spirits in dreaming has a history all its own, and one we do not need to go into here. But my observation is that in families where I know at least one person to have dreamed of a dead relative, the conflict over whether this type of dreaming is real or imaginary seems to develop immediately, often creating its own split in the family involved.

Having examined a number of cases in which shared family dreams seem to be happening, let's take a look at results of family dream sharing as reported by the few, brave dream workers who have attempted to restore the tradition of family dream work to their own families. Kelly Bulkely is probably the most articulate about the potential value of dream work to all families. Interviewed for the Spring 1997 issue of *Dream Time*, Kelly said:

> The most surprising thing has been how much help they've been [his children] in understanding my own dreams. I sometimes tell them dreams I've had, and they always have interesting and insightful things to say. The lesson I've learned from them is that family dream-sharing works best when it's a truly mutual process, when it's an open, back-and-forth dialogue. It's amazing to see how much children enjoy the opportunity to be the ones helping their parents with something, rather than always being on the receiving end of the care.[10]

Jill Gregory, a prime mover on a multitude of dream projects for many years, including the Novato Dream Center and Library, is another person who enthusiastically promotes family dream work. In a series of articles originally printed in *Dream Network* and later reprinted in *Electric Dreams*, Jill talks about the weekly dream group she did with a group of fourth graders at her daughter's school. In one of the articles, she recounts a dream that impacted her own family:

> My daughter Shamrock told me a dream, which involved a mother putting dirty diapers back on her three children instead of using clean diapers from the box of "Luvs" disposable diapers that she had with her in the living room. Shamrock said to me, "I think I know what this dream is telling me. I've been getting mad at my little sister a lot more than I used to. That's because I'm mad at her for a lot of things that she's done that bug me. I need to change and show her my love in a cleaner way. I need to forgive her for just being a little kid and doing things she's not supposed to do. And I think this dream is also telling you and daddy the same thing about how you treat me and my sister lately. When you come to tell us something we're doing

wrong, don't remind us of the times we did it before. It's just like putting dirty diapers on a baby. Show us your 'luv' in a clean way."

When I related this to my husband, he surprised me by saying that he had noticed the same thing and was getting ready to talk to me about it. The power and simplicity of the imagery of the clean and dirty diapers proved helpful to my husband and me in changing how we approached our children when they did something wrong. Shamrock's foundation in dreams and dreamwork enabled her to serve our family in a timely, non-threatening and profound way.[11]

Jill is adamant about the value of family dream sharing. "We protect our children from physical world dangers and traumas of even minor impact," she says, "but abandon them to horrific, repeated traumas in their dream world. This is not due to malice, but rather to ignorance."

Although again this dream of Shamrock's is not a shared or mutual dream, the impact on the family is clear. A common complaint among participants in group dreaming experiences is that because they have opened themselves to the consciousness of other members of the group, they sometimes pick up far more than they ever wanted to know about what's going on in the other dreamers' lives, at times even things about which the other dreamer is blissfully unconscious. This is an important issue to note in the sense that when families become working dream groups, open to all of the potentials of group dreaming, family roles, power structures, and emotions will have to be considered, possibly even with the assistance of a therapist or trained dream worker.

Linda Magallón said to me in private correspondence in 1999, "In 1985 I was still playing the role of Mom, the clean-up lady for other people. But nowadays I believe that folks should clean up their dirty laundry at home. Before they come to a communal gathering."

However, the family is the initial and primary community. In the context of the family, the effective practice of group dreaming requires a willingness to open to the message of the dream and the willingness to create a new balance between self and the family, self and the social group. There are many challenges to be met.

Chapter Ten - Dreaming the World

"We are a people who live on the roof of the world," Pueblo Indian elder Mountain Lake told Carl Jung, when the Swiss psychoanalyst visited the United States in the early part of the twentieth century. "We are the sons of Father Sun, and with our religion we daily help our father to go across the sky. We do this not only for ourselves, but for the whole world. If we were to cease practicing our religion, in ten years the sun would no longer rise. Then it would be night forever."

Carl Jung was no stranger to the idea that since the beginning of recorded history there have been many people in many cultures who have believed that human beings dream the world into creation. In recent years there has been a movement in dream work toward returning to this philosophy, but with certain new twists brought about by the integration of modern science.

At the 1999 conference of the International Association for the Study of Dreams, Dr. Stephen Aizenstat, a clinical psychologist and the President of Pacifica Institute in Carpenteria, California, told the story of a client who had come to him with a recurring dream. Aizenstat said the client had repeatedly watched from his dreams as a large and beautiful church was destroyed.

These dreams puzzled both Aizenstat and his client. They worked diligently, trying to uncover the dream's meaning. They tried Jungian interpretation; they tried Freudian interpretation; they tried pretty much everything they could think of. But still the dreams persisted.

Then the client, an attorney, decided to take a trip to the Mexican town where his mother grew up. There, to his amazement, he found the church, the one he'd been dreaming about all these months. And what was more, the church was in danger of being torn down by a developer who wanted the property. The man's aunt told him that his mother had been very fond of that church and had always worked to preserve it.

With this new understanding of the dream, Aizenstat said, the attorney went to work. He laid claim to the village and the church of his dreams, filed a suit against the developers, and saved the church—which he still supports to this day. The question Aizenstat asked his audience at the conference was, "In this case, just who or what is dreaming?"

"Dreams and myths are not static events of the past," Aizenstat told *Dream Network* editor Roberta Ossana in a 1998 interview. "They are alive in the present moment."

In the mid-90s, Aizenstat was invited to be part of the Earth Charter Initiative, a United Nations sponsored attempt to develop twelve to eighteen principles for sustaining the environmental future of the planet. He subsequently joined seventy other world citizens at The Hague in the Netherlands. The result was the Earth Charter. The question posed to the conference was, "What are the principles that we can develop to answer and insure a sustainable future for the planet?"

"The problem," Aizenstat told Ossana, "is that this question doesn't take us anyplace! As long as we keep asking what we can do for the planet, we are still imposing our set of values in a linear way on a static system."

At the Pacifica Institute, Aizenstat and his assistants have devised an "Earth Charter Project" as a way to hear the living story, the myth of the planet through dreams. "We've asked literally hundreds upon hundreds of people to hear into dreams and hear the planet speak to them...." Aizenstat says. "But in order to hear that, *we need to think differently....* We also have to allow the possibility for things of the world to speak on behalf of themselves."[1]

The new interest that modern dream work takes related to the idea of dreaming the world can be traced directly to the rediscovery of lucid dreaming in the 1970s. Himself a pioneer in the field of consciousness studies, Robert Ornstein points out in the foreword to the 1985 publication of Stephen LaBerge's book *Lucid Dreaming*:

> LaBerge's proof (of lucid dreaming) is important because it shows once again that the possibilities of human consciousness are greater than we had thought. Many scientists believed that dreams were in their very nature "irrational" and "unconscious." From this perspective, lucid dreaming was beyond the pale.[2]

Linda Magallón outlined the defining qualities of dream lucidity in her *Psychic Creative Dreaming* course where she says:

> Carl Jung theorized the collective unconscious to be the combined knowledge of all humankind in which every person is connected. For Jung the collective just is; we dip into it in order to form our dreams. It exists automatically, without any conscious effort on our part.... It took the lucid dreamers to fully comprehend dream mutuality; to realize first hand just how dream territory changes to accommodate the dreamer. The dream was found to be a reflection of the dreamer's inner state.... a shift in consciousness caused an instantaneous revision, or a switch to a different viewpoint or entirely new scene.[3]

Because dream lucidity seemed so new during the seventies and eighties, but also because it resembled other states of consciousness which were newly being studied, dream researchers began to compare lucid dream accounts with dream records from other cultures.

Harry Hunt, author of *The Multiplicity of Dreams*, a text published in 1989 and commonly used to teach about dreams in psychology courses, says,

> We are left to ponder the significance of the creation of a dream psychology (psychoanalytic and/or laboratory based) focused on a form of dreaming regarded as 'trivial' by societies whose cultures were created

around and even organized in their dreams. Perhaps it is our dreams that have become single-minded, private theaters of personal memory.[4]

At the time of lucid dreaming's reemergence, "channeled material" was being taken more seriously than ever before. Lucid dream researchers were familiar with the work of psychics Edgar Cayce, Jane Roberts and others, and were undoubtedly influenced by them. In the somewhat archaic language through which his readings were delivered, Cayce reminded his listeners to

Forget not that the creator, the gods and the god of the universe, speaks to man through his individual self. Man approaches the more intimate conditions of that field of inner self when the conscious self is at rest in sleep or slumber, at which time more of the inner forces are taken into consideration and studied by the individual.... It is each individual's job to understand his individual condition.[5]

Jane Roberts and Seth were even more succinct in Volume Two of *Dreams, Evolution, and Value Fulfillment*, published in 1986. "When I speak of the dream world," Seth says,

I am not referring to some imaginary realm, but to the kind of world of ideas, of thoughts, of mental actions, out of which all form as you think it emerges. In actuality, this is an inner universe rather than an inner world. Your physical reality is but one materialization of that linear organization. All possible civilizations exist in the realm of the inner mind.[6]

Thus when lucid dream researchers turned for confirmation toward other cultures and their histories of world dreaming, it was to find continuity as well.

Following World War II, when the Chinese invaded the mountain kingdom of Tibet, forcing the flight of the young Dalai Lama and many of his country's people to India, the eyes of the world became focused on the drama. In the years since then, with the Dalai Lama's leadership, hundreds of thousands of Europeans and Americans have, if not converted to Buddhism, at least begun to understand the tenets of Buddhist practice. One practice in which Buddhist monks and nuns participate is lucid dreaming, or dreaming the clear light.

Over five days in October of 1992, at the Dalai Lama's residence in Dharamsala, India, an unprecedented event took place. The fourth in a series of biennial meetings with the Dalai Lama called Mind and Life Conferences took place. This time the subject was "Sleeping, Dreaming and Dying."

The conference, organized by Dr. Francisco J. Verela, was like its predecessors designed for intimate and in-depth exploration of subjects which traditionally divide East and West. Only a handful of scientists and observers were allowed at the conference; the press was forbidden. Each morning, one of the scientists would present a paper, with careful translations being given. Each afternoon, the Dalai Lama would respond to the paper.

According to Varela, in his introduction to the book which resulted from the conference:

During the third day we would move to a more recent and controversial area within the study of dreams, the phenomenon of lucid dreaming. We chose this topic because on the one hand it has received some scientific attention in the West, and on the other hand it has been a very active field of study in the Buddhist tradition.[7]

Presenting the morning paper on dream lucidity was Dr. Jayne Gackenbach. That afternoon, the Dalai Lama responded from the foundations of Buddhist spiritual practice.

"In addition to practicing during the waking state," he told the assembled scientists and observers, "if you can also use your consciousness during sleep for wholesome purposes, then the power of your spiritual practice will be all the greater. Otherwise at least a few hours each night will be just a waste."

The Highest Yoga Tantra, which is the fourth and most profound of the four classes of tantra, speaks of the basic nature of reality. In addition to the nature of the Path and the culmination of the Path in Buddahood, this level of tantra discusses both the mind and the body in terms of three progressively more subtle states or levels: the gross, the subtle, and the very subtle states. In this context, one can also speak of gross and subtle levels of 'I' or the self.

In order to train in the path that would allow us to transform death, the intermediate state, and rebirth we have to practice on three occasions: during the waking state, during the sleeping state, and during the death process.[8]

That afternoon, the Dalai Lama even went so far as to offer some practical suggestions for lucidity, suggestions found in the Tibetan tradition. "Different factors are involved in the ability to recognize the dream as dream," he said. "One is diet…. If your dreams are not clear, as you're falling asleep you should direct your awareness to the throat center. In this practice…when you begin dreaming, it's helpful to have someone say quietly. "You are dreaming now. Try to recognize the dream as dream."[9]

Nor was Tibetan culture the only ancient dreaming culture Jayne Gackenbach explored. In the 1980s, after a move to Alberta, Canada, Gackenbach found herself teaching dream work classes not only at McGill University, but also teaching classes, through the University of Alberta, on the Alberta Cree Indian Reservation. She taught psychology classes for Cree natives at the Yellowhead Tribal Council and at Blue Quills Native College, finding them to be the "most lively I have ever had."

She also co-facilitated a number of workshops in the area with Ravenwoman, a Cree healer, with whom she had developed a close friendship. Ravenwoman told workshop participants that her grandfather believed, as did many of the elder generation that, "if you listen to your dreams you could learn things my ancestors knew how to do."[10]

While working with Ravenwoman, Gackenbach conducted many interviews with Cree natives. Many of the stories she encountered involved mutual dreaming and group dreaming.

Almost all Native American cultures in both North and South America involved strong dreaming traditions. For example, Curtiss Hoffman, an anthropologist and host of the 2006 IASD conference, recently located one of many ancient sighting stones—on the campus of Bridgewater State College in Massachusetts where he works. Hoffman has worked closely with the tribal people in that area, who are of primarily Algonquin ancestry, on the preservation of sacred sites. "They are concerned," Hoffman says in a yet unpublished manuscript,

> that the sites are part of an ancient system of balance between people, earth, and sky which is under threat of being upset, with what they consider to be potentially dire consequences for us all. The basis for this belief is traditional knowledge which has been handed down orally for generations in their medicine lodges, though not until recently revealed beyond the tribes for fear of ridicule, persecution, and vandalism....[11]

Like Henry Reed, who with his Dream Helper Project brought forward the type of dream ritual used in ancient Greece, many dream workers have incorporated elements of dreaming cultures in their contemporary work. Dream researchers such as Robert Moss, Stanley Krippner, and Maria Volchenko have carefully studied Shamanic practices of cultures from the Brazilian jungles to the steppes of central Asia, weaving these practices into a more modern perspective of consciousness.

In an essay "When We Become A Dreaming Culture," which Robert Moss has posted on his web site at www.mossdreams.com, he voices his hopes for the world, saying:

> Dreaming we remember our kinship with all living things and the Earth that sustains us. Dreaming we walk between worlds and remember that our spirits are starborn. As a society of dreamers, we will participate actively in the emergence of a more gifted and generous version of our species: the multidimensional human.[12]

In addition to the evidence of world dreaming presented by multiple ancient cultures, there is the evidence provided by a few attempts in recent years to study the dreams of specific populations. Interestingly enough, these collections of dreams also demonstrate the connections between dreamers, whether or not the dreamers have been aware – and in most cases they were not – of the possibility of shared dreaming.

One of the unsung heroes of World War II was author Charlotte Beradt, who literally smuggled dreams out of Nazi Germany. Beradt says in her book *The Third Reich of Dreams*:

It had occurred to me from time to time that a record should be kept of such dreams (dreams of totalitarian Germany), a thought that now became a plan. They might one day serve as evidence when the time came to pass judgment on National Socialism as a historical phenomenon, for they seemed to reveal a great deal about people's deepest feelings and reactions as they became part of the mechanism of totalitarianism.[13]

In the repressive atmosphere of Germany in the 1930s, Beradt kept her project secret from all but her closest friends. She inquired innocently of people she knew, if they mentioned a dream, what the dream had been about. She collected dreams from merchants, from shopkeepers, from the dressmaker, from her dentist. All of these dreams revealed remarkable similarities.

"I continued to gather material until 1939," Beradt says, "when I was compelled to leave Germany. It is interesting to note that dreams dating from 1933 differed little from those of later years. My most revealing examples stem from the very beginning of the Nazi period, when the regime was still treading lightly."[14]

How Beradt collected the dreams and eventually got them out of Germany is a story in itself, since the very act of making such a collection could have been seen as treasonous. "A number of friends who knew of the project," she writes, "helped me gather material.

The most important single contribution was made by a doctor who had a large practice and could query his patients unobtrusively. Altogether, the dreams of more than three hundred persons were obtained....

I tried my best to camouflage the notes I kept on these dreams. When writing them down or copying someone else's notes, I would call the party "family," an arrest "grippe," Hitler, Goering, and Goebbles became "Uncle Hans," "Uncle Gustav," and "Uncle Gerhard" respectively.... I hid these odd-sounding "family anecdotes" in the bindings of books which were scattered through my large private library. Later, I sent them as letters to various addresses in countries abroad, where they were kept until I myself had to leave Germany.[15]

The result of this brave activity on the part of Beradt and her companions is the single most thorough collection of dreams ever amassed from a war-torn country or from a totalitarian state. And they are eerily repetitive, from one individual to another, from one year to another.

"The dreams we are concerned with," Beradt concludes, "were not produced by conflicts arising in their authors' private realm, and certainly not by some past conflict that had left a psychological wound.... These dreams may deal with disturbed human relations, but it was the environment that had disturbed them."[16]

There has not been such a systematic study of dreams in times of war since this one. The Second World War was a time of profound human thought about the nature of war itself and provided numerous other examples of shared dreaming. For example, here is a statement that Carl Jung made to his friend Laurens Van der Post in his book, *Jung and the Story of Our Time*:

It was remarkable" he [Jung] told me once, "how as the war became more desperate and widespread, I found myself dreaming more and more of Churchill. It was almost as if there were a kind of dream telepathy and state of dream participation between us. I would wake up in the morning having dreamt of him and read, for instance, that he had just been on another long and dangerous journey by plane. That happened not once but lots of times.[17]

In more recent years, a friend of Jane Roberts, Susan Watkins, has provided another look at the dreams of an entire population in her book *Dreaming Myself, Dreaming a Town*. Watkins told *Dream Network* editor Roberta Ossana in a 1989 interview how she got the idea for the book. She was editor of the newspaper for a small town in New York while she worked on a book about Jane and Seth's Monday Night Class called *Conversations With Seth*. After a particularly difficult and frustrating morning of work on the book, she decided to take a break.

On impulse I picked my great-grandfather's memoir out of the book case and started paging through it. I remember that it was a warm day in March and air redolent of spring mud was wafting through the open apartment windows, hinting of things to come. I turned to my great-grandfather's description of the huge fire that had leveled Dundee's downtown 118 years before...the notion flitted across my mind that it was too bad nobody had recorded their dreams the night before that fire. How interesting it would be to compare! And then all at once, from one moment to the next, all of these projects clicked together, a crack opened in the sky and the idea to collect dreams from the people of Dundee and compare those dreams with daily life—to document unofficial history—fell out and hit me on the head: BONK![18]

Immediately Sue Watkins put a note in the *Dundee Observer*, which she edited, asking people to send her their dreams. As soon as she put her notice into the newspaper, Watkins said, she received "less than I expected and more than I could have imagined." Interestingly enough, Susan Watkins said that the individuals she least expected to care about dreams were often the very people who had the most vivid dream life and the most unabashed manner of relating their dreams. Such unexpected individuals included the CEO of the local bank, who also had past-life recall, and an unemployed hog farmer.

"I've been interested in my own dreams and dreams in general for most of my life," Watkins told Ossana. "As a child I had vivid, recurring, sometimes terrifying and often precognitive dreams that seemed to spill over into my waking life in the form of coincidences and 'odd' events. Even then I noticed connections between my dreams and tidbits in newspapers the next day."[19]

Although there were some clear cases of shared dreaming recorded by Watson in this unique process, she said that one of the problems highlighted by her collection method is probably more universal than we notice. "Less than any encultured notion that dreams were crazy or evil," Watkins said, "people who talked to me seemed to feel that because they weren't some kind of 'expert' their own dream interpretations couldn't possibly be any good." "Unfortunately," Watkins added to Ossana, "too many 'experts' share this belief."[20]

The literature around the idea of dreaming the world is difficult. Much of it comes from ancient traditions, poorly recorded or with broken histories. Other material, such as Watkins' book, provides a limited and inconclusive picture.

However, it must be acknowledged that if shared dreaming is accepted as a fact, and lucid mutual dreaming is a learned skill as it appears to be, then the possibility exists that we may well be dreaming the world—or making it up as we go along.

Part Three
The World Dreams Peace Bridge

Chapter Eleven - In the Wake of 9/11

On the morning of September 11, 2001, I awoke from a strange dream:
I am standing in the doorway to an air traffic control tower. This is a major airport, maybe Kennedy in New York, and there are a number of employees monitoring air traffic. One African American man stands up from his chair with a microphone in his hand. He is obviously shouting and agitated.

This was at 5:30 a.m., my usual wake-up time. I rolled over in bed, took a look at the clock, and thought, "Strange dream. I never dream about airplanes." Thinking no more about it, I went on with my morning routine. I walked in the park near the river down the street from my house, had some breakfast, and then sat down at the computer to check the messages on the IASD Bulletin Board, as I did every day.

This morning I had barely sat down when I received an email from a friend. "Turn on the television," was all it said. Given such a cryptic message, who could resist? I quickly stepped over and turned on the television, to see a twenty-one inch image of what looked like the World Trade Center towers in New York City. An announcer was saying, "There has been an explosion at the World Trade Center. An aircraft, maybe a private airplane, seems to have flown into the...."

As he spoke, the commentator's voice trailed off. We all watched in horror as a second plane, obviously a commercial jet, flew into the other World Trade Center tower, shearing off part of the building, creating a fiery explosion. The stunned commentator was saying, "It's another airplane. A second airplane has flown into the tower."

As the story of the day's tragedy began to unfold, I heard in my head, as clearly as if someone had said it out loud, "This day will change the world." My next thought was about the Boarders on the International Association for the Study of Dreams (IASD) Bulletin Board. What would they think? What would they be hearing? And then, oh my word! I wondered how many hundreds of people around the world had dreamed precognitively about this event, and how they must be feeling, seeing it unfold before their eyes. I knew I needed to go back online to tell people they could discuss their premonitions on the Bulletin Board.

Precognitive dreams are not synonymous with group dreaming. However, we have seen from several cases how precognitive dreamers will tune in on mass events such as the O.J. Simpson trial. In these cases, the group focus seems to produce the immediate appearance, in the dreams of multiple dreamers, of upcoming, emotionally charged events. Watching the events at the Twin Towers on September 11, I had a feeling for what might follow.

Later that day, other members of IASD's Board of Directors would begin to talk with me about how we might deal with the nightmares which were sure to come. My response was no; first we have to deal with the precognitive dreamers.

What touched my heart the morning of 9/11 was the swift response of other dreamers from around the world. Somehow, in the process of creating a Bulletin Board community, I had landed in the middle of a warm, caring and generous group of international dreamers. On the morning of 9/11, the first messages that came on my screen were messages of condolence, both for me and for the American people from Japan, Australia, Turkey, England, Canada, Mexico, Chile. Striking as they had, at the start of Manhattan's business day, the terrorists had found citizens in every part of the world awake and watching TV. The outpouring of caring and compassion from around the world was heartwarming and comforting.

Then came the dreams.

There are some things about precognitive dreams that all people who study them seem to agree upon. One is that spontaneous precognition most frequently involves something that is emotionally charged. Many people will dream precognitively about accidents or disasters, particularly if these involve family members or other intimates. Another thing about precognitive dreams upon which most researchers agree is that they can happen at any time before the event, sometimes days or years in advance. The events of September 11, I knew, contained an emotional charge at least as strong as any other dream-producing event in the past few years, maybe stronger. I wrote a message to the Bulletin Board inviting dreamers to share their feelings and dreams about the day's events on the Board and then forwarded the message to all the other dream groups I knew of: IASD online study groups, *Electric Dreams*, various list serves, and the oldest online dream group in existence, a Yahoo group called dreamchatters.

I was in the midst of having some remodeling done on the house that September, and before long the work crew arrived, banging ladders, shouting back and forth between vehicles. I stepped out on the front porch, not knowing if they had heard the news. John, the contractor, had a daughter at New York University, just a few blocks from where the planes had struck. I knew he would be worried. Yes, they'd heard the news. No word from John's daughter.

I found myself once again in front of the television, this time flanked on either side by burly workmen. We could not tear our eyes away from the sight of the towers bursting into flames, the sounds of shouts and sirens, heroic police and firefighters moving into place, people leaping to their deaths from impossible heights, and the controlled panic of people moving away from the explosions, helping one another, finding one another, looking for one another.

All day long I moved back and forth from television to computer and back again. John kept his cell phone close to his ear, calling for news about his daughter. And the workmen made half-hearted attempts to return to work.

One of the first precognitive dreams reported to the Bulletin Board was from Lou, a Board regular. "Did anyone else have a precognitive dream?" he wrote. "I think I did. I have been dreaming for weeks about plane crashes, but I didn't think anything of it until this morning. In my dream last night, a plane crash landed in a field."

At the time Lou wrote his post to the Bulletin Board, even though the news of the third airliner flying into the Pentagon had broken, nobody yet knew the plight of the fourth plane, which did indeed crash into a field, as passengers and crew on board brought down another terrorist team.

After that, the first trickle of dreams on the Bulletin Board became a stream and reports of dream precognition flowed in—not only to the IASD Bulletin Board, but also to all of the various dream-associated lists and sites online. Some dreams were only vaguely related to the terrorist attacks. Quite clearly there were some people who only wanted to feel part of the conversation. But other dream reports were very precise.

"I woke around 4:30 a.m. on 9/11," wrote one woman:

In the dream, a spiritual master from Nepal is telling my son, my friend, and me that if we return to this high rise building in Manhattan, there will be a big fire and explosion. The "we" we have been will die. We will be born into piety, he tells us. We are ready to become vessels.

IASD Board member, David Gordon wrote to the Bulletin Board mid-afternoon on the September 11:

Last night a friend of mine dreamed that he sat waiting high up in a sports stadium. Wondering what kind of event had been planned, he looked out into the distance; and to his horror saw a huge plane crash into a city and entirely destroy it. Next to him in bed last evening his partner dreamed that she was caught in a building in which there was a raging fire. Everyone was screaming and trying to get out.

Two people who had been backpacking in the Yukon wilderness, a married couple, later reported that they had been totally out of range of either radio or television when the terrorist attacks occurred. They had both slept badly the night before though and each of them had dreamed so clearly about disastrous events in New York City that the next morning they trekked out of the wilderness to find a boat captain with a short-wave radio. This was early in the morning on September 11 and the boat captain reported that nothing out of the ordinary was happening in New York, despite their dreams. Baffled, they were about to return to their campsite when the boat captain called them back. He had just heard the first confused reports of a plane hitting one of the World Trade Center towers.

The people who made their way to the online dream sites were not the only ones who reported precognitive dreams. There were phone calls all day from other people I knew. One of my closest friends called to say that she had spent the previous night dreaming that she was wandering the streets of a big city, with tall, canyon-like walls of buildings all around her. In her dream at one point, she came to an entire city block that looked as if it had been razed to the ground. In the dream she wondered if they were going to build a park there. Another friend, one who swore she had never had a precognitive dream in her life, dreamed that she was trapped in the elevator of a building where there was a big fire.

I got the funny feeling that my friend was not the only person to have a precognitive dream on September 11 who had never recalled dreaming precognitively before. I worried about all those dreamers who, in addition to dealing with the shock of events in waking reality, might be reeling under the impact of what their dreams had announced.

"I don't think I've ever had many precognitive dreams before," a Board visitor from the UK wrote. "Growing up, my family always said that dreams were just nonsense, but I think I might have dreamed about the World Trade Center disaster the night before it happened. I dreamed that I was in a plane that was crashing. I went up to the cockpit to see what was happening. The pilot was fighting with a man who had a gun."

Another person wrote,

Hello,

I came to this site after years and years of dreaming, many of them come true. I have always written them down. Two nights before the disaster, I dreamed my sister and I were on an American Airlines jet and it began to crash. I woke on the morning of the disaster filled with a horrible feeling of dread and confusion. I had no idea why I was feeling the way I was. I am getting a bit concerned about my dreams in general. I guess that is why I found this site. Last night I had a dream that made me wonder if there are other people like me, or if I am just going crazy! Actually I'm quite pleased to know there are others like me!

The days following the terrorist attacks on the World Trade Center and the Pentagon became a blur of activity as I and other dream workers began to discuss how to cope with the flood of requests for dream information. Quickly, various texts about trauma and nightmares were located, copied and put up on the IASD web site, which was getting more hits than ever before in its history. Therapist Robert Bosnak, a pioneer in online dream work methods, enlisted the assistance of his friend Jill Fischer, a psychotherapist from Connecticut, to create The Nightmare Hotline.

Jill and Robby together had created the Cyberdreamwork web site and the cyberdreamwork training program, a method of group work which combined online telephone conferencing, chat rooms and bulletin board to successfully connect dreamers from around the world in weekly dream groups. Now the pair set about designing a hot line that would be staffed twenty-four hours per day, seven days a week, by fully trained therapists to assist people in dealing with their post-9/11 nightmares.

In the midst of all this activity, the first tapes were released of Osama bin Laden and his Al Qaeda troops claiming responsibility for the Trade Center disaster. In these tapes, we clearly hear the voices of bin Laden's captains discussing the dreams they had about the suicide flights of the Al Qaeda martyrs, and how these men who went to their deaths along with so many others, were doing the will of Allah.

I was shocked and saddened, but not surprised, to see a conversation begin online, led by a well-known dream researcher, wondering whether bin Laden and the Al Qaeda had been utilizing dream state to plan their attacks on the United States and maybe even terrorize people in dreams. I followed this conversation with some interest, since my own belief is that we all utilize the dream state to plan the future.

I wondered if the people whose paranoia led them into thinking such crimes as terrorism might be planned in dream state could recognize that people on both sides of the conflict had been dreaming and scheming. Yet no such clarity emerged from the conversation, which quickly dropped back under the surface of the fast-moving information stream.

In retrospect, it is at least worth noting that the question of planning war in dream state arose. It is also worth observing in this context that generals—from Julius Caesar to George Washington to General Patton in World War II—have frequently recorded their dreams (often precognitive) of conquest and victory. In fact, it is surprising to me that no enterprising dream author has yet collected these military dreams into a book. The question of how war and other lethal conflict fits into group dreaming or world dreaming deserves consideration. But in these post-9/11 days there was little time to think about such things.

Mark Barasch, a New Yorker and author of the then best-selling book *Healing Dreams*, wrote to the Bulletin Board that he was collecting dreams about the Twin Towers for a lecture he had been asked to give in Manhattan. He acknowledged that he had more than a passing interest in the subject himself "having dreamed a week before the tragedy, about cars streaming from NYC in a rain of ash from some 'apocalypse' that had flooded the city."

An IASD Past President, Alan Siegel sent a note to the Board of Directors public discussion list that he'd been asked to appear on the Today Show early in October, to talk about post-traumatic nightmares in children. Reporters all over the United States, who seemed to have discovered the importance of dreams in light of the terrorist attacks, were now wanting immediate commentary from dream experts; and researchers such as Ernest Hartmann, M.D., Kelly Bulkeley,

Dale Graff and Robert Moss, on seeing the number of precognitive dreams presented online, had begun to ask for collections of these dreams to be sent to them for research purposes.

At home, the remodeling work continued. John's daughter had been located and was safe at home with a roommate in upstate New York.

One of the most impressive dream responses to the disaster came to my attention on the Bulletin Board several days after 9/11. A woman who signed herself simply "Emily" wrote: "In July 1999 I had the following dream which appears on page 154 of my book *Dream Weaving*:"

> I was lying in bed while a woman, a nurse, looked after me. She said it made her sleepy to watch me sleep! I stayed in bed, because it was so dark out that I assumed it was night. Then I looked at my clock and saw that it was 9 a.m., so I got up and went outside. The sky was predawn gray. Someone told me there had been a disaster in New York City that had created a lot of dust that was blocking the sun....[1]

The author of this post, and author of the book *Dream Weaving: Using Dream Guidance to Create Life's Tapestry*, released by the ARE Press in January 2001, was Emily Vanlaeys.

By the end of September, I began to feel a shift in the mood on the Bulletin Board. From excitement at the fact that there had been so many precognitive dreams, the Boarders slid toward a sort of morose acceptance that even if someone dreamed precognitively and got the event with absolute accuracy and then tried to warn someone, nobody would believe the warning.

One boy who, like John's daughter, attended New York University had dreamed, in the early hours of September 11, that there was some sort of an attack going on in Manhattan and that debris was falling on his apartment. Since this particular boy had a history of accurate precognitive dreams, he woke up his two roommates and told them they needed to all get out of there.

The roommates laughed him off, he said. They told him to go back to sleep. A few hours later the apartment was one of those in the area just north of the World Trade Center that had to be evacuated.

A New Jersey woman wrote that for weeks before the disaster, she and her sister and her daughter had all been having dreams so dire that they decided to go to the police about them. They were treated politely, but firmly told that there was nothing the police could do about dreams.

So what if we do have precognitive dreams, people began to ask? What if the dreams are accurate and nobody listens? What if the dream is not accurate, but I get everyone upset by it? Is there any way to tell if a dream is precognitive? Should I have let people know what I dreamed? Could I have averted the tragedy? Is there someplace online people can go to register their precognitive dreams?

These were all questions I had dealt with previously on a much smaller scale but the very real agony in the voices asking these questions broke my heart. Sometimes it seems that for every person who dreams a clear, precise, predictive dream, there are two or three others whose dreams are only illusory. There are many people who are enchanted by the glamour of being psychic, who will make the flimsiest of connections between their dreams and waking events, and who want to call these dreams precognitive. But there are still many, many others, who consistently have accurate predictive dreams, and who know that certain events are scheduled to happen. For these people, the impotence of knowing that something is going to happen but not being believed goes far beyond any definition of the Cassandra complex.

It was these people I wanted to address when I wrote the paper "Dealing with Precognitive Dreamer Guilt" in late September and sent it to Richard Wilkerson for *Electric Dreams*. In addition to putting it into the e-zine, Richard kindly formatted the article as a stand-alone document that could be accessed by the precognitive dreamers who came to the IASD Bulletin Board and other places online.

This paper is still readily available so I will not recreate it here. Still, I would like to talk about one or two of the points raised in this article. In the past, those who study dreams have been reluctant to cover psi dreams: that is telepathic, lucid, mutual, precognitive dreams, or any type of dream that deals with alternatives to our standard beliefs about space and time as anything but anomalies. Psi dreams were thought to be experienced by such a small percentage of the population as to be almost negligible. Yet here were all these dreamers appearing online, clamoring for answers.

In writing the article about precognitive dreamer guilt, I first wanted these people to know that it is possible to dream the future—not to mention performing several other acts from the dream state that are generally believed to be impossible.

Until this time there has been very little available, even on major dream-related web sites, to support or lend credence to psi dreamers or those who by precognition, telepathy, or other paranormal means receive information in their dreams about upcoming events. Since 9/11 this has begun to change. In addition to the numerous books and articles more seriously addressing the issues of psi dreaming published in the past few years, the IASD has begun one of the most popular online conferences available, its annual PsiberDreaming Online Conference, hosted by Ed Kellogg. This conference, the only one I have ever encountered where participants say they would gladly pay more for less material, provides two weeks of presentations from major researchers and practitioners of all forms of psi, It gives audience members the opportunity to interact with and question the presenters and even provides a gallery for dream-related art. It has become a fertile breeding ground for new thoughts and ideas about psi. However in 2001, information available about psi dreaming or the types of precognitive dreams so many people had experienced was limited.

One question about precognitive dreaming that needed to be addressed was the question of how to tell if a dream is precognitive prior to the event happening in waking life. Anyone who has ever dreamed of pending disaster wants to know the answer to this question. Do I just look at a newspaper in the dream? Ask someone what the date is?

People experienced in precognition will say that the precognitive dream has a different quality from other dreams. They say they can tell immediately if a dream is precognitive. When asked to describe the specific quality though, the answers given by precognitive dreamers vary widely. Some dreamers will say that the colors in precognitive dreams are sharper and brighter; some say the distinguishing factor is that the dreams have unknown people or places or events; some will say it's just a feeling they have when they wake up. My own belief is that each person's way of signaling precognition is quite individual but can be discerned by the dreamer who pays close attention.

The precognitive dream raises serious questions for the dreamer, as it should for all of us, particularly in cases like the Twin Towers disaster where hundreds of lives might have been saved by listening to dreams. And once we are past the question of whether precognition exists, there are myriad other questions, the first among them being whether a predicted or foreseen future can be changed.

I found it fascinating that one dreamer I knew actually dreamed her response to this question the night of September 10, as if she were giving herself a preview of the trouble ahead. The dream as it was told to me was this:

> I was in the home of some friends, not people I knew in waking life, but people I knew very well in the dream. We were all sitting around the living room talking. I knew that the next day would be Pearl Harbor Day. The Japanese were going to attack Pearl Harbor and the U.S. was going to get into World War II. Should I tell them?
>
> The mother of the family said to me, "You don't look very well. Would you like to go lie down for a bit?" So I did. I fell asleep. But when I woke up I was still there, in the same house, in the same dream, and Pearl Harbor was still going to be attacked the next day. Would it do any good to tell them?

In this dream the dreamer faces the dilemma of choice that any precognitive dreamer must make. There are dozens of examples of precognitive dreams that have come true. What many people do not know is that there are also numerous recorded examples of dreams in which telling the dream or changing some waking-life event seems literally to change the future.

A particularly good example of this was told to me once by a man who just happened to visit the office at Poseidia Institute. He was the copy machine repairman who came to fix our broken copier. While he spread parts of the copy machine around him on the floor, he talked about a dream he'd had just before taking his family on their summer vacation.

In the dream he was driving the family car, wife beside him, kids in the back, when he realized that he was driving too fast. Just at that moment he crested the top of a small rise. The sun's glare was in his face and a patrol car pulled out, lights flashing. The policeman pulled the dreamer over and gave him a ticket.

The next day, as the family left for vacation, he was driving. But when they came to an area that began to remind him of the scenery in his dream, he pulled over and asked his wife to drive. "Be sure to put on your sunglasses," he told her. Sure enough, before long, with his wife in the driver's seat, they crested a small rise. The sun's glare was on the windshield, and a police car was sitting at the side of the road. His wife, driving carefully at the speed limit as she always did, drove right on by the police car without even noticing it.

"I figure I saved myself sixty, seventy dollars on that one," the repairman said, shoving the newly repaired cartridge into place on the copier, a self-satisfied grin on his face.

Prior to 9/11, support for precognitive dreamers was rare. There have been precognitive dream registries, but nothing to date that is widely used. A Precognitive Dream Registry is a place where dreamers can register the fact that they've had what they believe to be a precognitive dream, date and time stamp it, and compare their own dreams with the dreams of others on the same subject. Harry Bosma of the Netherlands, who has done a great deal both for the online dream movement and for psi dreamers through his various innovative programs, has been working to create a viable dream registry that can be used by people of many different nationalities.

Another issue faced by psi dreamers is that many of them are uncertain about their abilities and would like to learn more about how to dream telepathically or precognitively or to just sharpen their skills.

Not long after 9/11, Dale Graff, who was one of the U.S. government's most capable remote viewing experts during the Cold War's Stargate Project, and an excellent precognitive dreamer as well, invited people who had dreamed precognitively of the disaster to join him in a Psi Dreaming project.

It was Dale's intention to work with a few of the most talented precognitive dreamers he could find in order to predict future disasters in some very specific ways. Unfortunately, he was inundated by so many dreamers who simply wanted to learn more about using their talents that he had to drop the project altogether, unable to cope with a major educational effort, while still working with those already proficient.

What is the value of a precognitive dream? I returned to my own dream of the morning of 9/11 many times during the post-9/11 discussions with other dreamers. As a vehicle for foretelling the future, my dream was a complete failure. Seeing a disaster only a few hours before it is going to happen, particularly in a dream such as mine, which showed only a fragment of the waking life event, allows no opportunity to use the dream as a warning. And the majority of dreams prior to 9/11 were just like this. Were such dreams only an intrusion from the emotions of the event to come, a way of seeing through a glass darkly?

Personally, I believe that all dreams can be viewed on many levels and offer information simultaneously at the personal level as well as the interactive or social level. When I looked at my September 11 dream in this manner, I found a clear personal message. In my dream I had been standing in the control tower, watching others respond to an emergency. Why, I had to ask myself, was I in the control tower? What metaphor did that offer? It seemed to me that I knew enough to be in control, but rather than acting, I was only observing.

In the paper "Dealing With Precognitive Dreamer Guilt," I talked about my own feelings of guilt as well. I did not feel guilty for not warning of the disaster ahead; there had been no time for me to do that, whether or not I would have been believed. Rather, I interpreted the dream as a message from my dreaming self to my waking self that I needed to stop observing and respond.

I presented to dreamers in this article that Edgar Cayce defined the word responsible as "response-able," that the only thing any of us needs to do in any situation is to respond. The ability to change directions, change paths, to become more able to respond, is one of the major freedoms which dreams allow us – a freedom which can transform our waking lives.

I realized in the days after September 11 that I, like many other people, had become complacent, believing that the affairs of the world were moving along just fine without me. I directed my attention to a narrow circle of personal matters and interests rather than paying attention to world events.

During the Civil Rights era of the 1960s and 1970s, I had marched in the streets against racism and violence. I had protested South African apartheid and the U.S. involvement in Southeast Asia. During the last years of the 1960s, I had attended a wonderful program created by the University of Pennsylvania and Crozier Theological Seminary to train community activists: Upland Institute. Two Quakers, George Willoughby and George Lakey, and two Baptists, John Williams and Ken Smith, introduced students to social activism, grass roots organizing and pacifism.

Between this training and the message of my 9/11 dream, I knew what I needed to do. I needed to stop watching and begin acting, in every way I knew how, to stop the tide of hatred that seemed to be rising in the world. I felt as if 9/11 had the effect of waking me from a long dream.

In the years that I moderated the IASD Bulletin Board prior to September 11, I had especially listened to the dreamers and dream workers from countries other than the United States. Because Internet technology was readily available in the United States, and for years the primary language used online was English, many non-English speaking people felt cut off from Internet use. Additionally, in the dream community, many dream researchers felt ignored or dismissed by their American counterparts. European dream researchers such as Brigitte Holzinger in Austria, who conducted seminal research on lucid dreaming, Roger Ripert in France, who was one of the first to do group dreaming online, Maria Volchenko in Russia, and many others felt overlooked when collections of writings were compiled or commentary requested.

Although I could not deal with all of the conflicts created in this situation, I did my best to make the IASD Bulletin Board a comfortable place for all dreamers, and invited non-English speaking visitors to communicate in their native languages if they so desired.

Past that, I addressed the question of people feeling ignored by inviting non-U.S. members of IASD to create an Online Guide to International Dream Work, which in some cases was presented in two or even three languages in addition to English. I also edited an International issue of *Dream Time* in 2001, which invited some of these same researchers and dream workers to contribute articles about their work. During this process, I developed friendships with a large group of international dreamers who were an active part of the online community.

When I looked at my precognitive dream from the morning of September 11, 2001, it seemed to me that the most important message the dream was giving me was to exercise some control in my own life, to take action, to confront the world situation illuminated by the attacks on the Twin Towers.

Reading through some of the posts on the dreamchatters list one evening in early October, I ran across a message from Victoria Quinton of Melbourne, Australia. In her dream, she had seen the image of a single white candle, lighted against the darkness. Victoria urged other dreamers to consider how each of us could bring a little light to the world.

Immediately my mind's eye zoomed in on the television show my mother watched every week when I was in junior high school. Bishop Fulton J. Sheen appeared as a spokesperson for the Christophers, a Catholic service organization. Each week at the beginning of the program, Bishop Sheen would glide across the stage in front of live television cameras, while in the background a choir sang the theme song of the Christophers: "If everyone lit just one little candle, what a bright world this would be."

Almost simultaneous with this vision the words popped into my head: "The World Dreams Peace Bridge." I was going to invite people to join me in creating a Peace Bridge.

"Dear Dreamers," the invitation read, "if you believe that we can dream precognitively, and if even beyond that, you believe we might together be dreaming the world, how would you like to join me in dreaming up some world peace?"

I acknowledged in the invitation that I had no idea what a Peace Bridge might look like, or what we might do on the Bridge, but I thought it was worth trying just to find out what might happen.

The invitations went out on a weekend. By the end of the next week, over fifty dreamers from fourteen different countries had responded by joining the Yahoo discussion list, which would become the World Dreams home. In the nearly five years since its inception, the World Dreams Peace Bridge has become the world's longest-lasting group dream journal, with dozens of dreams recorded each month, but it has also become far more than that, a model for what can be done with a combination of the desire for peace and attention to dreams.

What did this have to do with group dreaming? There is a type of research called "unstructured participatory research," in that the researcher who designs the experiment also participates in it. I knew that there had never been an international research group focused on dreams created for online interaction. My experience with group dreaming predicted to me that this group might well provide much interesting and useful evidence.

Chapter Twelve - Creating a Peace Bridge

When I invited people to join the World Dreams Peace Bridge, I also hoped that it might be an antidote to depression. Each day I saw the dreamers who had precognitively dreamed the World Trade Center disaster become more alarmed at the shift in world politics and more distressed at their seeming inability to do anything about it. I hoped that by creating a place where dreams could be discussed freely, along with thoughts and feelings about the world, we might also create a crucible for change, allowing dreamers to become proactive rather than reactive.

I should not have been surprised when people responded by dreaming about this new project.

"When I mused on your invitation," Jody wrote to me on October 21, 2001, "I had a dream surprise. Here it is.

I am talking with some people, dark haired, beautiful women, I think. They asked me to commit to the task of growing, harvesting and preserving a set of heirloom seeds. I hesitate, thinking of the task and that I might not be so successful with seeds as with plants. Big responsibility these rare seeds and I'm not completely confident of my skill to do this. Also, I know that it will require a long-time commitment and patience.

But in fact I do accept the commitment, and receive a small, brown envelope with seeds in it. On the package, it says: GOLDEN ERA. The name of the seeds! But I immediately realize what I have been given and what my task is: I have been given the seed forms, the "memes" or images of a "Golden Era," the golden or high time of culture, and it is my job to perpetuate these seeds, these memes or life forms.

By accepting the package, I accept the commitment.

"Here is a brief dream which I had the night after the September 11 attacks," Sandy wrote,

A close-up of the face of Beau Bridges. He looks directly at me (directly into the camera, if this were a movie) and I know there is something really important happening. He does something with his hands. It's out of frame, and so I can't tell what it is. And then he raises his hand up, and he has opened a lipstick tube. Once again, he looks directly at me, and then deftly applies the lipstick. He smiles and I know this is really important.

"Here is what I make of it," she said, "'Beautiful Bridges' (instead of burning bridges, which is how I was feeling after the devastation.) Here is a really strong man. A man who can take charge. He has power, but he needs something else. When he applies the lipstick, I think of it as a metaphor for feminizing his power, and I reckon this is exactly what we need in these times."

Not only was the idea that we could build a beautiful dream bridge and plant the seeds of change having an impact on the minds of the people contacted about The World Dreams Peace Bridge, but it seemed to be impacting others as well.

Generally I walk in the morning at sunrise by the river that runs through the city park near my home. One morning late in October, I encountered a couple I often saw walking at the same time there. Moving quickly toward me, the woman, Isobel, said, "I dreamed about you last night." By this time they were standing almost directly in front of me, the embarrassed husband looking ready to run if necessary. "I don't know if you believe in dreams," Isobel said. I assured her that I did. "In this dream," she said, "your entire house and yard were being remodeled. The house was bigger, lots bigger, and beautiful, with lots of windows."

"And you know that ditch by your house?" Isobel was referring to an old railroad right of way which abutted my yard. Maintained by the city, it was kept in low woods. A drainage ditch separated the property from my yard. I nodded, smiling at her excitement. "Well, that was all landscaped too. There was this little bridge that crossed over the ditch, and everything was landscaped into beautiful gardens. It was absolutely gorgeous."

Her eyes were shining, remembering the beauty of the landscape she'd seen in her dreams. "I probably dreamed it for you because I couldn't dream it for myself," she said sadly, the light suddenly gone from her eyes. She turned to walk away.

"Well, next time I'll dream for you," I replied.

Turning back to face me, walking backward, Isobel grinned. "But I don't want no house and garden," she said. I asked her what she would like me to dream for her.

"You can send me on a world tour," she laughed. "I want to go on a world tour, singing." She turned and hurried to catch up with her husband.

I shook my head in amazement. Beautiful bridges indeed. And little did Isobel know that her dream might actually take her on a world tour when I reported it to people on the Peace Bridge. Isobel died not long ago. I hope that she is somewhere singing.

Some people invited to join The World Dreams Peace Bridge declined the invitation because they saw dreaming for peace as an imposition on others. I was surprised at this, since my own belief is that if in fact we are creating the world around us from our dreams, hopes, and fears, much of the process is unconscious but happening anyway. Still, I was interested to hear the varying opinions from those I asked to join the Peace Bridge. "I would no more want to focus on creating peace than I would on creating war," one woman wrote to me. "Who am I to decide what other people need?" I did not bother to argue with her that democracy involves responsible decision-making. Many people refused participation in any peacemaking process because they saw making peace, like making war, as a process of subjugation. Nonetheless, I was glad when the subject of creating peace and how to do that became a point of discussion on the newly-formed Peace Bridge discussion list.

"Peace grows from within," said one Peace Bridge member.

"I can dream of peace for everyone in the world, including myself," said another. "What is Peace but every person's right to happiness and self-fulfillment?"

I was happy when not long after this discussion began, one member suggested that we adopt as our theme song, "Let there be Peace on Earth, and let it begin with me."

George, a retired minister, wrote:

I have known that song for years, and have heard it in church. I used to think of it as meaning peace has to begin with my being peaceful with others and working to make peace in the world. Now I see it as even more relevant to our purpose than that.

Through dreaming, we work through our own opposites or conflicts. We may speak of this as working toward an integration of consciousness with the unconscious, or working for peace within ourselves. These are the opposites which, when resolved, create a harmony that is seen in mandala dreams. When we resolve conflicts within ourselves through our dreaming, we are more psychologically ready to resolve old conflicts of ours with those around us in waking life. And so we work from our inner harmonizing to our outer harmonizing to we hope, being able to contribute to peace and justice and harmony in other parts of the world.

From the beginning, The World Dreams Peace Bridge discussion list was an active one, more active than any other online group I had ever encountered. For many people on the list, English was a second language. This sort of participation from people who sometimes struggled with the language, not to mention the concepts, warmed my heart—the heart of an American who, like many others who live in the United States, had never heard a language spoken other than English until I was in high school. For non-English speakers to be willing to communicate in this way was amazing to me. On the Peace Bridge from the very first months, it was not unusual to have two hundred or more messages in a week.

At first, many of the dreams reported to The World Dreams Peace Bridge were nightmares, the nightmares of people attempting to recover from trauma. Sara, who lived in New York City and volunteered with other members of her synagogue in the Twin Towers rescue efforts, suffered from terrible nightmares. The terrorist attack had affected her much more than it did many of us. One day, after posting a dream to the discussion list, she said, "These dreams are nightmarish when I awaken, but then I look forward to working through them. I am so grateful for the opportunity to share with you all."

Immediately following the terrorist attacks on the World Trade Center came the anthrax scares. Some unknown and as yet not apprehended, person or persons had sealed live anthrax material into an envelope and mailed it to the U.S. Congress. Security already tightened after 9/11, was tightened even further. The new Office of Homeland Security issued red alerts, amber alerts, occasionally even a code green, while hundreds of arrests were made of illegal aliens, many of them young people or students whose visas or green cards had expired.

In early November, Jeremy wrote from South Korea,

Just now I lay down to nap and dreamed I was awake in my study, and suddenly white dust, like thick snow, started falling from the ceiling. I got up and went down to the living room and saw it floating down there too. I alerted my wife, who was already aware of it, and she said we should get some masks. Our child was in the house too, and suddenly I filled with fear.

"Obviously this was about Anthrax," he went on. "Death could come so suddenly and soon. All the peace in my heart, that I've been carrying several days now, was swept away by the catastrophe."

Like many of us, Jeremy had been practicing daily meditation. The Internet was an interesting help there too, since the number of meditation sites had grown, and meditations like the "Healing Breath" meditation to which Jeremy sent a link, provided moving images and music for the meditation.

In the environment of shared dreams and shared thoughts created by the Peace Bridge, many of us worked hard to not only understand the images from our dreams but to apply this understanding toward improved self-awareness. "I tell you," one member wrote, "if my personality had known what I was signing up to with your Peace Bridge, she probably would have taken a vacation instead."

"What I realize I am doing in this group," wrote another dreamer "is staying fully in the flow with my authentic self. I am not censoring what my heart chooses to discuss and say. I am staying open and present to the energy of each person, and the group energy. I have not done this ever before in my life in an ongoing group setting."

Due to my previous experience with the Dreams to the Tenth Power experiments, I was not very surprised when the synchronicities began to appear on The World Dreams Peace Bridge. One of the earliest came in November when Jeremy wrote to a new member of the Peace Bridge from India, Radhika. He asked her a seemingly impossible question. He asked her if she happened to know (out of millions of people) a woman he'd met in India several years earlier, someone he liked very much and had not heard from in quite a while. As it turned out, not only did the two women know one another, but they were also friends and neighbors.

By now, there were U.S. troops in Afghanistan, rounding up Taliban soldiers and searching for Osama bin Laden. Radhika, who lived near the Indian border with Pakistan, wrote,

Today, and this has been building, I am tired of this war. The Taliban says that Osama is no longer their guest. Bush's picture is in our papers every day, looking really important. Apparently the same terrible war lords that had Afghanistan under their control before the Taliban took over are back in. These men had long tyrannized and destroyed Afghanistan for their power. So what if there is music in the streets for a while? What really is the fate of Afghanistan?

Already on the Peace Bridge discussion list there had begun one of the most important factors of cross-cultural interchange. Since members of the Peace Bridge came from many different backgrounds and many different countries, not only were dreams discussed, but world politics also came under scrutiny from many different perspectives. Often I learned about world events from the Peace Bridge before I ever heard them from the television or newspapers. In fact, as the American media moved toward the right, I often heard news on the Peace Bridge that I never heard at all in the media. Since all issues were up for discussion on the Bridge: books and articles recommended for reading, movies suggested, and poetry and songs quoted, I found my mind expanding in all directions.

In early December, for example, Sue wrote from California. "I don't really understand why the white buffalo are showing up in my dreamtime, but last night I had another dream." She went on to recount it.

I had been walking through a museum of sorts, looking at all the exhibits of animals. And I remember a kite exhibit. We went outside to another area that was kind of like a county fair. All of a sudden, I see this huge, beautiful white buffalo standing there, just waiting to be touched. I was so excited. I said to my husband, "Look. It's a buffalo exhibit." And then, as we got closer, I could see all sizes of white buffalo. Many were babies.

At the time of her dream, Sue was not aware of the Native American legend of the white buffalo. Many others in the group were. According to Lakota Sioux legend, White Buffalo Woman was the spirit who taught the tribes all they know of living on earth, including how to make fire, hunt, and smoke the sacred pipe. When she left the first people, she promised that one day she would return. In 1994, a white buffalo calf was born in Janesville, Wisconsin. Many believed the gene for the white buffalo had long been extinct, and the odds of a white buffalo being born were according to scientific assessments, about ten million to one. Many believe that the birth of this white buffalo will restore harmony to the earth.

When Sue sent her dream, one of the Peace Bridge members with Native American ancestry wrote of a vision she'd had four years earlier of White

Buffalo Woman saying, "I have always felt that the return of the spirit of the buffalo meant the return of the People, the return of the old ways that have been gone for much too long."

The Peace Bridge group continued to grow as 2001 drew to a close. From Mexico, Yvonne wrote,

> I have also been enjoying everyone's dreams and replies. Of course, I am still behind 249 messages…. I do not have any dreams though to share that would be worthwhile for the group, I guess…since they all seem to be more in the 'fighting' stage. Still, I promise to keep working so that (hopefully by the week of meditation) I can have something to share with this wonderful group!

Like many others, Yvonne believed that her dreams should be shared only if they contained messages of peace. But those in the group who had seen the value of working with nightmares disagreed. We were still feeling our way along, trying to decide who we were and what to do. A week-long meditation for peace was planned for the year's end.

As a dreamer, Yvonne had certainly qualified by my standards. Earlier that year, at the IASD conference in Boston, Yvonne, a young woman I had never met before, asked me to sit and talk with her for a few minutes. Her question was whether I knew anything about healing with crystals.

This was a bit of a surprise to me, since crystal healing was nothing I ordinarily talked about. In fact, I knew quite a lot about gems and stones and their use for healing purposes. When I asked Yvonne how she happened to make her request, she was suddenly shy. Before the conference, she said, I had come to her in a dream and told her she needed to learn about crystals.

I'm not sure that this dream counts as shared dreaming, since I did not recall being in Yvonne's dream at all. But we were discovering some new things on The World Dreams Peace Bridge. Freed from the restraints of traditional experimental format, allowed to go where it needed to go, the energy of dreaming seemed to provide a remarkable vehicle for sharing.

In January 2002, several visitors to the IASD Bulletin Board began sharing dreams of bridges, though they knew nothing about the Peace Bridge or what that group of dreamers had been doing. These dreams held many parallels to dreams we were recounting on the Peace Bridge and raised a question that I had never seen addressed anywhere in print—the question of the role of the Internet in developing psi skills through the construction of virtual reality.

What do I mean by this? On the Peace Bridge during the first months of its existence as a community, we often traded both dreams and insights about what the Peace Bridge and its environment might look like if this were a physical place. People described the bridge and its environs. There were dreams about the hotel or boarding house at the Bridge and about the kind of water the Bridge spanned. I think it is no accident that gamers, people who enjoy role-playing games, enjoy the Internet, because community on the Internet involves the type of imaginative play that gamers are so good at.

The Internet also calls upon the user to exercise a form of telepathy, in the sense that people online are often strangers to one another in physical reality, while being intimates in virtual reality.

When I looked at the dreams of the virtual community called The World Dreams Peace Bridge, what I saw was that people, in their dream states, often did what we had asked people to do more formally in the Dreams to the Tenth Power experiments. People on the Peace Bridge often quite accurately identified one another in dreams, although they were strangers in physical reality.

When the dreams about bridges continued on the Bulletin Board, some of the members of the Peace Bridge who were also Bulletin Board regulars began responding to them.

"My feeling when I read about these bridge dreams," remarked Birdy, "is that they are connected to the Internet, because a while back I had a teaching dream that told me the Internet was a bridge." She went on to say,

I found The World Dreams Peace Bridge through my interest in dreams but it was when I read Jean's purpose for the list that I became excited. It was not the word Peace that drew me as much as it was the word Bridge, and the realization that this was a place I could go where others believed in their abilities to dream a bridge to the world.

This business of "building a bridge to the world" is what another active Peace Bridge member, Sandy Ginsberg, called "honoring the dream."

In all of the varying attitudes toward dream work, dream interpretation and understanding the dream, the approach of honoring the dream is the one that most implies taking an action. Some approaches to dream work are quite passive, or involve only thinking or talking about dream content in order to achieve understanding. Among those who practice the technique of honoring the dream, many never seek to interpret the dream, being content to allow the dream its mystery. They prefer to paint a picture, write a poem, or create a piece of music from the dream's contents. Often in doing this, a deep understanding of the dream occurs.

Sandy wrote about honoring the dream in an article for the Spring 2000 issue of *Dream Time*. "We run the risk of postponing the gift from the dream when we fail to take action," she wrote in the article.

By honoring the dream creatively, we allow the dream's meaning an opportunity to be delivered to us. By honoring the dream, I am referring to the conscious effort to manifest a part of the dream in the waking world. This creative act can take the form of visual art, earthwork, food preparation, music, interaction with another, or an activity or journey that is calling to you.[1]

It was not surprising that many of the members of the newly-created World Dreams Peace Bridge were artists of one form or another: musicians, graphic artists, dancers, poets, because the idea behind the Peace Bridge was something they already understood and were comfortable with, the idea that dreams require action, that part of honoring the bridge between dreams and waking reality requires taking the message of the dream seriously and acting upon it.

One result of this shared commitment to action was that the artists on the Peace Bridge began to share their dream-related artwork. In the Yahoo group format, there is room for sharing files, putting up photographs, allowing a virtual glimpse of the non-virtual reality of the artist or dreamer. The artwork, in many cases, was stunningly beautiful, particularly when lighted by the jewel tones of the Internet. The photos allowed us glimpses into one another's lives. In some cases, like Sandy's, the artist was a professional; in other cases, even though the artist was not trained, the dream art was an expression of the creativity inspired by the dream. Because of this profusion of beauty, we began to talk about creating a web site. The idea grew under the nurturing hand of Liz Diaz, a professional web designer, until we developed www.worlddreamspeacebridge .org, the World Dreams Peace Bridge's official web site, which now hosts not only the art work of many Peace Bridge members but also information on our many projects.

Creative action was a natural part of the Peace Bridge, a shared language no matter the cultural backgrounds of the dreamers. Just how much of a role this creative, active approach would take in developing a Peace dreaming community became apparent in the winter of 2002, when Valley began discussing a dream she was working with, about a crow and a phoenix.

What Valley told us in her original message to the Peace Bridge list was that she had been making a book with her daughter, Delaney, using this dream about the crow and the phoenix. The first question that came from the group, of course, was, "Book? What book?"

Valley explained that Delaney, who was then six, had a whole library of books they had created from dreams, that in fact making dream books was one of Delaney's favorite pastimes. Then we asked Valley to tell us the dream.

The dream is the story of a little girl named Annabella, Valley told us, Annabella and her friend the umbrella. It seems that Annabella went out one day with her friend the umbrella and had an adventure involving a crow who steals the umbrella and takes Annabella to the underworld, where she is almost lost to forgetfulness. A phoenix, with the help of the umbrella, reunites the two friends and helps Annabella recover her memory of who she is.

At this same time another Peace Bridge member, Jody Grudy, was planning an IASD regional conference in Cincinnati, Ohio. She was planning a dream dance performance as part of the conference. When she read Valley's dream, she thought it would make a perfect dream dance. She wrote to ask Valley's permission to use the dream as the story to be choreographed by Cincinnati dancers. When Valley received this request, she revealed something neither Jody nor any of the other Bridge members knew, that she herself was a dancer and choreographer. She had been tapped at the early age of sixteen for a place in the Dallas Ballet Company, one of the premiere ballet companies in the United States, becoming their youngest member at the time. As she shared this with Jody, she also said, "I would like to choreograph the dream and dance in it myself." "The Crow and the Phoenix" became a stunningly choreographed dance, presented at the regional conference, with Valley dancing the role of Annabella.

This was my first experience of the synergy created by the dreams of a group of experienced dreamers, but far from the last experience of it. Somehow, the combination of dreams with the creative process unleashed in the group an energy that went beyond any specific dreamer. The whole was literally greater than the sum of its parts.

This same energy applied when one of the original members of the Peace Bridge, IASD Past President Rita Dwyer, began to create a workshop for the 2002 IASD conference with the help of her friend Rosemary Guiley. They called it a "Dream Activism" workshop, and the number of people at the conference who attended the workshop signaled to me that members of the dream community were now looking for a new level of dream work...a way to become dream activists. In her book, *The Dreamers Way*, published in 2004, Rosemary Guiley says,

> Dream activism is not an idea or theory—it is a fact, a growing movement in the dreaming community that is reaching out into the general population. In this post-9-11 world, it is more important than ever that we join together to use one of the most important tools of our consciousness—dreams—to change the world for the better. Dream activism builds on ancient dream wisdom and experience.[2]

In a chapter on dream activism in her book, Guiley talks about that initial Dream Activism workshop and the attempt of the twenty or thirty people who attended it to come up with a good affirmation, one which could be used in conjunction with a monthly group dreaming effort: "While people may generally agree in their desire to help make the world a better place," Guiley says, they want to go about it in different ways. We all have causes to which we feel drawn. The solution to this proved to be a general 'activation' affirmation that would unite many people in dreams toward a common goal—improving conditions in the world—while allowing individuals to emphasize specific priorities.[3]

The activism affirmation the group created was "Tonight I dream the awakened heart. Today I awaken the dreaming heart."

There are a number of people who have participated on both the Peace Bridge discussion list and the IASD Dream Activism list, and there has been discussion about the differing results when people use a broad affirmation like this one from when they use more specific intentions or statements such as the Peace Bridge has often used to incubate dreams about a particular topic or area of world conflict. We do not have to examine the content of these discussions in order to notice one obvious fact. Any discussion of such subtle distinctions points to an enormous growth in people's perception of group dreaming. There was a time, not so very long ago, when the concept of people sharing the intention to dream together was totally beyond imagination for most people, including dream workers and dream researchers.

Setting the intention for dreaming, as we have seen, is an important aspect of group dreaming. On the Bridge we solved the question of how to affix the intention for a group dream in a variety of ways. The "Peaceful Solutions Dream In" was one way we selected in 2002. Suggested by Kathy Turner from Australia, the intent of this type of "dream in" was to dream peaceful solutions to world conflicts and also ways we might participate in solutions. Not all members of the Peace Bridge were peace activists in the physical world, but everyone agreed that dreams themselves could be a useful avenue for action.

Sometimes, the intent of a group dream would come up spontaneously when some member of the group would mention a particular situation. A group member might mention, for example, a family crisis or a friend in the hospital. Then another member of the group would ask, "Would you like us to dream for you?" No member was ever expected to dream in a particular manner or for a particular thing.

Shortly after joining the group conversation in the spring of 2002, Pam wrote, "I wonder if anyone has noticed an increase in what I can only call psychic activity since being on the Bridge?" She told us about a recent event in which a friend of hers had incubated a dream. Without knowing this dream incubation was even happening, Pam said, "I had a dream which referred specifically to the question, which I didn't know she was asking. My dream even included the first name and last initial of the person she was asking the question about."

Pam was not the only person to feel the influence of the group's commitment to explore every aspect of dreaming. In January, Bob wrote that he and his wife Rita, both members of the Peace Bridge community, had shared a dream. Bob said that the two of them had often shared dream symbols or dreamed of the same basic themes "But this is the first time we have ever dreamt directly related dreams at the same time."

"So, Jean," he asked, "is this an oddity or what?"

The question made me laugh out loud. From what I had already learned about groups of people dreaming together, and from what I had seen of the World

Dreams Peace Bridge, I expected that group dreaming here on the Bridge would become the norm. "Or what." I replied.

Shared dream experiences increased in number as the months went on. After a particularly amusing interchange, during which Juhani had telepathically picked up that the dog in one of Jody's dreams was the famous Belgian cartoon character, Tintin, Jody replied that not only was he correct, but that she was a Tintin lover, and was also of Belgian descent. Juhani wrote: "Wow. What a surprise. Creepy. Tintin is a kind of Global Action Peace Maker. If we ever have trouble on the Bridge, then comes this dog and saves us." It was also Juhani who suggested that I might change my name from Campbell to Dream-bell, "because you really gong-gong shake people up."

The people on the Peace Bridge were curious to see what would happen if they simply kept dreaming, trying out new approaches, and exploring. After a discussion about monarch butterflies, in which several people shared butterfly dreams, Yvonne eloquently summarized what seemed to be developing as the group's philosophy about shared dreaming: "We, as collective souls, travel and 'migrate' to each other's consciousness. Some faster or deeper, some slower or more superficially."

"Butterflies do that," Yvonne said, "start as simple 'worms' but suffer a metamorphosis until they are ready to share their beauty, touching each other's souls."

"Oh golly," Donna enthused one day in April, "this world is so much stranger than I knew," and a day later, "Sometimes I think I could just live here on the Bridge and ponder everyone's dreams and all our synchronicities. But that doesn't do too much for my children."

In the world outside the Peace Bridge, the political situation continued to deteriorate. India and Pakistan fought each other to a standstill in a border conflict that threatened to resort to nuclear retaliation. North and South Korea were again embroiled with nuclear threats. We worried for the safety of Jeremy and Radhika and their families.

On July 26, 2002, Jeremy had a dream that set off a series of synchronistic dreams and events that have continued to this day. Here is the dream he sent us:

> I was dreaming, and in the dream I was in a vast, fairly empty land outside a small village, but this was in Midwest, America. Others were with me walking about and one of them came up to me and said, "A train has arrived."
>
> I looked around and there was a long, black locomotive. We all got on, and rode all the way across the country to Washington, D.C., the city of my birth. The train rolled on and stopped below the stairs of the Capitol Building, housing the U.S. Congress. The President (who happened in the dream to be Al Gore) was there in a suit applauding us, and other wel- dressed men on the steps were clapping as well. I looked around at the train and saw a large white

banner around the smokestack, with elegant black lettering which read PEACE TRAIN.

Among other things, this dream of Jeremy's sparked many other dreams about trains, including one from me, in which I dreamed a room full of miniature locomotives. Rosa Anwandter of Chile who, though she was not a member of the Peace Bridge discussion list, was one of many friends of the Bridge. She told me, "I dreamed that train! I dreamed it just last week." And she sent the dream on to be posted to the discussion list.

More importantly than the dreams in this case may have been the discussion. People on the Peace Bridge began wondering what might happen if people around the world would start to create peace trains. And what might happen if these trains got sent on to other people? And what if people who received the peace trains added cars, or created new peace trains? Before long, the musings became a plan, and the first of the Peace Trains was created by Jeremy's students in an English as a Second Language class at Hankuk University of Foreign Studies. His students took this idea out into the community as well, asking people to draw their ideas of what Peace might look like.

In Australia, Victoria Quinton asked her children to create a Peace Train, and through her contacts with the Nervousness.org community, contacted a teacher in Seattle, whose students created a Peace Train that wound around the walls of the hallway of their school.

The Peace Train had begun its journey just as the World Dreams Peace Bridge was finding its identity as a new form of Peace Action group. This was group dreaming with a new twist.

What I believe to be true about The World Dreams Peace Bridge can be summed up nicely by a funny little dream I had in 2002:

I am standing in the doorway of my house. I want to get to the house next door, but the way is being blocked by a big dog, a Boxer. There is a woman standing in the kitchen doorway at the back of the other house, looking over at me. She is the person I want to go see. She looks a lot like me, same long hair, same body build. I look at the dog, which is fierce. My own dog, Song, is afraid of him. I take another look at the dog, then start toward the front door of the house.

I seldom title my dreams, although many people do. But I gave this one a title: "Thinking Outside of the Box(er)." For me, this dream was a commentary on what happens on the Peace Bridge. The Bridge is the natural extension of the Dreams to the Tenth Power experiments in that it addresses the subject of group dreaming; yet released from the constraints of experimental format, it is dreams to the hundredth power, or the power of however many people want to join in the process.

In the PowerPoint presentation developed in 2004 to illustrate the work of The World Dreams Peace Bridge, the question is asked: "What Do Dreamers Do On The Peace Bridge?" The answer given is that:

We discuss our dreams.

We listen to the information in our dreams.

Always we listen for messages of Peace,

Or how we can work toward Peace.

Sometimes we discuss politics,

Or events making news,

Or how the news is reported differently in different parts of the world.

And we try to honor the dream.

We are building a Global Community.

Chapter Thirteen - DaFuMu Dreaming at the Reservoir

By January 2003, membership in the World Dreams Peace Bridge discussion list had more than doubled from its original size a few months earlier. Over one hundred dreamers from fifteen countries were on the Peace Bridge as massive, worldwide protests were launched against a buildup of troops in the Persian Gulf. There was threat of war in Iraq. It began to appear that the Peace Bridge would have the opportunity to dream of Peace during a full-scale war.

Yet the feeling on the Bridge was that this particular war was unnecessary, and we prayed that there would be a reprieve. During the first week of February, we scheduled another Peaceful Solutions Dream In. This time we invited all of the dreamers we could locate to join us in a week-long search for peaceful solutions to global conflict. We requested that they send their responses to a dialog box on our newly-created web site. Kathy sent a dream that seemed to offer the perfect solution:

I'm driving in a counterclockwise direction along a narrow road winding around the base of a mountain. Some road work is being done, but all traffic (including me) is moving very quickly. I see a large white truck and am afraid. Surely there'll be an accident. But we both seem to pass each other with no problem. Next a white, four-wheel vehicle is coming. Oh no. At the same time a construction worker throws a twisted steel rod across the road. I know it is hopeless now, as either the four-wheel drive or I will drive over one end of the bar and crash into the other vehicle. There seems nothing we can do. Then both I and the other vehicle STOP. Now we move the bar. That was the solution. It surprised me how simple and obvious it was.

A few weeks earlier, much to my delight, Stephen had joined the Peace Bridge—the same Stephen who participated in the very first Dreams to the Tenth Power experiment. It was fun having someone else on the Bridge who shared in those first experiments. We often commented to one another about the free-wheeling and magical spirit created by the Peace Bridge group.

During the Peaceful Solutions Dream In, Stephen reported a dream that asks an important question:

I had this dream the night President Bush made his State of the Union speech. I'm lucid.

I see a panorama of war, fire, chaos, blood, savage energy unleashed. The panorama shrinks to the size of a human face, with images of war moving over it, as though projected on skin.

The face literally devolves into progressively earlier stages of man, ending in a Neanderthal shape whose mouth is wide open in a primal scream. I think, "This is the face of war." Immediately I am asked, "What is the face of peace?"

I realize I have no vision of peace except as an absence of war. I can't name any actions that fill the face of peace. I am clear the face of war is a man. I wonder if the face of peace is a woman.

There were many other dreamers, both from the Peace Bridge and other online places like the IASD Bulletin Board, who responded to this week of attempted solutions. Walter, a Bulletin Board regular, wrote only, "Maybe the answer is in our children. Let's teach our children that evil can be eliminated with kindness and awareness." Kat-Peters Midland, who was new to the Peace Bridge and had never seen Jody's original dream of the New Age Seed Company, picked up on the theme of seed planting and carried it forward:

I am planting seeds in my garden outside, digging in the soil, putting seeds in the ground and covering them up. I go inside my house. I am in my bedroom sitting on the bed. I look outside through my circular bubble window, and I can see the plants have grown, and they look like they have grown into the beginning of a Medicine Wheel. I see three statues in the center of the Medicine Wheel, and one of them is a Buddha statue facing me. I see it very clearly and I am fascinated by it. I get up from the bed and start putting little statues in every pot of potted plants in my room.

Sharon, who was so new to the Peace Bridge when the Peaceful Solutions Dream In began that she was not even aware it was happening, said she'd had three or four dreams of conflict resolution that week, then added, "I think the dreams had specific messages for me, and maybe a greater one for the world. Ever since September 11, I have had a hard time not becoming cynical, especially with the US Government. I am in tears when I take a moment to think how many bombs I have paid for with my taxes…. So for me, the dreams give me hope."

Rosemary Watts of St. Louis, Missouri, a wonderful actress, singer and dream teacher, was teaching about dreams during this time in her daughter's sixth grade classroom. She described, in a message to the Peace Bridge, the images she'd seen. "One sixth grade girl drew a picture of the earth," Rosemary said,

with various continents shown with different colors/types of faces on the continents. There was a mask covering part of the earth with a hand on the mask beginning to hold it away from the earth. I asked her to tell me all about her piece. She said, 'Well, I believe the governments mask what the people want. If we can lay down the masks of these governments, then the people's voices will be heard, and it will be the voice of peace.

Many members of the Peace Bridge participated in the massive anti-war marches and rallies around the world during February and March this year. In San Francisco, May lit a candle in her window each day. In Turkey, Ilkin reported, the tradition was to bang on pots and pans every hour on the hour.

Since over ninety percent of the population of Turkey was protesting the war, it was hard to sleep with all the noise in Istanbul.

Sandy, who took her five-year old granddaughter to the peace demonstration in Los Angeles, asked the little girl after her first peace rally what she thought of it. With the kind of aplomb only a five-year old can muster, Sandy's granddaughter gave full commentary on her puzzlement. She asked again what war was, and then said, "But if we kill people, we can't play with them."

There was a great deal of other activity on the Peace Bridge during these early days of 2003 as well. In a burst of creative energy, Liz Diaz created designs for Peace Train tee shirts and for Children's Peace Train shirts, both to be sold online through the Peace Bridge store. We were beginning to develop a real web site.

Once Peace Bridge members began talking about the IASD annual conference, which would be held that year in Berkeley, California, we recognized that several members of the Peace Bridge were planning to attend and would, for the first time, get to meet in physical reality rather than dream reality or virtual reality. We agreed to arrive at the conference wearing signature Peace Bridge shirts, in order to recognize one another. With the proceeds from shirt sales, we collected enough money to send $100 to Radhika in India for an education program she wanted to start. In early March, a message arrived from Rhadika.

We used $100 to finance our first workshop with school principals. Since then, and based on our feedback from them, our work has expanded. This first interaction helped us know what we wanted to do—our theme was/is "living with differences," and we are now working with schools at all levels—students, teachers and parents on issues of violence, peace, prejudice, history, multiculturalism, etc. Our efforts toward a peaceful world. It feels good to know that the seeds for this work came from you and the feeling of dreaming the world into peace.

The days of "Shock and Awe," the invasion of Iraq by the United States and its allies in late March, riveted world attention. On the Peace Bridge, where the dreams were ongoing, many of us dreamed about the children of Iraq. In any war, it is the children who suffer most terribly. We decided as a group that we wanted to do something for the children, no matter how small our effort. Ever the wise woman of the group, May Tung counseled: "We are not a large group, but we can do something small and personal. We can provide toys and art supplies for the traumatized children of Iraq." Having lived in war as a child, May knew the value of a soft toy for children to confide in, and crayons and paper to picture the world. In this way, the Aid for Traumatized Children Project of the World Dreams Peace Bridge was begun.

For months the group of people within the Peace Bridge who chose to participate in the Aid for Traumatized Children Project collected funds, while at the same time looking for some way to send packages to war-torn Iraq. We wanted to make contact with therapists and others who were working with the children. Even though we were turned back time and again by UNICEF and other organizations, who told us that our project was too small, too insignificant to merit their attention, we began to establish a network of contacts within that country—again thanks to the Internet, which allows for e-mail to travel even though bombs might be dropping in the next town or next block.

"What do the wolves say as they race to the Reservoir?" I wrote in the May, 2003 edition of "The View From the Bridge" the monthly newsletter we had begun to produce. "Dafumuuuu!" I answered, as any Peace Bridge member would know.

In April, after two months of intensive peace dreaming, Kathy Turner had asked, "Is there a name for this type of focused, intense, peace dreaming we are doing?" And although the answer to her question was no, the people on the Peace Bridge set out to create a new word. There was much bantering on the Bridge at this time, a sort of playful antidote to the horrors unfolding in the world around us, and many words were batted about in a variety of languages, until we settled on DaFuMu, which is a marriage of words in Japanese and Chinese.

"It should be Da-Fu Mu," May wrote, "as 'Da', meaning 'big', describes the Fu. Mu (meng in Chinese) means 'dream.' Fu is the Chinese word for the greatest of good fortune. To wish someone FU, especially at the Chinese New Year, is to wish them good fortune." Thus our new word was a dream of the greatest of good fortune.

Kotaro Mayagi, an advertising executive in Tokyo, and a new member of the Peace Bridge, carefully wrote out the characters for this name he had helped to create, sending them to us in several different fonts.

Me, you
Will do
Everything
Make it
Come true
DAFUMU

Juhani wrote on April 9. "A bit weird, a bit unusual."

"Us!" May replied.

Later, Kathy summarized her thoughts on DaFuMu Dreaming in a more serious manner, which explains how the type of dreaming we were doing differed from any other dreams, group or individual. "A DaFuMu enters by conscious intention into the collective consciousness," she wrote, "and seeks to shift the possibilities held there."

It seems to me it is a practical application of the ideas inherent in Jung's collective unconscious and the Eastern idea of universal awareness. But what is revolutionary, and perhaps even evolutionary, is that rather than merely seeking to experience the Collective Unconscious (as in the traditional Jungian view of dreams) or seeking to align our consciousness with universal consciousness (as in the Eastern view) the DaFuMu actually uses the conscious intent to shift the possibilities held within the collective consciousness. Now clearly the shift cannot be dramatic and won't deliver "what we want" as actualities. But it will shift possibilities, and that opens up something new.

Unlike traditional means of shifting possibilities (e.g. prayers to God— understood by me as another name for this field of collective consciousness) the DaFuMu actually uses one of the Prime Means by which the collective consciousness is more or less directly available to us. I suspect that makes our conscious intent more powerful in effect. To me, all this means the DaFuMu is a revolutionary tool of lucid living.

Second, the DaFuMu also creates the possibility of new ways for the individual of relating to the world. I have not forgotten the DaFuMu dreams from before the Iraq invasion. I've read them over many times to see what about them I find so interesting. What I notice is that almost every dream is either an experience of peace or displays ways to find peace. Now that means we were able to lay down in our minds the possibility of a new pattern, that of peaceful relating, or to confirm that pattern within us, giving it more strength.

DaFuMu Dreaming, or big dreams of great good fortune, can be applied to any situation. They are group dreams initiated with the intention of understanding and improving a specific situation.

Like DaFuMu Dreaming, the Reservoir was a concept that grew from dialogue within the Peace Bridge discussion group. During the 1970s, Seth told members of psychic Jane Roberts' Monday Night Class that when they dreamed together, they should dream "the city." This dream location, he told them, would become a beacon, a dream location for other dreamers to find, both then and in the future. After weeks and months of talking and dreaming about what a Peace Bridge might look like, the dreamers of the Bridge were carrying out Seth's suggestion quite spontaneously. They were beginning to imagine and dream the environs of the Peace Bridge. The first location added to the landscape was the Reservoir. It was May who first verbalized a description of the Reservoir we had been discussing.

The idea is to have our own Peace Bridge Reservoir of healing energy. We can concentrate on this central place, sending our individual healing energy to this Reservoir. Whenever anyone wants or needs to, they can go there. We may even meet each other there!

The Reservoir is formed by each of our thoughts and emotions. I suggest a concrete ritual to send our energy there. Each time, when any of us lights a candle (I happen to do it almost daily.), we make a conscious wish and send the caring light and energy to our Reservoir….

The Reservoir is located north of the Peace Bridge. It is a naturally formed pond, surrounded by boulders, rocks, trees, green grass and wild flowers. No one has ownership of it. Birds and animals frequent there.

Why north of the Peace Bridge? That comes from my dreams. I had many dreams when I was either there or returning from a 'far away Northern region.'

May referred to an ancient Taoist text concerning the True Person, Cinnabar-of-the-North, the child of the Queen Mother of the West and her consort, Father of the East. The Essential Being is this child, "my true self."

"I see our Reservoir of Healing Energy," May concluded, "as north of our Bridge, pale blue mist floating above. We can be there any time we want or need to be."

The response of Peace Bridge members to the Reservoir of Healing Energy in a time of war was profound. Valley's dream from this time was typical, one of many dreams of the Reservoir. She wrote during a time of personal illness:

I am following a river upstream. It begins in America and flows down into Mexico and Central America. I follow the river up to the mountains where there is a beautiful waterfall surrounded by incredible beauty. It is so beautiful and alive in this place, I find it almost difficult to accept.

I acknowledge that I belong in this place and then find myself in the doorway of an ancient cave where I can see a large carving of a goddess inside. I enter the cave.

I lose my recall of the dream after this, but in the morning I wake up completely energized and completely well, with no sign of any physical ailment.

In response to Valley's dream, another member of the group sent the John Muir quote, "The light shines not on us, but in us. The rivers flow not past, but through us."

Liz, who was inspired to create a meditation slide show for the Reservoir page online, made from photos she took at a physical-world reservoir in Austin, Texas, wrote the following poem.

Silent serenity
Flowing to me
And through me
Above me
And
Below me
Leaving the thoughts
That fill my mind
To go to the waters

The Reservoir of Time
So that I
May be at peace
This moment

And then, just in time for our third monthly DaFuMu dreaming in June, Juhani wrote: "this conflict is growing to be a hormone-based scream show. I'll try to dream a Dream Answer Animal, a symbol, an animal that lives here and now. If there is a free path to a better life, it surely will take it without saying."

From Germany, Ralf, who had been practicing lucid dreaming since he studied years earlier with Stephen LaBerge, replied with a "lucid map" to be used before sleeping in order to incubate the dreams.

I will remember to meet the wise Dream Answer Animal.

I will remember to follow its path.

I will remember to get lucid and ask for the meaning of the path.

I will invite that DAA to WDPB

I will remember to enjoy the ecstatic awareness of being in a dream.

Ralf, who is trained as a nurse and also a naturopath, noted: "I dream peaceful solutions more often since I am on the bridge." But additionally he made this comment,

We don't know much for now of how this thing works. But information may be an important part of the psychodynamic (in the sense of energy). So it may be that new thoughts, ideas, solutions may have a unique power. This is an important factor in homeopathy too. The system changes when the right information is applied.

There have been many dreams of Dream Answer Animals since Juhani's original suggestion; but one dream which arrived during the June, 2003 DaFuMu Dreaming came from Nick, a college student in Australia. In his dreams that night, Nick said he found himself looking at a stack of pages about all different kinds of animals. The last page though was about a plant, salvia or sage.

Kathy replied:

We are definitely creating our own dream world up north around the Reservoir. I'm glad sage is there, Nick. May, your Reservoir is definitely growing—a song, sung by Kev Carmondy, an aborigine, about the first strike by the aboriginal people in the 1960s and how that led to the land rights movement, has a title I feel applies to the Reservoir: "From Little Things Big Things Grow."

This could also be said of the World Dreams Peace Bridge Peace Train Project, which started from Jeremy's dream and continued to grow during 2003 like the "Little Train That Could." In February, Jeremy's colleague at Hankuk University, Tim Watson from Canada, introduced the Peace Train Project in a workshop at the Fifth Annual Non-Violence Conference in India. He reported that many teachers in the workshop planned to take the concept back to their classrooms. The first week in April, Victoria Quinton brought the Peace Train Project to a workshop at the annual conference of the Victoria Association for Philosophy in Schools in Amdale, Australia, where kids created an entire train.

For Children's Day in Turkey that April, through a woman Ilkin synchronistically met at a party, children all over Turkey created Peace Train pictures. Of all the countries in the world which celebrate family days: Mother's Day, Father's Day, Valentine's Day for lovers, Turkey is one of only a few countries that has a day specifically to celebrate children, who are much loved and cared for. The International Peace Train pictures glowed with jewel-like color and the imaginative ideas of children asked to picture peace.

In June at the IASD conference, in a hotel at the Berkeley Marina, it was hard to imagine the war, even though Children's Peace Train art work from Korea, Turkey, China and Australia filled the walls of the conference products' room. The California air was balmy; sunlight reflected off the waters of the bay where the hotel's harbor tour boats rocked. Water splashed in a courtyard fountain. It was fun to watch Peace Bridge members suddenly glance at a nametag and realize the person they had been standing next to was another member of the World Dreams community.

On the last day of the conference, reality surged back at the Dream Ball, an annual closing event, which allows dreamers to come costumed as characters from their dreams.

Initially we were concerned that Liz, creator of the World Dreams web site, would not be able to attend. A single mom, she and her two little boys had recently moved and she was hesitant to leave them. But finally she arrived, bringing with her a surprise—the Peace Dragon Train costume.

This costume, modeled in part after Jeremy's original dream and in part after the joking conversation we'd had on the discussion list about a DaFuMu dragon resembling the dragons in Chinese New Year parades, boasted a ten-foot length of gold cloth long enough to drape over the heads and shoulders of at least half a dozen Peace Bridge members. It also had a smokestack, with a dragon face and eyes that actually lit up, which Liz had created at home and hand carried on her flight.

All afternoon before the Dream Ball, Jody, Jeremy, May, Liz and I worked to create wheels for the train out of poster board and to apply felt letters reading "Peace Train" to each side of the gold cloth. Liz had even brought garlands of plastic flowers to run the length of the train and bamboo sticks to hold the dragon train aloft. By the time the doors opened on the Dream Ball, we were ready. Jeremy would wear the dragon-faced smokestack, which had eye holes as well as flashing red eyes; the rest of us would follow.

May, who had prepared for the possibility of Liz's arrival by bringing a tape of train sounds, went ahead of us into the hall, telling Master of Ceremonies Bob

Hoss that she needed the microphone. He was so surprised at the request that he gave it to her without delay. Immediately the sounds of a traveling train filled the room. Those of us forming parts of the Peace Train made a grand entrance, touring the tables surrounding the dance floor to the sound of train whistles and loud applause.

This might have been enough to satisfy any dreamer but when time came for the costume judging, we donned the train again. Jeremy told his dream, his nine-year old daughter, Ellie, smiling from the sidelines. We won the costume contest that night but the most astounding thing was what happened when we all trooped on stage to collect our blue ribbon. Slowly, softly, from the back of the room, I heard Dr. Ernest Hartmann's voice begin to sing, "All we are saying is give peace a chance." His voice was joined by another, and then another. The volume swelled, and before long the entire room full of dreamers from all over the world was alive with the sound of people asking for peace. This sound would have to sustain us for the rest of the summer, as events in Iraq continued on a downhill slide.

In August, following the bombing of the United Nations headquarters in Baghdad, I wrote to Veronica Avati, the UNICEF Child Protection officer in the northern city of Erbil, one of the many who had been helpful to us in our search for a way to send comfort items to the children of Iraq. Her brief response told the story of the bravery of many people.

Dear Ms. Campbell:

Many thanks for your sincere thoughts and words. Unfortunately we lost a dear colleague and friend in Baghdad with so many others working for the UN. It is a tremendous shock for all of us, but I truly hope that for Chris, Jill, and many others who lost their lives, we will be able to continue and pursue our work for the well-being of Iraqi children.

Sincerely, and with so many thanks from the UNICEF office,

Veronica.

On November 20, 2003, I woke before five a.m. and went directly to my computer. Because the World Dreams Peace Bridge spans the world, someone is always awake. I found a message in my e-mail from Ilkin, saying that bombs were exploding again in Istanbul. Earlier that day, four terrorist bombs had exploded in populated areas of the city, including one in the subway. At the time, Ilkin's twin sons would have been on their way home from college classes. The boys were all right, we found out later, but a girl who was a close friend of theirs died in the hospital after the subway explosion.

Immediately after Ilkin's first message, I sent out a request to the Peace Bridge and other online dream groups for a DaFuMu dreaming for the people of Istanbul. There were several dreams sent to the Bridge that day, but I will start with my own, since it seemed to be the beginning of a group arabesque.

> I am sitting in the dining room of a big house where IASD is having a workshop. Yvonne Baez from Mexico and I are sitting cross-legged on the floor, facing one another. I am explaining to her about permeable and impermeable boundaries in dreams. Then later all of the people in the house lie down on the floor to go to sleep.
>
> We are awakened not long after that by Alan Siegel and Bob Hoss coming in the front door. Soon everyone is awake again.
>
> In the next scene in the dream, I am flying in a helicopter that Bob Hoss is piloting. We are flying across a bay spanned by the Bosporus Bridge.
>
> I look to my right. Ahead of us is a convoy of helicopters. I am worried that they are US helicopters getting ready to bomb someone. Then I look to my left and see a winged figure back winging to alight on the land below. At first I think it is an eagle, the US eagle, and I'm afraid again. But then I realize it is an angel. Bob smiles at me like we are sharing a secret.

There were many other shared images that came from this night of DaFuMu dreaming, but the one that most closely connected with mine came from a dream sent by Yvonne Baez, who was present in my dream. Yvonne wrote that she forgot to set her intention for the DaFuMu dreaming before she fell asleep, but two hours later something woke her up. "I felt Jean's presence right in front of me," she said, "and immediately began to send peace and love around the world."

Yvonne also sent a dream in which she is in a swimming pool with a friend who is having a crisis of faith. Suddenly in the dream, Yvonne said, the clouds started taking on the shapes of big angels all around. "I tell my friend, 'Look up to the sky. There are many angels above us,'" Yvonne said. "She looks up, but she sees nothing."

After the bombing crisis passed, Ilkin sent a message to the group, thanking us for being with her and her family during the bombings. She told us that the DaFuMu dreaming had fallen on the same night as the Muslim feast of Qudar. "It is believed in Islam," Ilkin said, "that tonight is the sacred night on which God sends all his angels to the world to listen to the prayers and forgive sins."

Despite the continuing tensions of the war, there were still events to be enjoyed by online dreamers. At the end of the summer, Harry Bosma began the first of his online courses for lucid dreamers called More Lucid Dreams. Several members of the World Dreams Peace Bridge participated, though I did not. Not long after the class began, Kathy Turner sent me a message saying,

Jean, I think you must be popping in to see what is happening at Harry's More Lucid Dreams Project. THREE of us have dreamed of you in the last two days!!! Jill (who was totally unknown to me) dreamed you sent her a check for $5; Laura dreamed you walked through her mansion in a Green Peace tee shirt. I dreamed I returned your photo to you…. So, Jean, what do you think of this??

I have never known quite what to make of it when people dream of me in this way, at a time when I have no corresponding dreams to qualify the matter as shared dreaming. It could be that, in these cases, I am operating as an ordinary dream symbol, an aspect of self that dreamers choose to portray as an accomplished dreamer. Or it could be that I have visited people's dreams and simply do not recall this in waking consciousness. To deny that anything is happening at all though does not make sense to me, especially in light of the fact that a number of dreamers, like Yvonne Baez for example, have recognized me on first meeting from having earlier dreamed about me.

The impact of long-term, intercultural group dreaming was clearly demonstrated in a series of events that took place on the Peace Bridge in November of 2003. Particularly in time of war, it is useful to confront the question of just who is the enemy. Naturally, if people share their lives with one another daily, as happens on The World Dreams Peace Bridge, there is ample opportunity to deal with this question, often with remarkable results. At times there was enough conflict among Bridge members, just like the members of any family, that it was necessary to find patient and creative ways to deal with it. It was necessary to become bridges of peace ourselves.

Following the observance of Hiroshima Day on August 6, Jeremy wrote a post to the Bridge with the subject line, "My Mother Died in Hiroshima." In this e-mail, he detailed the cause of his mother's death, which happened when Jeremy was five. Her death, he said, proceeded from the fact that his father was at the time Manager of Budget for the U.S. Atomic Energy Commission, and the family lived at the Nuclear Testing Facility in Oak Ridge, Tennessee. The type of breast cancer from which Jeremy's mother died was later found to be the most common cause of death from cancer to result from the nuclear bombs tested at Oak Ridge, and also dropped on the Japanese city of Hiroshima at the end of World War II. It was easy to understand how Jeremy's attention turned to the use of depleted uranium in U.S. armaments in Iraq. These weapons have proved to be the cause of birth defects and increased cancer rates for Iraqis and Americans alike.

The response to Jeremy's post was enormous, particularly among active members from China, Japan, Germany, Australia, and the United States, all countries involved in World War II, though not on the same side. As people began to discuss the implications of Jeremy's message, May Tung wrote from San Francisco: "Don't forget the Chinese when we talk about Hiroshima. I grew up in World War II; remember the fear and hatred we had for the Japanese. Though my family was fortunate enough to move to the safe region, the Japanese were pushing closer and closer. That kind of fear and panic, feeling your back is against the wall with no more ground to retreat.... WE CELEBRATED when the bombs were dropped and Japan surrendered."

Kotaro, who had often expressed his concern about militaristic sentiment growing in Japan, wrote a response to May. In it he spoke about how, as a young man, he had often thought about what he would have done had he been asked to fight for his country during World War II. "There is no 'if' in the history," he wrote, "but I think I would be certainly one of them if I was born in those years. I would try to be a good soldier for Hirohito and God blessed country. This imagination always terrified me."

Dearest Kotaro," May wrote back:

Here we are, a Japanese and a Chinese, with genuine affection for each other. As a matter of fact, dear friend, you alone have made more basic difference in my feelings toward the Japanese than any other single factor. I have felt close to you, respected you, since the beginning.

She added to this: "How do we promote peace? By posts like these on the Bridge. None of our hands are totally without blood."

Ralf responded with a dream, which he told the group. In the dream, Ralf is an agent. His job is to kill Hitler, who is speaking in an auditorium in front of a group of people. The dream is long and complex. Time after time Ralf, as the agent, comes close enough to the Fuhrer to kill him, only to have something happen which prevents the fatal shot. Finally, in the dream, Ralf is able to kill Hitler. But not long after this, exactly as if the dream were a computer game, Hitler appeared again, doing exactly what he had been doing before.

In his commentary on the dream, Ralf wrote,

I see that we need to fight for democracy itself all over the world, even in the so-called 'democratic countries' like the US and Germany. We need to fight for democracy and peace in our personal relations and we need to fight for a peaceful way of living together globally and locally. We can't wait for any administration to do that.... We need to modify our operating system. Any killing of dictators seems to be no use in the long run. Global Windows XP needs an update, urgently.

Chapter Fourteen - Kids on the Bridge and the Children of Iraq

When the war in Iraq began, the people of the World Dreams Peace Bridge dreamed of the children. This was not an isolated phenomenon. Almost every active member of the group dreamed about the children, and did so repeatedly.

There were several factors that undoubtedly led the dreamers and their dreams toward the children of Iraq. One was the knowledge that by World Health Organization account, over seventy percent of the population of Iraq is under the age of seventeen. For a country half the size of Texas, that is a huge number of children. Another factor in this particular group is that unlike many other groups in which I'd done dream work, many members of the Peace Bridge were parents of young children. Not only were there many parents on the Bridge, but they were parents who listened to the dreams of their own children, parents who encouraged their own children to dream, and people who were sensitive to the dreams of children. They were tenderhearted.

The impact of an environment such as the Peace Bridge cannot be discounted as a factor in group dreaming. The model that the Peace Bridge provides is well worth studying in the context of dream research.

During 2003, within the environment of growing global disaster, the members of the Peace Bridge became a family, a community of support. This connectedness colored our conversations and provided a sense of security resembling the security found in the clans or extended families of older, safer times. Not only did people on the Bridge inquire about each other, they listened to each other's daily joys and woes as well as dreams. In February of 2003 for example, when Ilkin suffered a financial crisis, members of the Peace Bridge responded with physical help as well as dreams. Due to a financial error, Ilkin's twin sons lacked tuition funds to cover their next term of college education. Of grave concern was the fact that boys not in college in Turkey would be conscripted to serve their mandatory six months of military training and at the time, no one knew which direction the war might take in the Middle East. Turkey shares borders with both Iraq and Syria, so Ilkin had every reason to be worried. Members of the Peace Bridge sent tuition money for the boys.

On the Peace Bridge, the care people were developing for one another extended to caring about one another's children, not in superficial ways, but ways that were as deep as the dreams themselves. It was not unusual for members to send one another packages or small gifts in the mail. Victoria's e-mail in early March demonstrated the impact of the Peace Bridge on the children. "I said to Blake (her three year old), 'Look at the pictures of snow in the country called Turkey,'" Victoria wrote. "To which he replied, 'How do we get there, elephant or aeroplane?'"

A few days later Jeremy sent a note saying, "Ellie has just opened and poured a bottle of Aloe Vera gel juice over my keyboard. Oh well, no anger, no blame, unless shared; and let's get back to work. Better a wet keyboard than a broken mind or heart."

Stephen wrote back: "Want to be my dad next life?"

There was enough conversation about the children that before long, we coined the term Kids on the Bridge to refer to them collectively. And all of the kids were encouraged to dream. Immediately after the crash of the space shuttle Columbia in February 2003, Liz sent a note saying her six year old, Michael, woke up that morning with a dream. Liz said that Michael told her, "Mom, I had a terrible dream." He dreamed that the world was ending, that the bad guys in airplanes bombed all the earth and all the good guys. He said that only one "good guy plane" was left and some people were safe. He told his mother that he would draw her a picture of the dream and bring it home to her from school. Later, when he brought her the picture he'd drawn, he said to Liz, "Mom, I didn't tell you. Something worse happened in the dream. You died, but that one good guy left came to heal you."

In an easier time, this type of dream might have been dismissed as nothing more than a little boy's heroic fantasies. Under the circumstances of impending war, this dream can be seen in a different light, the light of what happens even for children who live in relative safety and comfort. We talked on the Peace Bridge about what must be happening in the dreams of Iraqi children.

My own dream on the eve of "Shock and Awe" was as disturbing as it was sweet, in that it had the feel of a shared dream although there was no way to verify it. When I say the "feel" of a shared dream, I mean just that. Not only was I lucid, but my own way of telling whether or not I am sharing a dream tends to be particularly tactile. In dreams I have shared with another person where we both remember the contact and are thus able to compare dreams, what I have discovered is that I am more likely to feel the effect of the contact physically, like a touch on the arm, than I am able to do in non-mutual dreams.

In my dream that night,

> I walked up to the yard of a small house. A man squatted in the darkened doorway with his arms around a little girl four- or five-years old. When the little girl saw me, her eyes lit up. She grinned, laughed, said something to her father, and raced to meet me, arms outstretched.

Whatever explanation I might find for the sensation of the physical contact in this dream, the child herself stole my heart and stole into my dream state as well. This little girl, who I seriously doubt to be only a figment of my imagination, has appeared in my dreams regularly ever since the beginning of the war in Iraq. Like waking-life children, she has matured in the years since I first dreamed her.

On the same night that I first dreamed this little girl, Victoria wrote,

I was somehow on a fact-finding mission to think of ways in which bridges could be built and transportation created that did minimal damage. Later groups of people made their own "tents of peace" and there was fun discussion of ideas, plus art and music centered around the tents.

She added, "(Note: Last night my daughter and her friend slept in a tent in the back yard.)"

Ilkin, dealing with thoughts of her own children going to war, dreamed repeatedly about the children of Iraq, and Nick, who was barely the age of her sons, replied,

Ilkin, I feel that we can definitely support the children of Iraq in dreams. In my personal belief, dreams can be a gateway to a deeper reality, condensing exchanges which can affect people's lives very greatly. I remember as a young child I had a dream in which I found myself on an island. My bubble of perception was blasted open by a sorcerer. The colours were more intense than I could imagine. I felt myself blast out into this spray of colour and light. Such an experience lingers in the depths of my memory, and really reminds me how lucky I was.

Dreams of the Iraqi children sparked a wave of creative output from members of the Peace Bridge community. Kotaro, no doubt thinking of his own teenage sons as well, sent a photo of a laughing, chubby baby (himself) which we have used repeatedly as a website graphic. The photo is captioned: "I was not born to kill. I was not born to be killed."

Many people shared poetry. A favorite poem among Peace Bridge members became "Let's Give the World to the Children" by Turkish National Poet, Nazim Hikmet, that reads,

Let's give the world to the children for just one day
like a balloon in bright and striking colours to play with
let them play singing among the stars
let's give the world to the children
like a huge apple like a warm loaf of bread
at least for one day let them have enough
let's give the world to the children
at least for one day let the world learn friendship
children will get the world from our hands
they'll plant immortal trees

In the same spirit as Hikmet, Ilkin sent a poem of her own to the Peace Bridge. Like several others on the Bridge, she had a first-hand experience of the horrors of war, having spent time in prison as a teenager during the military coup in Turkey. Her words so affected many of us that two years later, when Kotaro traveled to Hiroshima for Hiroshima Day, taking mementos and prayers from several Peace Bridge members, hers were the words he recited.

To All the Children of my Dreams
forgive me children
forgive me the children of my dreams
forgive us the children of Iraq
forgive us the children of the world

you were hungry, thirsty
you were naked, in pain
you were alone with your huge eyes
you were begging for help in my dreams

when I tried to visit your dreams every night
when I tried to give you courage and take your fear away
when I tried to meet at least one of you every night
I was still hopeful, believing the power of humanity

forgive me children
I didn't understand you
I didn't understand the look in your huge eyes
I didn't understand what you want to tell with those eyes

I am aware of my part
but what a shame I am not alone
forgive us for not seeing how short the time was
for not wanting to believe how powerful the evil is

thank you, Mr. Bush
thank you, Mr. Saddam
for teaching us how evil man can be
and damn you both
for killing the children's dreams.

did you ever hug your twins with all your heart, Mr. Bush?
how was the feeling of murdering your own grandchildren, Mr. Saddam?
can you touch your little ones without shame tonight, Mr. Blair?
thanks to you, how will we look at the eyes of those children now?

forgive us children
not the dead ones, you are already gone
and going on every minute now in Iraq
but ones wounded, ones who lost parents

ones who are losing futures, losing hope, forgive us

do you know where Baghdad is?
do you know what Baghdad is?
it was the city of civilizations born in centuries
it was the city of stories told children for centuries
it will be a ruin, a giant grave of innocents by tomorrow

I wish I could tell the children there are fireworks shining in the sky
I wish I could tell them there are fires of celebrating
if a child asks with all her innocence, with all his excitement
how can a mother answer, they are not stars falling down but death is coming

I can't ask you to forgive me children, to forgive us
all I can do is watch you dying on TV screens
technology of 21st century is showing how technology is killing
I will never stop in my heart, day or night, hearing your screams
though I will never lose my belief in humanity
I am ashamed of the failure to stop this hell
I am ashamed of my country taking part in this massacre
I am ashamed of insensitivity

oh Hitler, you must be turning in your grave
they are already getting so many steps ahead of you
you were at least open in your goal
they are hiding their goal behind "the sake of humanity"

I can't ask you to forgive us children
I was a child once
then I grow up, as you will in time
and learned that it is always the children who suffer most

Although members of the Peace Bridge continued during the months after the invasion of Iraq to search for a connection inside the country through which to send comfort items to the children, there were frustrating weeks of failure. Despite the fact that we could exchange e-mails with Dr. Karzan Ali at his clinic in northern Iraq, all mail was stopped except for military post, and packages could neither be shipped in nor out.

At long last, our search took us to Kathy Kelly at the Chicago-based nonprofit organization, Voices in the Wilderness. During the years before the invasion, when strict sanctions upheld by the U.S. and other Western powers deprived Iraqi children of essential medical aid, Kathy and her colleagues broke the sanctions repeatedly to bring relief. Although Voices in the Wilderness has now been closed due to a Justice Department fine of $200,000, which Voices refuses to pay, members of this organization have moved as a group to Voices of Creative Nonviolence, and continue to protest the war. Kathy has twice been nominated for the Nobel Peace Prize.

Ever willing to extend support to others, Kathy wrote back to us immediately after an initial e-mail. She was not in Iraq at the moment she said, though she and other Voices workers, including seventy-year old New Englander Cynthia Banas, had stayed through the bombing of Baghdad. However, she could put us in contact with Emad Hadi Abbas, co-founder of one of the only totally Iraqi non-government organizations (NGOs). Childhood Voices-Iraq, founded in the first days of the war by a group of University of Baghdad arts faculty and young artists, operated a pre-school/after school program for children called Seasons Art School.

Kathy Kelly, herself a dreamer, would go to federal prison soon after we first met her to serve a six-month term for demonstrating on Federal property at Fort Benning, Georgia's School of the Americas, where special troops are trained for torture and other activities. From jail, she finished writing her book *Other Lands Have Dreams*, published in 2005. She wrote to me that prison was also a great place to find the time to study Arabic.

Ilkin took the lead in our new communication with Emad Hadi and others at Seasons Art School. At that point, a year into the occupation of Iraq by U.S. and allied troops, there was hope of a speedy recovery and a rebuilding of the tattered city of Baghdad. We were first able to send cash to Seasons Art School through the complicated network of Voices workers and their friends, but before long the postal ban was lifted between Iraq and Turkey and Ilkin was happily shopping with her friend Tatiana for teddy bears, drawing paper, crayons and paints. A guitar and an aud, the traditional stringed instrument of the Middle East, were also sent with this first shipment to replace instruments destroyed during the bombing.

Around this time, in February 2004, Ilkin had a final dream about the children of Iraq. She had only recently decided that she would be able to attend the IASD conference being held that year in Copenhagen, Denmark. This is the dream as Ilkin wrote it. The "whisperer" is the name she gives to the voice that whispers to her in her dreams.

I am finding myself on an airplane. We are flying to or from Copenhagen. The man sitting beside me (who she later recognized at the conference) is asking about "Aid for Traumatized Children Project" of the World Dreams Peace Bridge…. I am speaking nonstop and the man is listening to me in amazed silence.

Suddenly all my connection with the real world is stopping. I am seeing myself still speaking with the man, but in fact I am not there. The whisperer says, "We created (made real) the most valuable dream-inspired novel of history, and the me sitting there, telling the man all about it is not aware that I am <u>writing</u> it, in fact not telling."

I am objecting to the whisperer, laughing and saying, "History is full of valuable, dream-inspired novel examples."

The whisperer says, "Humans make so many activities. They make protests against wars, globalism, for children, women, human rights, ecology and everything. But tell me how many of them can take the opportunity of seeing the result? The wars are still going on; children are still working in factories; women are in violence; rain forests are being destroyed. Everybody can dream; many can be inspired from their dreams and make paintings, compose songs, but how many can live their dreams in real life?"

I am sitting down, cross-legged, in the emptiness. Suddenly I realize that what we are is not dreaming or only being inspired from our dreams, but making dreams real. I am feel a great happiness fill me. "We did it. We realized the dreams, didn't we," I call to whisperer.

The whisperer replies, "Yes, you really did realize them. Even one tiny feeling of one child living in the world must be enough for you. You people created the world's most real, most lived in dream story. And you wrote it, even if nobody can read."

The other me is still speaking to the man. I am feeling words coming out of her mouth are flowing into a whirling source which is invisible to her. I am seeing in my mind scenes from Jules Verne's books for children about the future, and Dante's *Inferno*.

For the researcher in me, the speculative part of me that never stopped saying, "What if...?" the Peace Bridge provided an unending feast of information on the subject of group dreaming. Here was Ilkin's dream whisperer saying that the Peace Bridge had achieved something unique in the annals of dreaming and I did not really doubt it.

One of the discussions that spring on the Peace Bridge had to do with what Nick called "The Voice." He was speaking about the words a dreamer may hear spoken on the edge of waking, not a dream, but a function of hypnopompia, or that area between sleep and waking. The Voice, Nick claimed, spoke only words that should be believed, words that were the deepest of messages.

Because I tend to doubt absolutes of any kind, I questioned this idea. I had experienced The Voice myself, but had never heard a real discussion of the subject among dreamers. Other members of the group agreed with me that The Voice was like dreams, nothing to be believed absolutely, but that there was possibly useful information to be found there. In an issue of "The View from the Bridge" written by Kathy, she said, "So far The Voice has said in its tender, ironic manner:"

Valley: "Not all butterflies make it to Mexico."

"There is a new star on the horizon that has never been seen before."

Nick: "Elvis dreams of Peace."

Jean: "May the life of the sweeper change the width of the broom."

One thing that was true of the Peace Bridge was that its members, as a group, were much more interested in the nature of consciousness and more willing to ask difficult questions about the function and operation of consciousness, than any other group I had ever worked with or been part of.

The Peace Bridge and most particularly the Kids on the Bridge provided me with another opportunity for research in the spring of 2004 when several of the Peace Bridge members with children allowed their kids to participate in the beta testing of a program I had been working on for some time, The Dreams Scouts International Program.

The Dream Scouts are only obliquely a part of the information on group dreaming, so I will keep the discussion of this subject brief. However, the Dream Scouts have a group dreaming history of their own which contributes to the body of knowledge on this subject.

The reason I began writing the first Dream Scouts Adventure Book, *Under the Crystal Tree,* in 2003 was because the group of teenagers involved in the plot had been appearing in my dreams for years. The plot involves a group of teens from a variety of cultural backgrounds who live in Washington, D.C. and who meet in dream state under a crystal tree in a meadow. But the Scouts who did not know one another previous to dreaming together, meet in waking life and begin a series of adventures together.

The characters of the Dreams Scouts are fictional but this does not appear to stop them from having lives of their own. I am not the only person to have dreamed about them, something I discovered when I first began to talk about writing the adventure books several years ago. My niece Carol had dreamed the Dream Scouts, as had some of her friends.

As I began writing the manuscript for the as yet unpublished first book and mentioned the Crystal Tree to people I knew, it also received an immediate response from dreamers who said to me, "I've dreamed that tree!" They would then describe to me both the tree and the meadow that contained it.

Given my background in group dreaming, I was not particularly surprised that other people would dream the characters or the dream location of my novel but I had some particular group dreaming questions in mind when I decided to test the potentials for the Dream Scouts International Program at precisely the time members of the Peace Bridge were dreaming about the children of Iraq. I had conceived of the Dream Scouts as a way to not only teach children about dreaming, but I also wanted to see how young people might respond to the type of online activity in which the adults were engaged on the World Dreams Peace Bridge.

So I invited the adults of the Peace Bridge to ask their children if they would like to participate in testing the program. Before long, there were fifteen kids between the ages of six and sixteen, along with at least one parent each, ready to participate in the program. To make it easier for the kids to communicate, we provided a bulletin board on the Dream Scouts test site. I asked Nick if he would moderate the board, not only because he was close in age to the kids involved, but also because of a life-changing dream he sent to the Peace Bridge when we first began dreaming about the children in Iraq. Although he was still in college, Nick, a computer major, had been studying dreams for years. He had created an online dream forum "Sea Life" which he managed on his website www.dreamofpeace.net. The dream Nick sent to us in March, 2003, was

In another lucid dream, I was just lying in my bed. And the walls started being covered with messages ranging from hieroglyphic patterns to icons, to all different kinds of languages. Finally I made out a message: "Teach the children." I sat there for a moment, waiting for what it was I was to be taught, and then suddenly realized that I could certainly help by "teaching the children" about dreaming.

Asking for more advice, I decided to reenter the dream to discover who it was I was supposed to teach. I found myself in a room with Janette's youngest son, Micah. He is about five and now seems to appear quite often in my dreams. I know that he is a great friend, who I am meant to encourage. It is great fun getting him interested in the world of dreams.

Because of this dream, Nick not only generated a conversation on the Peace Bridge about dreaming with children, especially the little boy who persistently shared his dreams, but he also decided to change his college major. He is now completing a degree in education.

Of the fifteen young people who formed the test group for the Dream Scouts International Program, two were brought into the group by Nick. One was a sixteen-year old boy from Sydney, Australia, Richard, who had been active on the Sea Life forum. Richard's first comment to me, even before we began the beta test of the Dream Scouts program was, "Why do I feel like I've met you, even before I met you? I think I must have dreamed you before." The other person Nick brought to the group was six-year old Micah, who insisted on being part of the program.

I was curious to see how kids in different age groups would respond to the manuscript of *Under the Crystal Tree* that they were given to read, but even more curious to see how they would respond to online interaction and more specifically to sharing dreams online. The first thing I discovered was that although three of the Kids on the Bridge were nine-year old girls, not a single one of them was interested in the online program. The mother of one of these nine-year olds who kept in touch with me during the beta testing offered an explanation, which made sense to me. At nine, she said, girls are more interested in sharing with their best friends than they are in sharing with strangers on the computer. This mother also told me that at the same time, her daughter was very interested in dreams and had asked her mother to buy her a dream journal. She had also started dreaming mutually with her closest friend at home and mom had overheard the two of them talking about the dream space they shared "under the tree."

Although interactive sites for kids abound, there are not many sites online through which children interact with one another and none where they are invited to discuss their dreams. The majority of the young people in the Dreams Scouts test group fell between the ages of ten and fourteen. There were more boys than girls in the group and it was interesting to me that the boys seemed more easily able to share both conversation and dreams than the girls. This may be due to the fact that boys are generally more interested in Game Boys and other computer-related action games than are girls, so that boys tend to develop ease and familiarity with computers at an earlier age.

The first thing that became evident in the Dream Scouts test group was that some of the parents were feeling threatened by the possibility of family dreaming. "I dreamed that I was on a sailboat last night with my father," Stephen told me at the beginning of the test program. "He was rushing to dock before dark, critical of me like he always was when he was alive." In the dream, Stephen felt like a little boy, and once he woke he realized he was concerned about showing that aspect of himself to his son. Other parents in the group reported similar anxious dreams.

The kids themselves responded with a touching mixture of curiosity and tentative outreach. They were not so much afraid to tell their dreams, as they were self-conscious and hesitant. There were, however, a sufficient number of shared dreams to convince me that the program was worth pursuing. The availability of an online venue for dream sharing for kids and families could in my estimation, revolutionize our understanding of group dreaming.

Throughout the year of 2004 we continued to work on the Peace Bridge with the children of Iraq. Through regular, almost daily, e-mail contact with Emad and others at Seasons Art School, we exchanged photos and learned about each other's families. Ilkin became Mum Ilkin for many of the students at the school. We asked the children if they would contribute drawings to the Peace Train.

That summer, because the annual conference of the International Association for the Study of Dreams was being held in Copenhagen, European members of the Peace Bridge, along with many from the United States, would have the opportunity to meet. Ilkin, Ralf, Juhani and Jeremy, accompanied by his daughter Ellie, attended the conference. We mounted a large display of Peace Train art, including children's artwork from Turkey and Iraq at the conference, attracting many new members to the Bridge. One of these, Brenda Mallon from

Manchester, England is the author of by far the best dream book available for working with the dreams of young children, *Dream Time With Children.*

From the beginning, the communication exchanged with the people in Iraq was for me a source of excruciating emotional turmoil. To be both an American and on principle opposed to the occupation of Iraq, while at the same time being in daily contact with those suffering the brunt of the occupation, was at times almost unbearable. Yet as time went on, it became clear that the programs started by Childhood Voices-Iraq were in serious need of our help, a need that overrode any personal concerns. The school's programs had been funded by a one-year startup grant from UNICEF and though negotiations were underway for a grant extension, for several months the efforts of the World Dreams Peace Bridge were all that stood between the end of current grant funding and the program being closed.

Seasons Art School applied a radical formula to education in Baghdad. Because all students were in public school for only half a day, Seasons Art School filled the gap by providing two half-day sessions. Boys and girls were taught together. Students in the program came from poor families, and middle-income families. Some were street children orphaned or abandoned during the war. Some were handicapped. All were given music, art and drama classes, and instruction in both English and computer use. Emad and others at the school were eager to ameliorate the effect of military training imposed on even very young children during the regime of Saddam Hussein as well as the trauma of having grown up in a country continuously at war.

I found myself suddenly at the center of a major fund-raising effort. Synchronistically, I received an email from the mother of a fourteen-year old girl who attended a Vermont Compass School. This mother was asking if the students in her daughter's school might be allowed to develop a fund-raising program for the students at Seasons Art School. It was a sad commentary on the state of aid for children when she told me that putting the words Iraq and children into her Internet search engine resulted in The World Dreams website coming up at the top of the page. If we felt we were doing too little for the children, it appeared that much larger organizations were doing even less.

Through the efforts of ten high school students, their advisor and one parent, a program was ultimately developed by the Vermont students which raised over $1,800 for Seasons Art School. That this fund-raising effort accomplished considerably more can be seen from the comments of the students who conducted the program. A statement typifying the responses of the students was made by fifteen-year old Sarah, who said, "Before, I didn't want to think about Iraq, because everything seemed to go wrong. Now I feel like I can do something, so I don't feel hopeless."

Dreams were at work in the fund-raising process just as they were in other aspects of the World Dreams Peace Bridge. In the spring of 2004, Harry Bosma created an experimental psi dreaming program online, which he called Psi Angels. The purpose of this group would be to auction off chances on the IASD online auction. Winners would be allowed to ask a question of the Psi Angels, who would then try to dream the answer. Ilkin, in addition to being one of "Harry's Angels" was also the winner of the initial auction bid. Her question? How can we raise funds for Seasons Art School? To be sure of an answer, she participated in the group dream herself. Several of Harry's Angels dreamed about music or musical performances that night, and the discussion among group members after the dreaming exercise concluded that maybe a concert would make a good fund-raising project. Ilkin dreamed about Carlos Santana.

During this time, Ilkin had also been conducting an Internet search for potential benefactors for Seasons Art School. When she received a positive response from Carlos Santana's Milagro Foundation, no one was surprised. The fund-raising and grant-writing activity involved an enormous amount of work. I filled the days of September with grant applications and proposal writing.

During all of this time, conditions in Iraq had grown steadily worse. Electricity was sporadic, fuel costs skyrocketed, people waited for hours in long lines for bottled water, propane for cooking, and gasoline for automobiles. As the cost of living went up and family incomes disappeared, tensions increased. Foreign employees of NGOs were kidnapped, some for political reasons, some for ransom. Children were also being abducted for ransom, making attendance at school hazardous. Emad received a death threat note under his door at home.

In November of 2004, when we had not heard from Emad for over a week, Ilkin and I were extremely concerned. Ilkin sent an e-mail, asking him to please respond. He replied,

Mum, my friend is died. Some people kill him. I don't know why. I am very sad after that. I wish in that time those people kill me, because this is my best friend, Mum. I hate this life after that. You can imagine a good person, and he have children. Died for what? Nothing. Oh my God, what happened, for this world is changing in so many things.

A few weeks later, after a period of renewed contact, we again did not hear from Emad. This time I was so worried that I asked the members of the Peace Bridge group to hold a special DaFuMu dreaming session. Athough he knew nothing about the dreams being dreamed for him, Emad's reply was immediate. The next day I received a message from Emad, asking me if everything was all right. He had dreamed about me the previous night, he exclaimed, and I was crying. I was surrounded by a lot of people, but I looked so sad. He also said he was sorry not to have written to us, but he had been in Amman, Jordan attending a workshop. In this case, group dreaming worked where Internet communication failed.

By the end of the year, with a $5,000 grant from Carlos Santana's Milagro Foundation and another $5,000 from private donors added to the Compass

School funds, the Peace Bridge was able to send over $13,000 to Seasons Art School to keep them in business until new funding was located. We had also begun talking with Emad about another program, "Dreams and the Children of Baghdad," a way to do dream work with children at Seasons Art School.

In autumn of 2004, through a series of e-mails, May Tung had established contact with Dr. Ali Rasheed, one of three doctors in Iraq trained to work with Post Traumatic Stress Disorder (PTSD) in children. Dr. Rasheed conducted workshops in Iraq and throughout the Middle East with teachers, hospital staff and others, attempting to teach them how to recognize the signs of PTSD and to work with children. He was assisted in this work by Dr. Wisal Aldouri of the Iraq Department of Education. When we first met Ali, he was thoroughly disgusted with funding sources from the U.S. State Department who asked for results of his program after six months. This project could take years, he told them, at least ten years to be developed and see results. They took away his funding.

When Ali, at May's request, joined the Peace Bridge discussion group, the first thing he encountered was the photograph of a perfect white rose, sent from Kotaro in Japan. Kotaro had begun the practice several months earlier of taking flower photos with the digital camera in his cell phone as he walked to and from the subway ride to work.

Ali was enraged. How could flower photos do anything for world peace? It was only after other members of the Peace bridge explained how Kotaro's daily photos affirmed beauty and life to us all—and after Ali told us that a day earlier he had witnessed a ten-year old boy being shot and killed in the street in front of him—that we could resume any sort of conversation about dreams.

After the bombing of the Iraqi city of Falluja, members of the Peace Bridge sent $500 to Ali to buy toys and other items for the children. As a doctor, he was one of the few people allowed near the city, including journalists. Ali wrote that when he went to a toy store in Baghdad to buy the toys, the store owner gave him everything at cost, saying: "Take the toys for the children."

The Peace Bridge continued to dream, but was also continuously busy with attempts to put the dreams into action. Through reading and correspondence we educated ourselves in the effects of war on children. One of the saddest facts to discover was that very little has been written about the effect of war on civilian populations. In fact, so little material was available in 2001 that an international group of psychotherapists, who had presented papers to the American Psychological Association on the subject of the effects of war on civilians, approached Dr. Stanley Krippner, asking him to edit a book of their papers. The resulting volume, *The Psychological Impact of War Trauma on Civilians: An International Perspective*, co-edited by Teresa McIntyre, was published by Prager Press in 2003. Stanley, a former president of IASD as well as a former president of APA, graciously donated a copy of the book to the Peace Bridge so that we would have it available to pass around. More than any other factor of war, post-traumatic stress in civilian populations of children has received the least attention.

In an article published in 2006 in the *Washington Post*, the results of a recent survey conducted by the Iraqi Ministry of Health are mentioned by foreign correspondents Jonathan Finer and Omar Fekeiki. Out of 1,000 individuals, randomly selected across five Baghdad neighborhoods, 890 reported repeatedly witnessing violent incidents, the majority of them since the 2003 invasion. Most of these individuals, including many children, report symptoms of PTSD.

In the spring of 2005, Ali and Wisal began to send us some of the children's drawings they collected in their teaching workshops, drawings of planes dropping rounds of missiles on villages below, and the repeated drawings made by one little girl of the same perfect, beautiful bride over and over again.

Meanwhile, plans for the "Dreams and the Children of Baghdad" program moved forward. Even though Emad found it necessary to move Seasons Art School from the location where it began to a safer area of the city, a group of twenty-one children were selected to participate in the dream program. The program, Emad wrote, would have a room of its own and (knowing nothing about the Dream Scouts or their meeting place under the Crystal Tree) he said it would be called the "Crystal Birds Dream Program" because children were like crystals with the light shining through.

The first of the children's dreams reached us not long before the summer IASD conference, again being held in Berkeley, California. At the conference a silent auction hosted by the Peace Bridge would raise over $3,000 for programs in Iraq. The children of Iraq had joined the dreaming Kids on the Bridge. A look at one or two of their dreams provides an example of the importance of dream work with children at war:

Zenab, age 12 dreamed:

I am planting some flowers and small trees, making my own garden with great effort. But the war came and I had to leave my house with my family. After that, returning, I found that my garden had been completely destroyed. I didn't give up. I started to plant and remake my garden once again.

Muhamud, age 13 dreamed:

I dreamed I am an engineer. The first work I did on returning to my neighborhood was to rehabilitate my damaged school, "The future school."

In the hearts of Peace Bridge members, the dreams of children have come to be seen as one of the world's most valuable resources, to be protected at all cost.

Chapter Fifteen - Riding the Peace Train

The year of 2005 opened with one of the worst disasters the world had ever seen. On December 26, 2004, an undersea earthquake rocked the floor of the Indian Ocean, setting off a tsunami of such magnitude that over 200,000 people were instantly killed in Indonesia, Sri Lanka, southern India, Thailand and other countries with ocean borders. The devastation was so widespread that the entire world community was in shock.

The year continued to produce one horrifying disaster after another with dizzying speed. The month of August seemed to be the apex of the year, a month reflecting both the best and the worst of the human condition. This was true on the Bridge as well.

On August first, Olivia wrote from England, "One of my dreams last night had lots of emus! (the Australian ostrich)."

In the dream I had moved out of my accommodation, a rented room in some obscure town, and considered camping on a desert-like "field" (sand with neat dunes in rows) surrounded to the west by suburban housing, to the north by mountains, and to the east a forest. To the south was the obscure town.

I stood there in the "desert" when I suddenly saw a few emus, and then more and more, and then I couldn't understand why I hadn't seen them immediately, for they stood everywhere—all but one or two, standing, sleeping, or even hibernating in that position.

Olivia said to the group, "As I woke up, I really wondered about the emus. Does anybody have any insight into what emus might stand for?"

Ilkin immediately replied from Turkey,

I don't know if this can help you, but we call emus camel bird in Turkish and I think it is the same or similar in Middle East. Both camels and camel birds (emus) are strong animals against hunger and thirst. They can smell sandstorms before they come, can use the fat and water they store under bad conditions etc. Camel birds' eggs used to hang to protect from spiders in houses and other places. There are hundreds years old camel bird eggs hanging in beautiful hand made carvings in Hagia Sophia and many churches, mosques and antique places against poisonous spiders.

The day after this, Kathy reported that the emu is known as the "law bringer or enforcer" to aboriginal tribes.

A day later, Kathy said to Olivia, "Your Emu Dreaming has captured my dreaming mind!! I hardly ever have dreams of aboriginal people, but after your dream I've had two!" Kathy also suggested that Olivia contact Australian-born shamanic dream teacher Robert Moss to see what he had to say about the emus.

Olivia sent an email off to Moss, and received a response within days. "Perhaps the Emu People are dreaming YOU," Moss countered. "The ancient ones of different traditions come looking for us through dreaming."

A few days later Olivia had a second dream set in the desert. "Oh wow!" she reported to the Peace Bridge, "I had a dream last night, a rather abstract one, where I received instructions about water holes in the desert and how keeping the water together in holes, rather than it permeating the soil, prevented it from evaporating."

At this time the world news was full of the draught and famine in Niger, Africa. Children were dying by the score from lack of water, and the dreams begun by Olivia sparked a conversation about the importance of water. In Iraq, we heard from Ali and Wisal, many children were dying from dysentery caused by untreated water.

A few months earlier we had decided on the Peace Bridge to conduct a monthly DaFuMu Dreaming for World Peace on the fifteenth of each month, and that date was coming up. Kathy created a page for the World Dreams web site as a way to do fundraising for the people of Niger, and we agreed to make the August DaFuMu Dreaming date a meditation on water. Olivia suggested: "Every time we take a drink of water or use the loo…," we could imagine all of the people of the world having safe, clean, drinkable water, and water filling the Reservoir at the Peace Bridge.

In the midst of this discussion, Kotaro was planning for a trip to Hiroshima for the observation of Hiroshima Day on August 6. Ralf turned his attention to creating a poem—in English—for Kotaro to take with him to represent the Peace Bridge. Ralf wrote,

War—so easy to set the trees on fire

Peace—so long to grow the seeds

Now let's plant the forests for our children

A few days earlier, at the August second convention of the Veterans for Peace group in Dallas, Texas, Gold Star Mother for Peace, Cindy Sheehan had announced her intention to go to the Bush White House in Crawford, Texas and hold vigil there until President George Bush, who was on a five-week vacation at his "Texas White House," his ranch in Crawford, would talk to her. Cindy, whose son Casey was killed in Iraq, demanded to know from the President why her son had died.

And suddenly Valley, who had been part of the World Dreams Peace Bridge from its beginning, found herself amid a firestorm of activity. Along with her partner, Hadi, Valley was one of the early planners of the Crawford Peace House, created at the beginning of the war in Iraq to establish a peace presence in the sleepy town of Crawford, near the ranch where the President spent much of his time.

According to Cindy Sheehan, if the President could vacation for five weeks while boys were dying in Iraq, she could wait for him to talk to her. She took her stand in a weed-choked ditch outside the ranch, and was soon joined, despite searing heat, dust, and fire ants, by several thousand others.

On August thirteenth, two days before the DaFuMu, Valley wrote to the Peace Bridge.

Greetings from a mom on the front lines of peace in Crawford at the Crawford Peace House with Cindy Sheehan and her strong stand for peace....
My daughter has been here with me, and she is in love with Cindy. She is a hero to her. It's so wonderful for her to be involved with all of these strong women activists out here....

The same day that Valley wrote to us from Crawford, Ali sent the following message from Baghdad.

I would like to convey the pain and agony of my people here in Iraq, and in particular Baghdad.

Death tolls going up and daily bombings are getting more brutal and savage. No description can draw the bloody scene...3 successive bombings this morning in the same location, and the wounded people who survive the bombings had another one at the entrance of the nearby hospital. More than 50 were killed and about 80 wounded.

These bloody events are to be recorded and I find no words to describe the pain and sadness everyone here feels.

In Iraq the number of suicide bombers—driving vehicles, walking with explosives taped to their bodies—had increased dramatically along with attacks from occupying forces, an explosive brew which trapped the ordinary citizens of the country in ever-increasing danger.

Jeremy, returning to the activity of the Peace Bridge after a week at the International Peace Conference in Poland, wrote to the Bridge.

I am thinking of joining the Southern Peace Train, to Washington, D.C. for the September 24 protest. So many lies behind the war and nobody accounting—the DU (depleted uranium) is what scares me most, and what I would speak out about. Even people at the conference hadn't heard about it before, even the Attorney General of Delaware, a receptive woman whom I discussed it with.

Almost exactly three years after he first dreamed of the Peace Train, Jeremy was planning to ride his dream into physical reality. From all over the United States trains were being scheduled to bring antiwar protestors to the American capitol for a massive protest scheduled for September 24, 2005. The train Jeremy planned to ride would be leaving from New Orleans two days before the event. Jeremy would visit the home of a friend and former classmate from Tulane University where he received his law degree, and then the two would ride the Peace Train to Washington. As it happened, the Monday following the planned protest was also Jeremy's birthday. It was a combination impossible to resist. Other Peace Bridge members began making arrangements as well, to go to the September protest and celebrate Jeremy's birthday with him. On August 16, Valley wrote that Cindy Sheehan too planned to ride on this Peace Train from New Orleans and that Valley and Hadi would be with her.

The protest in Crawford, now being called Camp Casey, had mushroomed in a matter of days from a few people occupying a ditch to thousands, with press from around the world – grieving parents and relatives of dead soldiers, celebrities and well wishers – all being coordinated by volunteers through the Crawford Peace House. "Crawford is a place of miracles," Valley wrote:

> The people and resources that are needed show up…. This is another instance of a dream realized. When we first thought about Crawford as a Peace House, I had a dream of a long, white banner that was from far away, and it led to Crawford. The banner said, "Peace is the Way." Now so many people are making their way to Crawford to speak out against this war and work for peace. My son and I made a banner together from that dream that has been to many rallies since the war began.

We continued to dream of water, both on the designated DaFuMu Dreaming day and later, and we continued to dream for peace. On August 27, May wrote,

> Dear Jeremy, Olivia, Valley, Victoria, Ron, Louise, myself and everybody. When I read the posts from some of you this morning, I felt 'what a group!' I was impressed and inspired by what you have said. The question came up to me after reading. Is there a legitimate place for hatred, anger, disgust, condescension, despair, distrust? What and where is the 'best in us' and how do we balance—is that it?—and make room for these human qualities? What is the alchemical process we need? Then I recalled last night's dream and it is,

> Bearing the Best: I am in a procession with a small group of people, probably all women, walking downhill on a street. I happen to be the first (no leadership implied). It's all very grey, the pavement and the sky. We each hold a box as if in ceremony, respectfully. In the box (size of a shoe box but shallower) there are maybe six objects (artifacts), carefully partitioned to keep them in place. They are precious objects for some reason. We are careful that they stay in place and safe. I look at mine and others also notice that I have the "best" of whatever it is. I feel good, realizing that I am fortunate to have the best. I wonder for a moment if perhaps the reason of why or how come I happened or worked for what turned out to be the best. There is a mild realization that I worked for this end result.

Ali, responding to all of the dreams, prayers, and thoughts emanating from the Peace Bridge toward the people of Iraq, wrote on the same day.

> Dear Victoria and all friends and dreamers,

I believe there are many things we can do. Exchange of ideas can evoke others to think and brainstorm their minds…what to do? Who do what and when?

Each one can dream of peace and tranquility. Each one can pray and ask His Lord for more stability and peace for Human beings to behave in Human way. Every one can light a candle that might light the pathway in our dark hostile paths that are full of criminals and merciless mercenaries…. The wish list will never end.

But dear friends, I feel so good to have your reflections and that is really impressive. I usually print out these electronic encounters and show them to my colleagues in the hospital and elsewhere, to prove that we are not alone.

Two days after May's dream and Ali's post, on August 29, the largest hurricane to make landfall in the United States for well over a century struck a savage blow at the Gulf Coast of Louisiana and Mississippi. Hurricane Katrina, a category-five storm, rolled over New Orleans, breaking down the levees which shielded the city from flood waters, killing and displacing thousands, cutting short the President's vacation, and ending the vigil in Crawford. Members of the World Dreams Peace Bridge sprang into action. Because there were members of the Peace Bridge discussion group living in several of the cities to which hurricane victims were moved, we created a People to People campaign through which we funneled donations made by people in other parts of the country and the world.

In Austin, Texas, Liz purchased clothes, pajamas, underwear and toys for children who had lost everything to the floodwaters. Valley, in Dallas, reported to us on conditions faced by people who had been bussed to the Civic Center there. In Cincinnati, Jody used the funds from the Peace Bridge to purchase groceries for a family displaced with no assistance other than that provided by other employees of the company for which the mother worked. The family, thankful to be together, had a story as horrifying as many others coming out of New Orleans, which Jody relayed to us on the Bridge.

Unfortunately, the day after the family's arrival in Cincinnati, there was an electrical storm which knocked out power to the family's temporary home. Jody recounted the pitiful cries of the children, "Will the water come?"

Watching television as rescuers struggled to save what was left of the population of New Orleans, I heard one man remark, "I've been in Iraq, and this is worse than anything I saw there. I guess it's different if it's your own home though." This comment covered the tragedy. Most of the National Guard troops which, in other times, would have been turned to disaster relief, were serving in Iraq, assuring that rescue work would be too slow to save lives that otherwise might have been saved. The billions spent on maintaining the U.S. military presence in Iraq had, in part, been taken from funds requested by the U.S. Corps of Engineers to rebuild and strengthen the system of levees keeping flood waters out of New Orleans, one of the few major world cities built mostly below sea level. On the Peace Bridge people saw the irony in what the soldier on TV referred to as "worse than Iraq."

Of course, the Peace Train scheduled to travel from New Orleans in September was cancelled. The web site bulletin board set up for the New Orleans Peace Train however, was not. Several Peace Bridge members had watched this bulletin board with interest, reading the messages from people who planned to ride the train to Washington in September. It was natural to return there following the hurricane to see how people fared.

What I read on the bulletin board was infinitely heartwarming. Many of the war protestors collected at Camp Casey in Crawford had fled not away from the storm but toward it. In an area near Lake Pontchartrain, just north of New Orleans, members of Veterans for Peace had created Camp Casey Two, set up a soup kitchen and begun broadcasting (with generator powered electricity) a list of immediate needs for the people there. Filmmaker Michael Moore had also closed his Chicago office and driven, with his staff and loads of supplies, directly into Louisiana.

As the bumbling efforts of the Federal Emergency Management Agency (FEMA) became increasingly obvious to the shocked citizenry of the United States, the mood of the nation darkened. The number of people planning to attend the September March on Washington increased daily. Simultaneous protests were planned in San Francisco, Los Angeles and other cities where the majority could not afford a cross-country trek to Washington. At first indecisive about whether the Peace Train would run at all or whether, if it did run, he would be on it, Jeremy decided to fly from South Korea to Atlanta, Georgia and take the Peace Train from there. I joined other members of the Peace Bridge – Jody, Valley, Regina, Wendy, and others – in plans to combine peaceful protest with Jeremy's birthday excursion.

In the time since Jeremy's original dream of the Peace Train, the Peace Train Project had continued to grow. Online we had a Peace Train mission statement, the Peace Train Song (written by Jeremy), and a growing gallery of Peace Train art collected from around the world. There was even a Peace Train certificate designed to be presented to anyone who created trains, with a list of the "stations" Peace Trains could be sent to: Jeremy's address in South Korea, Victoria's in Australia, May's in San Francisco, and mine in Virginia. The number of hits to our web site had also increased. Trains came to us from people we didn't know and had never met – a church group in Baltimore, a summer camp program in Michigan, a school in Mexico City.

As Jeremy wrote in his "Call for Peace Trains," published on the World Dreams web site,

> Whereas our planet is in jeopardy—children live in poverty; violence is everywhere; the air is filthy; and the ice caps are melting—we call upon

ordinary people of the world to join us in a cry for peace by reaching out with your hands and building a carriage for the Peace Train, or even an entire train.

"A Peace Train is an art form," he continued, "with an engine, carriages, and caboose."

The IASD's annual PsiberDreaming Online Conference, for which I generally act as a volunteer as well as sometimes-presenter, was scheduled to begin just days before the march on Washington. I was eager to get in as much time as possible at the online conference before leaving for the weekend. The conference had grown under Ed Kellog's management, to include consciousness experts of all kinds and I was looking forward to the interchange. But then, on September 21, almost as soon as the online conference began, news came that another category-five hurricane, this one named Rita, was aimed at the Gulf Coast—almost too much to be believed. The hurricane was scheduled to make landfall the same day, September 24, as the March on Washington.

This time I shocked the credulity of even some Peace Bridge members. I left a message on the PsiberDreaming Conference bulletin board and sent it around to all of the various dream groups, asking dreamers if they would like to join me in an attempt to "dream down the storm."

My request was met with everything from amusement to agreement. I was accused of magical thinking and attempting to mess with Mother Nature, but the size of the storm began to dwindle.

I would not have taken this step if I had not experienced the weather-working discussion several times before. I was reminded of a day in 1989 when Poseidia Institute was hosting the weekly radio show *Psychic Dimensions*. Then there had been a severe drought in Virginia and other southern states. We had asked the radio audience to discuss the question of whether it was possible to change the weather. In one of the liveliest discussions ever heard on the program, listeners assured us that it was indeed possible to change the weather and told us stories of when they had seen it happen or had done it themselves. So we suggested that, during the week between this broadcast and the next one, listeners turn their attention toward praying, dreaming, or meditating for rain for the drought-parched area.

The next week when we arrived at the studio, it was pouring down rain. "Did you do this?" we asked our audience. It was only then that we heard from many of our listeners that yes, they'd prayed or dreamed or meditated on rain but only God could change the weather.

The day after I posted the message about dreaming down the storm, Hurricane Rita was downgraded to a category-four storm and then to a category-three.

Kotaro wrote:

"Dear May,

As I cannot control my dream, while I am awake I am trying a very short mantra this time, "Be in good balance, in harmony of nature."

There were jokes made, of course, that in August we had focused our DaFuMu Dreaming for World Peace on a hope for water. Maybe we weren't clear enough, someone said. Maybe we should have been more specific, said another—water over here, not over there; clear, clean, drinkable water, not death by floodwater.

On September 22, Jody sent the following dream:
Laissez les bonnes temps roulez!

I dream I am swimming in turbulent water, waves rolling over me, and I am trapped under a huge mass of concrete or other building detritus. I try to push my way up under it and realize I cannot escape by pushing up directly. Instead, I must "roll" over and over and over in a sideways swimming to bob up from under it.

I think then of the New Orleans jazz culture's slogan: Laissez les bonnes temps roulez!, which expresses the irrepressible energy and love of life of that culture. And it is the way to deal with wave upon wave of disaster.

She added. "It is my dream but it feels like it is for all of us. Water is not our enemy, nor are the challenges in life. Rolling with them is the thing to remember and practice."

The morning of September 24 dawned clear and blue in the nation's capitol. Hurricane Rita, downgraded to a category-two storm, made landfall east of New Orleans midday. I heard an interesting story later from one of the dreamers who decided to participate in dreaming down the storm. He had been conducting a dream workshop in northern New Mexico, he said, and when the workshop was over, he asked the workshop attendees if they would like to help with the experiment. They said they didn't feel too comfortable with the idea of trying to exert power against the storm, the workshop facilitator told me but they would be glad to ask the storm to carry some of its rain to New Mexico and Arizona. The next day it was raining in both states, in areas that had not seen rain for months. This sort of group dreaming is thoroughly unverifiable, of course, but interesting to experiment with all the same.

In Washington, even though we were far too excited to remember our dreams that weekend, members of the Peace Bridge provided themselves with one synchronicity after another, enough to keep us laughing for weeks.

I arrived in the capitol before ten a.m. via one of the busses rented by our local Peace and Justice group. Already thousands of people thronged the Smithsonian Mall and the park near the Jefferson Memorial from which the March would begin. Banners and flags whipped smartly in a cool breeze. From the bus the white crosses of Camp Casey could be easily seen, filling the grass in row upon row, one for each of the nearly 2,000 American soldiers who had died so far in Iraq, some with photos, many with flowers.

Though I planned to meet Jody and Jeremy at the Corcoran Gallery before the March began, I was so close to the scene of the action that I called to tell them I would meet them later. I said to my companions, "I need to go find Valley." I turned around, crossed the street and there, surrounded by the multitudes, spotted Valley walking toward me. "Oh good," she said, as if she saw me every day here, "I needed someone to hold the other end of the Crawford Peace House sign when Hadi speaks." Laughing, she led me to the backstage area behind the huge outdoor stage, where March leaders and media gathered. She told me she'd said to Hadi a few minutes earlier, "I have to go find Jean," and left to locate me. We laughed about how much easier this was than trying to hear a cell phone conversation in the mob.

For his part, Jeremy took the Metro into the city from Takoma Park, Maryland, where he was staying with a friend. Not entirely sure how to find the Corcoran Gallery from where he exited the subway, he stood for a moment looking at his map. Ahead of him, he said, he heard a man who had gotten off the same train, asking for directions to the Corcoran. The man mentioned that he had to meet his friend Jody.

"Excuse me," Jeremy said, walking up to him. "I'm going to the Corcoran Gallery myself. Maybe we could get lost together." The other man was Jody's friend Mike from Cincinnati.

Not to be outdone by all of this synchronicity, at breakfast that morning at the hotel where Jody and I were staying, Jody met a man she knew from Cincinnati who was in Washington for an environmental conference. When she mentioned she was about to meet up with friends from Australia, he was astounded, as they were long time friends of his as well. He changed his plans and came to the March. Needless to say, by the time we all met one another again, late that afternoon at the Crawford Peace House tent, the members of the Peace Bridge had plenty to tell one another.

The synchronicities continued throughout the weekend. Jody, Valley, Hadi and I had decided to stay through the weekend to celebrate Jeremy's birthday with him on Monday. Jeremy recounted how, the day he was born in the hospital that was then across the street from the White House, the nurse had presented him to his parents with the words. "He's going to be a great man. This one may grow up to be President." "She didn't know," Jeremy said with his blue eyes twinkling, "that I was going to grow up to be an anti-president."

On Sunday evening during dinner at a Lebanese restaurant on Connecticut Avenue, all of us were sore and tired from the March, but happy to be together. We were entertained by Hadi's description of the first days of the Crawford Peace House and his tales of Najurdin, the Sufi fool of God. Hadi, a Muslim who grew up in Pakistan but became a U.S. citizen after college, met Valley at a dream workshop she was teaching in Dallas.

"We always expected big crowds to come to Crawford," Hadi told us over steaming plates of kibbi and baba ghanooj. All of us were howling with laughter by the time he finished telling how he and his friend Johnny had set out from Crawford one day in Johnny's pickup with a topical map of the Crawford area. This was before the Peace House was purchased, two years before Camp Casey, but Johnny and Hadi wanted to study how 500,000 people might be safely accommodated in the area.

It was near dark, Hadi said, when Johnny stopped for a last look at the map, dark enough that Hadi, who was riding in the passenger seat, couldn't see the map clearly. Johnny told him there was a flashlight in the glove box, but when it didn't work, switched on the dome light. Suddenly Hadi thought of something. "Maybe this isn't such a good idea," he told his friend. They were parked just outside the Bush ranch. "What do you think the Secret Service might make of two guys in a pickup truck, one of them obviously Middle Eastern, looking at a map outside the ranch, eh?"

"The Peace House has always been a magical place," Valley chimed in. "Before Camp Casey we had no money. The phone was about to be cut off."

"But now," Hadi said, "we finished paying off the mortgage, all from contributions people made."

Before we left the restaurant that night, I asked Jeremy what he wanted for his birthday. He had elected to celebrate with lunch in the cafeteria of the new Museum of the American Indian on the Mall. "Oh, I guess an Indian maiden to sing, "Happy Birthday" to me," he replied.

Back in our shared hotel room, Jody and I had months of news to catch up on. Like Valley, Jody and I and others on the Peace Bridge had found ourselves increasingly involved in local issues over the past year, in addition to our work on the Peace Bridge. Just days before her trip to Washington, Jody had been taped, along with Iraq war veteran and congressional contender Paul Hackett, for a CNN special called "Voices From the Home Front." Jody's son David was serving a second deployment to Iraq as a U.S. Army Reserve emergency physician.

By this time other members of the Peace Bridge, all opposed to the war, were also suffering the agony of having their children serve in the military. The Peace Bridge offered a refuge and support. When the CNN show aired in October, it was seen all over the world. In addition to friends telling her they had seen her live on the big screen as they walked through airports, Jody received a message from Ilkin on the Peace Bridge discussion list saying excitedly, "Is that you?" The program had aired in Turkey as well.

Jeremy's birthday party was all that Peace Train riders could ever have wished for. A tiny lounge, hidden away upstairs in the museum, provided a place for us to gather for a meditation undisturbed by museum visitors. We shared a brief moment of song. "Peace is Flowing Like a River" did not seem at all out of place in the quiet of the museum. Then downstairs to the cafeteria, where we heaped our plates with Native recipes. At the end of our lunch, one of the cafeteria workers came to brush off a table nearby. She commented on how much fun we were having. "It's Jeremy's birthday," Jody told her.

"Are you the Indian maiden?" I couldn't help but ask.

Turns out she was. This beautiful woman became an instant part of the group. She shared with us her Native American lineage to back before slavery, helped us to sing "Happy Birthday" to a disbelieving Jeremy, and then commented that in Louisiana, where she grew up, people said a person's age should be measured not in years, but in the number of friends he had. Life is but a dream, we reminded Jeremy as his Indian Maiden walked away.

I had the opportunity to introduce the World Dreams Peace Bridge to my local group of Peace activists, the Tidewater Peace Alliance, in December when we produced a month-long "Light in the Dark: A Festival for Peace" in Norfolk, Virginia with films, seminars, discussion and dance. The Festival was a feat of back-breaking labor, entirely created between the first of October and the first of December, but worth every minute of the work when I introduced Valley and Hadi to an audience of sixty-five or seventy people at the Studio for the Healing Arts, owned by another Peace Bridge member, David Gordon.

I was proud when Hadi explained after a screening of the new DVD, "Skip for Peace," created to picture life at Camp Casey, that it was the women who had organized and managed things there. "Strong women," he said. "Women should always run things. They are better at it than men."

And I was proud when Valley mentioned the World Dreams Peace Bridge and its role in creating peace. But I was completely satisfied when I saw the expression on Tench Phillips' face. Tench is the owner of the Naro Theater. He had introduced the idea of the Festival and provided films for discussions and seminars. At dinner following Valley and Hadi's presentation, Tench turned to me and said, "So how long have you known Valley? Seems like the two of you know each other pretty well."

"I met Valley in 2000, at the International Association for the Study of Dreams conference in Washington, D.C.," I told him. "We'd never seen each other, but she told me she had dreamed me before the conference. We've been good friends ever since then. We often dream together."

The Peace Train keeps rolling, filled with dreams. As part of the Peace Festival, we sold Peace Train place mats, laminated Peace Train art from around the world to raise funds for the children in Iraq. After the Festival was over, I agreed to conduct a Peace Train workshop for the lower-school children at the Virginia Beach Friends School.

This particular Quaker school was a model of what the Peace Train can accomplish. In 2003, Victoria Quinton created the Lorikeet Peace Train. The lorikeet is a beautiful, colorful bird indigenous to Australia. Along with her own children's Peace Train cars, Victoria sent a small, stuffed toy lorikeet and a notebook for messages when she sent the train to a friend in the United States. Following that, the train was sent to me. I asked a friend who taught at the Friends School if her sixth-grade students might be interested in creating some train cars.

Not only were they interested, but after the train cars were made—rainbows on wheels in many cases—and the students had been photographed with the lorikeet, their teacher carried the growing train home with her to Trinidad. There another sixth grade class added their cars to the train, photographed the lorikeet playing the steel drum and doing other fun things, and sent the package back to Virginia Beach. This was the Peace Train I brought with me to the Friends School workshop. Students could see what had happened to the lorikeet in its travels and also create more cars for the train. In the process, the children thought about what peace might look like if they could really send it around the world. They watched the World Dreams PowerPoint presentation, which contains photos of children making Peace Trains and photos of children in Iraq. They asked provocative questions.

The World Dreams Peace Bridge is not a very large group by any standard but it is filled with dreams and dreams are big. A group of people dreaming together can accomplish quite a lot.

Chapter Sixteen - The Dream Goes On

When I began to write this book, without thinking much about it, I invited one hundred of my closest friends to read the manuscript online, chapter-by-chapter, as I produced it. This made sense to me, since I was talking about a lot of people in the book, and wanted to make sure that I got things right. What I had failed to consider was that the Book Club, as I began to call the seventy or so people who accepted my invitation to read, would begin dreaming with me, dreaming the book along together, as if to underscore the importance of group dreaming.

The night I made the decision to write the book, I had the following dream:

I am working in the East Coast office of the International Association for the Study of Dreams. (In fact, there is only one IASD office, located in Californiat). We are preparing for a conference. A woman comes into my office, someone I don't know in waking life but knew well in the dream, and had not seen for some time. We embrace enthusiastically. Then we are joined by another woman, who hugs us both. Music begins to play, and the three of us begin to dance, a triad. We move out into the outer office, where other people form triads and begin to dance as well.

As a group, we move out into the hallway, a long hall in an office building. We pick up more people along the way. Approaching us, a man is pushing a heavy, industrial paper cutter. The dancers part to let him by, but he is coming directly toward my triad. We catch the man and his paper cutter up in the dance, and easily move the heavy piece of equipment down the hallway.

The group dances out the front door of the building, down the stairs, and into a city street. Soon all of the people in the city are dancing in triads, thousands of them, as far as the eye can see.

Now, it is not particularly unusual for me to dream of dancing. Members of the World Dreams Peace Bridge have been submitting dancing dreams for a long time. In fact recently there has been an increased number of these dreams due to a new member of the discussion group, Lana from Amman, Jordan. Lana is a graduate student who supports herself by dancing, particularly belly dancing. There had been a recent discussion in the group, which I found fascinating, about the many different words for love in the Arabic language, and how these words relate to sacred temple dances, which evolved into belly dancing.

I met Lana in one of those moments of synchronistic clarity when, pushed into the same corner at a crowded IASD conference volunteer reception, we exchanged polite information about our backgrounds. As soon as she said she was from Jordan, I asked, "You speak Arabic, right?"

"Yes."

"Would you be interested in doing some translation work?" I was about to begin sending the instructions for the eight-week Crystal Birds Dream Program to Baghdad. Lana enthusiastically agreed to translate. She told me one of her own dreams is to get funding for a program she has named, "Dancing Around the World Barefoot for Peace."

So I attributed my dancing dream to the ongoing Bridge conversation until the next day when, after I sent out the book invitations I received a phone call from my friend, Wendy Pannier. Wendy has been a Friend of the Bridge from the beginning, but too busy to participate in group discussion. "Oh, so that's why I dreamed last night about women dancing," she exclaimed when she heard about my dream. Later that day, in conversation with another friend, I learned that she too had dreamed the night before of the dancing women.

What was the significance of this shared dream? I can think of two immediate meanings or messages that are social rather than personal in their implication. One is a message that has been part of the World Dreams Peace Bridge since its inception, first appearing in Sandy Ginsberg's dream of Beau Bridges wearing lipstick. "Beautiful bridges," Sandy had said, but also "the need to feminize the masculine." This message has been repeated in one dream after another. More than one Bridge member has dreamed of the golden circle of women even before joining the Bridge. There has been so much written about the dance of life that this symbol barely needs explanation, but the need for women to become the peacemakers, to become the leaders seems an important one.

The other message in the dream is one that Anna put quite succinctly in her post to the Peace Bridge after seeing an earlier version of the dancing dream. "I can't help it," she said. "Every time I see the word abundance now, I read a-BUN-dance! All these dancing women!"

The subject of abundance, and the importance of abundance to world peace, has come up repeatedly on the World Dreams Peace Bridge, because what dreams offer us, no matter what type of dreams they might be, is abundance—an abundance of information, an abundance of alternatives, and an abundance of flexibility. Particularly if one happens to believe that together we are dreaming the world, it is important to connect with this message from dreams. Our dreams tell us that solutions to problems can be found and that health can be regained if we only pay attention to the suggestions of the dreamer. In fact, in a joking way, early in the days of the Peace Bridge, I suggested that maybe we should each sleep with a dollar, a peso, a yen under our pillows to see what would happen. Several people did it. And several people reported beneficial results. The abundant nature of dreams was discernable immediately in the process of writing this book.

On January 12, 2006, a day or two after I began writing, Diana sent me the following note:

Last night I dreamt a group of people, including myself, were playing a game that used cards. The deck was oversized, like tarot cards, with standard backing. On the front of the cards were colorful art works, all objects, like a memory game. It was played in a couple of rounds. Some cards were repetitive, so holders could have similar cards. Six cards were distributed, and each holder had to create an impromptu story of the objects in their hand, in the order they were received. The winner was the one who told the best stories.

A few days later, Diana dreamed about the cover of the book:

...at this point I realized that it is a train (we are riding on). I'm not sure if it was Liz or you who accompanied me, but I know it was a member of the World Dreams Peace Bridge, a feeling of strong female presence to my right. We are seated in a car directly opposite Richard (Wilkerson) from IASD. There is a book on the table. The title has the word Peace in it, and the book is blue (to tell me it is an important item). Then Richard grabs my hand and the hand of the person seated to the right, and proceeds to say an eloquent prayer/blessing of this purpose and journey. When he is done speaking I say "Amen."

It was not at all surprising to me that Diana could not tell whether the other person in her dream was Liz or me, as I had just asked Liz to create the cover for the book.

I knew that I had found exactly the right publisher in Susan Andrus at Wordminder Press when we got together for the first meeting about the book. Even though I had not yet told her about my ambitious goal to complete the manuscript in six weeks, and we had never dreamed together, Susan said to me, "I had a dream last night." In the dream, Susan and another woman (Guess who my candidate for this dream character was?) were being chased by men with dogs. The two women came to a high wall that completely blocked their passage. At first, Susan thought they were doomed, but then she decided to try climbing the wall. It was much easier than she thought it would be. When she got to the top, she said to the other woman, "Here, let me lift you up." With Susan's help, the other woman climbed to the top of the wall and the two went forward into safety.

As soon as I began sending out chapters of the book to the Book Club, people began to respond with their dreams. "Did I ever send you the dream I had about a first contact between the Powhatans and the English?" Curt Hoffman wrote to me in mid-January. "The Ten Little Indians dream at the end of Chapter Two reminded me of it." Curt is the archaeologist hosting the 2006 IASD conference, whose discovery of the sighting stones is mentioned earlier in the book. He and I have dreamed together more than once. Recently Curt sent his friend, Mary Whitefeather, to the Peace Bridge. Mary and I began immediately speculating about the further unfolding of this particular set of dreams and arabesques, as each of us feels that something important is happening.

In February Yvonne sent me a note.

Yesterday while reading, a question jumped to my mind. "Do you recall your dreams of last February?" I didn't, so I went to my dream diary and opened it to February '05. And I realized I'd dreamt about visiting you: I am walking around a pond and decide to sit down on a big rock next to a lovely tree. Someone approaches from the back. When I turn around, it is you. I am so glad to see you and happy to be in an endeavor together again.

In early March, I received a note from Evelyn Duesbury, one of several Book Club members who were kind enough to do a line-by-line editing of the manuscript. She apologized that she would not be able to line edit the final chapters as thoroughly as the first ones, because not only was she busy with a book project of her own, but she was also getting ready to move. Having done some copy editing professionally, I wanted to tell Evelyn what a gift she had already given me. She also sent along a dream from March 6, which revealed her feelings even more clearly:

I have two table-like desks along the wall here. Two women workers come over and are working at one of my desks. They are friendly with me, and I am friendly with them, but they keep taking more of the room here in my area. I am pushed over so I have only a portion of one of the desk tops. I kindly ask them to move back. Uncertain whether they do move back though.

The chapter "The Family That Dreams Together" prompted a number of dreams and dream stories from the Book Club, particularly that section of the chapter that deals with dreaming of unborn children. I should mention that one reader asked me if we shouldn't categorize these dreams as dreaming about rather than dreaming with. But I disagree. To the extent that group dreaming implies the fact that time and space may be more flexible than we currently believe, it implies that dreaming across the boundaries of time and space may be quite possible. Of course, at that point, there is an entirely separate discussion to be had about the relationship between the born and the unborn, but we won't go there.

Kotaro wrote on January 26, "As I read this, a personal memory came up to my mind. It is an event at the time when I requested a reading from Poseidia Institute. It was the spring of 1984."

In those days I had read the books related to Edgar Cayce again. I began to keep a dream diary at the same time. After several months, my wife got pregnant. It was a certain summer. In the dream, early morning, I saw my wife's red bicycle knocking down sidewise. It was a vision to make me scared even in the dream. I woke up and soon arrived at the office; however, the dream was not forgotten. Then it was too shocking to keep silence. I called her up and told her not to handle luggage today, because I saw the warning sign in the dream that morning.

By the time Kotaro returned home, his wife was crying. Even though she had paid attention to his warning and been careful and gentle with herself, she had to be hospitalized and then confined to bed for a month in order to carry the baby to full term. "Moreover," Kotaro continued, "the dream at the last few weeks of that year is not forgotten."

I was in the meadow that had been assumed to be spacious. The sky was clear completely in deep blue, and a strong wind blew. I see when there was intuitively Mongolia. At the left hand the brigade of people was seen to move to the right hand. The wagon that holds the tent and furniture and household goods, a lot of sheep and people were moving slowly. I noticed though that I was watching a small girl, who stood in the group that moved. I approached the girl and watched her face. It was very cute. She had on the clothes of Mongolia and a hat of blue and red wool. She looked up with a smile. I asked her in my mind, "Is it you?" She was only smiling.

When Kotaro's baby son was around a year old, the family went on a shopping excursion, the baby tucked into his wife's backpack, wearing a knitted cap his wife had made. "Then I saw my son's face with the wool hat," Kotaro wrote. "It was the face of the girl from my dream."

In February, Laura wrote: "In January 1989, when I was nineteen years old, I dreamed of giving birth to a healthy, blue-eyed, blonde-haired boy. Less than a week later, doctors confirmed that I was pregnant. Months later—wahh-lahh—a nine pound, blue-eyed, blonde-haired boy."

Her own baby, Laura said, was not the only infant she dreamed in utero.

I've dreamed my close friends having children (accurate to the weight of the baby) and told a handful of close women friends they were pregnant before they announced it publicly, so much so that I was un-invited to participate in baby pools at work! The most fun and significant dreams I had of a co-worker. In one dream, she was pushing a stroller with a little girl in it. I went to work and told her. The next night, a dream of the same woman, but she was picking out little blue outfits. I apologized to her, saying I guess my baby psi-dreams were off. Well, to our mutual pleasant surprise—TWINS—a boy and a girl.

The chapter on family dreaming produced another surprise, not just for me but for one of my readers. In selecting the people for the Book Club, I wanted to invite a few people who were not part of the book, and not even especially interested in dreams, just to see how they would respond to the material. One of these, a woman I met through peace activities rather than dream activities, responded enthusiastically from the beginning, and told me she had started recording her dreams early on in her reading of the manuscript. Not long after reading the family dreaming chapter, she told a dream to her college-age son. "Oh, yeah," he replied. "I used to have that dream all the time."

The number of dreams related to the manuscript could fill a small book all by themselves, but there were other events happening as well. I was happy to locate many of the participants in the original Dreams to the Tenth Power experiments to invite them to read the manuscript. Some, like Scott Sparrow, I had not been in touch with for a long time but they were easy enough to locate via the Internet. I was glad to find Tony Crisp who, since his participation in the dream researcher aspect of the Dreams to the Tenth Power experiments, had written numerous books about dreams, including a very popular dream dictionary. There were several people I could not locate, of course.

At the end of February though, halfway through writing the manuscript, I received a surprise e-mail from someone who had been instrumental in the work on Dreams[10], with whom I had lost contact over thirty years earlier, when we closed Poseidia Institute. She just happened to find me. Suzanne Keyes, whose connection with the Dreams to the Tenth Power experiments is discussed in Chapter six, wrote:

Hello Jean!

I was part of your Dreams[10] experiments at Poseidia Institute in the 80s. I've moved and moved and moved and am just getting to some boxes that have been shuffled around. One of them is full of dream paper work....

Suzanne found me through a Google search. "I wanted to say hello and get back in touch with you and thank you for your encouragement and the interesting ideas and experiences you brought me," she said. Little did she know the interesting experience she had just walked into. Naturally, I sent her the manuscript, along with a good laugh.

What conclusions can be drawn from all of the stories told here in this book?

Does group dreaming really exist?

Based on the evidence presented here, not to mention the volumes of uncollected data that we can assume to be available, I think it would be foolish to deny the existence of group dreaming though some will undoubtedly continue to do so. The implications of group dreaming for our understanding of space, time, the nature of consciousness and the nature of reality itself are clear and extensive, requiring a true paradigm shift.

Can anyone learn to do group dreaming?

The answer to this question seems to be that there is no learned skill in group dreaming. Apparently shared social dreams occur spontaneously and frequently. The real skill is in becoming conscious of the dreams. This is the difference between believing that all dreams rise from the unconscious and believing that dreamers have the ability to become conscious of the dreaming process.

Even then, we must remember that there are two distinct types of shared dreams: what Linda Magallón calls "meeting" and "meshing" dreams. In the first type of dream, not only do dreamers dream of one another, but they share a waking memory of having dreamed together. In the second type of shared dream, which seems to be the more common of the two, shared dream symbols mesh to create a broader picture or a deeper understanding of the facts.

Dream lucidity is not a function of shared dreaming, but by its nature can be utilized by the dreamer as a tool for developing consciousness. Dream lucidity is a skill that dreamers can learn. Another tool that can be utilized is dream incubation, or focusing on the intention of the dream while awake.

Are all characters or people we meet in dreams just other people we don't know when we're awake, but might meet later?

Although apparently some people we meet in dream state are people we know or can meet when we are awake, I do not believe that reduces or significantly alters the need for dreams to be understood or interpreted. The foundation of group dreaming appears to be agreement. That is, at some level of consciousness, generally unconscious to us, we can agree to share dreams with others and conversely, we can disagree to do so.

To the extent that this is true, the agreements are made for a reason, often because the dreamers want to learn something or create something. Examining the dream, exploring and interpreting it, can give us insight into our own meaning making. This aspect of group dreaming is no different from any other type of dreaming, as all dream content reflects personal information, no matter the social context.

We must not forget the flexibility and creativity allowed by dreams, which in many cases can be used to rehearse or explore waking-life solutions. There are also, I believe, due to this very flexibility, dreams which are simply for fun and for en-joyment, or learning how to be joyful. The people in our dreams may or may not be people we know now in waking life or will meet in the future, but all dream characters who appear in our dreams seem to do so with our agreement.

Does group dreaming mean that anything we dream could come true?

Essentially the answer to this question is yes, or as singer James Brown would say, "In order to believe, we must first conceive." But as the DaFuMu dreaming of the World Dreams Peace Bridge demonstrates, applying dream solutions to waking-life problems does not always produce a direct or straight-line result. Self-understanding and self-awareness are the keys to this process. For example, it does no good to dream of being an astronaut if some part of the construct called the self is afraid of flying. Before a dream can come true, it is necessary for all aspects of the self to be in agreement. Of course, this is the challenge of dreaming itself – to integrate the personality.

If this is true on an individual basis, then think how much more challenging it must be on a social level, where—if in fact we are dreaming the world—all dreamers sharing the thought or idea of doing something must agree, both individually and on the social level.

Yet, as Kathy Turner points out, DaFuMu dreaming may be revolutionary, even evolutionary, as it allows the individual dreamer a way to share with the group a conscious intent for change.

What is the value of group dreaming?

Once we have accepted the existence of group dreaming, the value of this type of dreaming in any social interaction becomes readily evident. Whether in the context of the family, a business, or a Peace Bridge, the addition of dream sharing and shared dreams immediately brings all interaction to a deeper level, what one might call the level of the heart, or feelings. No matter what our thinking mind might tell us about a particular situation or what to do in that situation, the awakened heart of the dreamer, once encouraged, generally does not lie.

In the Dreams to the Tenth Power experiments conducted at Poseidia Institute, participants, even those who had never met except in dreams, tended to become close to one another and felt they knew one another more deeply than they knew people in more mundane interactions. In an extended group setting like the World Dreams Peace Bridge, where dreams are shared over a long period of time, this depth of emotional contact is even more marked. If more groups of people in more social situations were to begin to share dreams in this manner, I believe that the change in social patterns could be dramatic.

Another factor to be considered is the synergy of group creativity. One dreamer, acting alone, can accomplish a lot; but dreamers working together, sharing their dreams, honoring their dreams, perhaps can change the world.

I would like to thank all of the people who have contributed to this book, all of the dreamers who have shared their dreams and all of those who have added to the knowledge of the dreaming process. I would like to extend a special thanks to the readers of the Book Club for editorial comments, copyediting, and hand-holding. When I first decided to ask so many people to read the pre-publication manuscript, some of my writing friends were shocked. How would I ever be able to deal with so many comments, so many editors, they asked? I would surely be spending all my time just writing to readers. But they didn't know dreamers, I would tell them, at least not the dreamers I know, who not only offered helpful words and encouragement, but supported me with their very dreams.

The people of the Peace Bridge have been generous with their time and with their love as always. There are many people on the Peace Bridge who have not been mentioned even once in this book, since I was using only some stories from the group to illustrate a broad spectrum of ideas. Also, some members of the Peace Bridge seldom speak, even on the Bridge. For these people, I would like to say: "Listening is the highest form of hospitality."

Special thanks go to Harry Bosma, who pushed me over the edge by insisting that I start writing. Harry recently sent me a note saying,

I think my next dream project will blend day-to-day politics with dreams. Years ago I had a dream where a woman sighs that it's better to be a man. This dream woman looked a lot like a real world woman, smart, strong, creative, well ahead of almost anybody else. In the dream I disagreed with her, but it got me thinking, and the dream has been haunting me ever since.

I hope this idea results in a book too.

And very special thanks go to Liz Diaz, whose remarkable graphic skills created the design for this book, while with her usual steadiness she accompanied me through this project, as she has through many others. Thanks to my publisher Susan Andrus for her willingness to produce a book in a fraction of the time it generally takes for book production and thanks to you, the reader.

The dreaming on the Peace Bridge continues, of course. All dreamers are welcome there. Just as the Peace Bridge began with a dream from Victoria Quinton, it seems appropriate to end with one of her recent dreams, sent to the Bridge at the beginning of March 2006.

> I had an odd snippet when I had a sudden headache and needed to rest briefly over the weekend. I was in a cave, perhaps in the desert, and I entered despite my fear, because Osama bin Laden was there. I put up my right hand and said, "Stop—don't act in fear." Then I undid the turban from his head and used it as a blindfold and said, "Now slow down and try seeing with your heart, not your eyes."

> The snippet ended; so did my headache and the "sudden tiredness."

You may have noticed that a percentage of the sale price of this book will go directly to the Aid for Traumatized Children Project of the World Dreams Peace Bridge. This work is supported by The iMAGE Project, the nonprofit which I direct. Tax-deductible contributions to the Aid for Traumatized Children Project are welcome, and can be made directly to The iMAGE Project at www.imageproject.org, helping dreams come true for the children of the world.

End Notes

Chapter One: The Experiment Begins

1. Zweig, Connie. "'See You In My Dreams' Test Works." *Brain Mind Bulletin* 10:1, Oct 1984, 3.

Chapter Two: We Meet at the Clock Tower

1. Noumenon is the Greek term for the nonmaterial, just as phenomenon is the word for material existence.

Chapter Six: Some Unexpected Results of Dreams[10]

1. Donahoe, James. "Exploring Mutual Dreaming." *Psychic* Nov./Dec. 1975, 23.

2. Reed, Henry, Interview, *Dream Network Journal.* http://www.starbuck .net/henryreed /new/documents.

3. Barasch, Marc, "A Hitchhiker's Guide to Dreamland," *New Age Journal* Oct 1983, 39.

Chapter Seven: The Language of Group Dreaming

1.Whorf, Benjamin, "Language, Mind and Reality," *The Theosophist* 1942: 63, 284.

2. Capra, Fritjof. *Uncommon Wisdom: Conversations with Remarkable People.* (New York: Bantam, 1989), 65.

3. Pearson, Cynthia. "Earwigs and Arabesques: Dreaming in the Multiverse. Paper presented at the Association for the Study of Dreams Conference 1998 <http://www.nauticom .net/www/netcadet/asd98>.

4. Magallón, Linda L. *Psychic Creative Dreaming: An Explorer's Guide to the Dream Net.* (LL Magallón, 1997), <http://members.aol.com/caseyflyer /flying/dreams04>.

5. Donahoe, James. *Dream Reality.* (Oakland: Bench, 1979), 5.

6. Magallón, Linda L. *Mutual Dreaming.* (New York: Pocket Books, 1997), 25.

7. LaBerge, Stephen, Paul Tholey, and Brigitte Holzinger. Conversation Between Stephen LaBerge and Paul Tholey. July 1989. Association for the Study of Dreams Conference, 1989, <http://www.sawka.com/spiritwatch /conversa>.

8. Sparrow, G. Scott. "Letter From Scott Sparrow." *Lucidity Letter.* Online posting <http://www.sawka.com/spiritwatch/letter_from_scott_sparrow>.

9. Kellogg, Ed. "A Mutual Lucid Dream Event." *Dream Time* 1, no.2 (Spring 1997): 32.

10. Ibid., 34.

Chapter Eight: Spontaneously Shared Dreaming

1. Wilkerson, Richard. "Dream Cyberphile." *Dream Time* 17, no. 1 (Winter 2000): 31.

2. Hicks, Chris. "Dream Line: O.J. Simpson Dreams." *Electric Dreams* 2, no. 13 (October 1995) . http://www.dreamgate.com/dream/ed-articles/ed2-13h/.

3. Roberts, Maureen, "Dreams, Death, and Diana: Lessons in Personal and Collective Healing." *Electric Dreams* 4, no. 9 Sept. 28, 1997. <http://www.dreamgate.com /dream/ed-articles/esl4-9rob>.

4. Wolf, Fred A. *The Dreaming Universe.* (New York: Simon & Schuster, 1984), 43.

5. Ullman, Montague. "A Group Approach to the Anomalous Dream." *Dream Telepathy* 2nd edition. (New York: Macmillan, 1973). Appendix D.

6. Roberts, Jane. *Dreams, "Evolution" and Value Fulfillment, Vol II.* (New York: Prentice Hall, 1986), 64.

Chapter Nine: The Family that Dreams Together

1. Taylor, Jeremy. *Where People Fly and Water Runs Uphill.* (New York: Warner, 1984), 129.

2. Epel, Naomi. *Writers Dreaming.* (New York: Carol Southern, 1983), 20.

3. Schwarz, Berthold E. *Parent Child Telepathy.* (New York: Garrett, 1971), 15.

4. Epel, 48.

5. Siegel, Alan. "Presidential Interview: Rev. Jeremy Taylor." *ASD Newsletter* 11, no.. 4 (Fall, 1994), 6.

6. L'Engle, Madeline. *Walking on Water.* (New York: Bantam, 1980), 102.

7. Bynum, Edward Bruce. *Families and the Interpretation of Dreams.* (New York: Harrington Park, 1993). 101.

8. Magallón, Linda L. *Mutual Dreaming,* 256.

9. Gackenbach, Jayne. "Thoughts about Dreamwork with the Central Alberta Cree." http://www.sawka.com/spiritwatch.

10. Siegel, Alan. "ASD Presidential Interview of Kelly Bulkeley, Ph.D." *Dream Time* 14, no. 3&4 (Summer/Fall 1997), 38.

11. Gregory, Jill. "Bringing Dreams to Kids." *Electric Dreams* 1, no. 18. <http://www.dreamgate.com/dream/ed-articles/ed1-18jg>.

Chapter Ten: Dreaming the World

1. Ossana, Roberta. "Dreams and Mythology Alive!" *Dream Network* 17, no. 3 18.

2. Ornstein, Robert. In forward to LaBerge, Stephen. *Lucid Dreaming.* (Los Angeles: Tarcher, 1985).

3. Magallón, Linda L. *Psychic Creative Dreaming: An Explorer's Guide to the Dream Net.*

4. Hunt, Harry. *The Multiplicity of Dreams.* (New Haven: Yale, 1989).

5. Seachrist, Elsie. *Dreams Your Magic Mirror.* New York: Dell, 1968, 28.

6. Roberts, Jane. *Dreams, "Evolution" and Value Fulfillment,* 43.

7. Varela, Francisco, ed. *Sleeping, Dreaming and Dying.* (Boston: Wisdom Publications, 1999), 7.

8. Ibid.,128.

9. Ibid, 129.

10 Gackenbach, Jayne. "Thoughts about Dreamwork with the Central Alberta Cree." http://www.sawka.com/spiritwatch, 1996.

11. Hoffman, Curtiss. Unpublished manuscript.

12. Moss, Robert. "When We Become a Dreaming Culture." <http://www.mossdreams.com>.

13. Beradt, Charlotte. *The Third Reich of Dreams.* Translated by Ariadne Gottwald. (Chicago: Quadrangle, 1966), 8.

14. Ibid., 8

15. Ibid., 10

16. Ibid., 10

17. Van der Post, Laurens. *Jung and the Story of Our Time.* (New York: Random House/Pantheon, 1975), 123.

18. Ossana, Roberta. "Dreaming in Dundee, New York: Interview with Susan Watkins." *Dream Network* 15 no.1. http://www.dreamwork.net/watkins.

19. Ibid.

20. Ibid.

Chapter Eleven: In the Wake of 9/11

1. Vanlaeys, Emily. *Dream Weaving: Using Dream Guidance to Create Life's Tapestry.* (Virginia Beach: ARE, 2001), 154.

Chapter Twelve: Creating A Peace Bridge

1. Ginsberg, Sandra J. "Honoring the Dream." *Dream Time* 17 no. 2 (Spring 2000), 9.

2. Guiley, Rosemary Ellen. *The Dreamer's Way: Using Proactive Dreaming to Heal and Transform Your Life.* (New York: Berkley, 2004), 224.

3. Ibid., 233.

Works Cited

Anderson, Walter Truett. *The Upstart Spring: Esalen and the American Wakening*. Reading: Addison-Westly, 1983.

Barasch, Marc Ian. "A Hitchiker's Guide to Dreamland." *New Age Journal* Oct.1983, 39-50.

_____, *Healing Dreams: Exploring the Dreams that Can Transform Your Life*. New York: Berkley, 2000.

Beradt, Charlotte. *The Third Reich of Dreams*. Translated by Ariadne Gottwald. Chicago: Quadrangle, 1966.

Bro, Harmon. *Edgar Cayce on Dreams*. New York: Werner, 1968.

Bynum, Edward Bruce. *Families and the Interpretation of Dreams*. New York: Harrington Park, 1993.

Campbell, Jean. *Dreams Beyond Dreaming*. Norfolk: Donning, 1989.

_____. "Dealing With Precognitive Dreamer Guilt." <http://dreamtalk .hypermart.net/campbell/dreamer_guilt.htm>.

_____. "Dreaming Together." *Dream Network Bulletin*, Sept, 1983, 2.

_____. "Dreams and the Children of Baghdad: Dream Activism from the World Dreams Peace Bridge." *Dream Time* 22, no. 1, (Spring 2005), 20-23.

_____. "Group Dreaming Research Report." *Dream Craft*. 2:2:1, 3-4.

_____. "The View From the Bridge." <http://www. worlddreamspeacebridge.org>

Capra, Fritjof, *Uncommon Wisdom: Conversations with Remarkable People*. New York: Bantam, 1989.

Castaneda, Carlos. *The Teachings of Don Juan: A Yaqui Way of Knowledge*. Berkeley: Univ. of California. 1969.

Danna, Theresa M. "The Children of Our Dreams." *Electric Dreams*. 4, no. 2, Feb. 1997 <http://www.dreamgate.com/dream/ed-articles/ed4-2 chi.htm>.

Domhoff, G. William. *The Mystique of Dreams: A Search for Utopia Through Senoi Dream Theory*. Berkeley: U of California, 1985.

_____. "Senoi, Kilton Stewart and the Mystique of Dreams: Further Thoughts on an Allegory about an Allegory." <http://www.sawka.com /spiritwatch/senoi>.

Donahoe, James. *Dream Reality*. Oakland: Bench, 1979.

_____. *Enigma*. Oakland: Bench, 1979.

_____. "Exploring Mutual Dreaming." *Psychic* November/December, 1975: 23-25.

Elgin, Suzette Haden. *Native Tongue*. New York: DAW, 1984.

Epel, Naomi. *Writers Dreaming*. New York: Carol Southern, 1983.

Farady, Ann. *Dream Power*. New York: Berkley, 1973.

_____. Letter to the author. December 28, 1981.

Finer, Johathan and Omar Fekeiki. "Iraq's Crisis of Scarred Psyches." *Washington Post.* March 26, 2006, A1.

Freud, Sigmund. *New Introductory Lectures on Psychoanalysis*, Translated by Strachey et al. New York: Norton, 1990.

Gackenbach, Jayne. "Princess Diana's Death as a Ripple in the Collective Field of Consciousness: Personal Ruminations in the Context of my Work with the Cree." *Electric Dreams* 4, no. 9 September 28, 1997. <http://www.dreamgate .com/dream/ed-articles/ed4-9gac>.

_____. "Thoughts about Dreamwork with the Central Alberta Cree." In ed Kelly Bulkeley. *Among All These Dreamers: Essays on Dreaming and Modern Society.* New York: SUNY Press. <http://www.sawka.com/spiritwatch>

Garfield, Patricia. *The Dream Book: A Young Person's Guide to Understanding Dreams.* Toronto: Tundra, 2002.

Garfield, Patricia, Judith Malamud, Jean Campbell, Anne Sayre Wiseman, and Gordon Halliday. "Mental Health Applications (of Dreams): A Panel Discussion." Presented at ASDII 1984. <http://www.sawka.com/ spiritwatch/mentalhealthapplications>.

Ginsberg, Sandra J. "Honoring the Dream." *Dream Time* 17, no. 2, Spring 2000, 9-11.

Grant, Joan. *Eyes of Horus.* New York: Avon, 1969.

Gregory, Jill. "Bringing Dreams to Kids. *Electric Dreams* 1, no. 18. <http:// www.dreamgate.com/dream/ed-articles/ed1-18jg>

Guiley, Rosemary Ellen. *The Dreamers Way: Using Proactive Dreaming to Heal and Transform Your Life.* New York: Berkley, 2004.

Hicks, Chris. "Dream Line: O. J. Simpson Dreams." *Electric Dreams* 2:13 October 1995. <http://www.dreamgate.com/dream/ed-articles/ed2-13hl>.

Hunt, Harry. *The Multiplicity of Dreams.* New Haven: Yale, 1989.

Jung, Carl G. *Memories, Dreams, Reflections.* Translated by Richard and Clara Winston. New York: Vintage, 1989.

Kellogg, Ed. "A Mutual Lucid Dream Event." *Dream Time* 1, no. 2, Spring 1997, 32-34.

Kelly, Kathy. *Other Lands Have Dreams: From Baghdad to Pekin Prison.* Petrolia: Counterpunch, 2005.

Keyes, Suzanne. "Letter From the Editor." *Dream Craft* 1, 6-8.

Krippner, Stanley, ed. *Dreamtime and Dreamwork.* Los Angeles: Tarcher, 1990.

Krippner, Stanley and Teresa McIntyre, eds. *The Psychological Impact of War Trauma on Civilians: An International Perspective.* New York: Prager, 2003.

Kuhn, Thomas. *The Structure of Scientific Revolution.* Chicago: U of Chicago, 1987.

LaBerge, Stephen, Paul Tholey, and Brigitte Holzinger. "Conversation Between Stephen LaBerge and Paul Tholey in July of 1989." Interview at Association for the Study of Dreams Conference, 1989. <http://www.sawka.com /spiritwatch/conversa>.

LaBerge, Stephen. *Lucid Dreaming*. Los Angeles: Tarcher, 1985.

L'Engle, Madeline. *Walking on Water*. New York: Bantam, 1980.

Lowen, Alexander. *Bioenergetics*. New York: Penguin, 1973.

Lusson Twins. *The Beginning or the End: Where are we Going?* Virginia Beach: Donning, 1975.

Magallón, Linda L. "Goodbye Group Mind: Dream Trek Column." *Electric Dreams* 4 no., 5, May 28, 1997. <http://members.tripod.com/~rickc250/ed4-5mag.htm>.

_____. "Mutual Dreamers Reunion." http://members.aol.com /caseyflyer /flying/dreams23.

_____. *Mutual Dreaming*. New York: Pocket Books, 1997.

_____. "Play Day and Fly In: Waking State and Dream Group Project." <http://members.aol.com/caseyflyer/flying/dreams24>.

_____. *Psychic Creative Dreaming: An Explorer's Guide to the Dream Net*. LL Magallón, 1997. <http://members.aol.com/caseyflyer /flying/dreams04>.

Magallón, Linda L. and Barbara Shor. "Shared Dreaming: Joining Together in the Dreamtime." In Krippner, S. ed. *Dreamtime and Dreamwork*. Los Angeles: Tarcher, 1990.

Mallon, Brenda. *Dream Time with Children: Learning to Dream, Dreaming to Learn*. Philadelphia: Jessica Kingsley, 2002.

Moss, Robert. *Conscious Dreaming*. New York: Crown, 1996.

_____. *Dreamways of the Iroquois: Honoring the Secret Wishes of the Soul*. Rochester: Destiny, 2005.

_____. "When We Become A Dreaming Culture." <http://www .mossdreams.org>

"¿Nos Somnos Esta Noche?" *Integral* 7, no. 62, (December, 1984), 2 corres del sol.

Ossana, Roberta. "Dreaming in Dundee, New York: Interview with Susan Watkins." *Dream Network* 15:1. http://www.dreamnetwork.net/watkins

_____. "Dreams· and Mythology Alive!" *Dream Network* 17, no. 3, 18-20.

Pearson, Cynthia. "Earwings and Arabesques: Dreaming in the Multiverse." Paper presented at the Association for the Study of Dreams Conference 1998. http://www.nauticom.net/www/netcadet/asd98.

Reed, Henry. "Interview Published in *Dream Network Journal*." <http://www. starbuck .net/henryree/new/document>.

_____. "Dream Incubation." *Sundance Community Dream Journal*. 2, no. 1, Winter, 1978, 9-26.

Reich, Wilhelm. *Character Analysis* 3rd Edition. New York: Noonday/Farrar, Strauss, 1990.

_____. *Psi, What is It?* New York: Harper and Row, 1975.

Roberts, Jane. *Dreams, "Evolution" and Value Fulfillment, Vol II*. New York: Prentice Hall, 1986.

_____. *The Nature of the Psyche*. New York: Bantam, 1984.

Roberts, Maureen. "Dreams, Death and Diana: Lessons in Personal and Collective Healing." *Electric Dreams* 4:9, Sept 28, 1997. <http://www. dreamgate.com/dream/ed-articles/ed4-9rob>.

Sacks, Oliver. *An Anthropologist on Mars: Seven Paradoxical Tales*. New York: Vintage, 1995.

Schwarz, Berthold E. *Parent Child Telepathy*. New York: Garrett, 1971.

Seachrist, Elsie. *Dreams Your Magic Mirror*. New York: Dell, 1968.

Siegal, Nancy L. *Entwined Lives: Twins and What They Tell Us About Human Behavior*. New York: Dutton, 1999.

Siegel, Alan. "ASD Presidential Interview of Kelly Bulkeley, Ph.D." *Dream Time* 14, no. 3&4, Summer/Fall 1997, 1 & 37-39.

_____. "Presidential Interview: Rev. Jeremy Taylor." *ASD Newsletter* 11, no. 4, (Fall 1994), 1-7.

Sparrow, G. Scott. "Letter From Scott Sparrow." *Lucidity Letter*. <http://www.sawka .com/spiritwatch/letter_from_scott_sparrow>.

_____. *Lucid Dreaming: Dawning of the Clear Light*. Virginia Beach: ARE, 1976.

Stevenson, Robert Louis. "The Land of Counterpane." Ralph L. Woods, ed., *A Treasury of the Familiar*. Chicago: People's Book Club, 1952.

Stewart, Kilton. "Mental Hygiene and World Peace." *Mental Hygiene* xxxviii, no. 7, (July, 1954), 387-401.

Tart, Charles. *Altered States of Consciousness*. San Francisco: Harper Collins, 1990.

Taub-Bynum, E.B. *The Family Unconscious*. Wheaton: Theosophical, 1984.

Taylor, Jeremy. *Where People Fly and Water Runs Uphill*. New York: Warner, 1984.

Ullman, Montague. "A Group Approach to the Anomalous Dream." *Dream Telepathy* 2nd edition. New York: Macmillan, 1973, Appendix D.

Ullman, Montague, Stanley Krippner and Alan Vaughan. *Dream Telepathy* 2nd edition. New York: Macmillan, 1973.

Van de Castle, Robert. *Our Dreaming Mind*. New York: Ballantine, 1994.

_____. "Precognitive Dreaming." *Sundance Community Dream Journal* 2, no. 2, 174-190.

VanderPost, Laurens. *Jung and the Story of Our Time*. New York: Random House/Pantheon, 1975.

Vanlaeys, Emily. *Dream Weaving: Using Dream Guidance to Create Life's Tapestry*. Virginia Beach,: ARE, 2001.

Varela, Francisco, ed. *Sleeping, Dreaming and Dying*. Boston: Wisdom, 1999.

Watkins, Susan. *Conversations with Seth Vol.1*. Englewood Cliffs: Prentice Hall, 1980.

——————. *Dreaming Myself, Dreaming a Town*. New York: Kendall, 1989.

Whorf, Benjamin. "Language, Mind, and Reality." *The Theosophist* 63 1942, 291-91.

Wilber, Ken. *Eye to Eye: The Quest for the New Paradigm*. Garden City: Anchor, 1983.

Wilkerson, Richard. "Dream Cyberphile." *Dream Time* 17, no. 1, Winter 2000, 30-31.

Wolf, Fred A. *The Dreaming Universe*. New York: Simon & Schuster, 1994.

Zweig, Connie. "'See You in My Dreams' Test Works." *Brain/Mind Bulletin* 10, no. 1, Oct 1984, 3.

Zukav, Gary. *The Dancing WuLi Masters*. New York: Morrow, 1979.

Share Group Dreaming with others while helping children.

Use this order form to order additional copies of *Group Dreaming: Dreams to the Tenth Power*. Groups or institutions wishing to order 10 or more copies qualify for a substantial discount of 60% off the retail price of $19.95, or $7.98 per book.

For every book sold, $2 will benefit the Aid for Traumatized Children Project of the World Dreams Peace Bridge.

Please send me _____ copies of *Group Dreaming: Dreams to the Tenth Power*.

Enclosed is a check or money order made out to Wordminder Press for $_____.

# of books	Price	5% tax (VA)	Shipping	Total
1-9	$19.95 each		$4.00	
10 or more	$7.98 each		$8.00	

Shipping Address (please print):

Name _____

Address _____

_____

_____

Phone _____

Email _____

                   (to notify you of shipping date)

Send order form and payment to:
Wordminder Press
PO Box 10438
Norfolk, VA 23513-0438

NEW YORK MILLS PUBLIC LIBRARY
399 Main St.
New York Mills, NY 13417
(315) 736-5391